AFRICANS AND SEMINOLES

Recent Titles in
Contributions in Afro-American and African Studies
SERIES ADVISER: HOLLIS R. LYNCH

Slavery and Race Relations in Latin America
Robert Brent Toplin, editor

No Crystal Stair: Black Life and the *Messenger,* 1917-1928
Theodore Kornweibel, Jr.

"Good Time Coming?": Black Nevadans in the Nineteenth Century
Elmer R. Rusco

Race First: Ideological and Organizational Struggles of Marcus Garvey
and the Universal Negro Improvement Association
Tony Martin

Silence to the Drums: A Survey of the Literature of the Harlem Renaissance
Margaret Perry

Internal Combustion: The Races in Detroit, 1915-1926
David Allan Levine

Henry Sylvester Williams and the Origins of the Pan African Movement,
1869-1911
Owen Charles Mathurin

Periodic Markets, Urbanization, and Regional Planning: A Case Study
From Western Kenya
Robert A. Obudho and Peter P. Waller

Frederick Douglass on Women's Rights
Philip S. Foner, editor

Travail and Triumph: Black Life and Culture in the South Since the
Civil War
Arnold H. Taylor

Red Over Black: Black Slavery Among the Cherokee Indians
R. Halliburton, Jr.

New Rulers in the Ghetto: The Community Development Corporation
and Urban Poverty
Harry Edward Berndt

The FLN in Algeria: Party Development in a Revolutionary Society
Henry F. Jackson

Old Roots in New Lands: Historical and Anthropological Perspectives on
Black Experiences in the Americas
Ann M. Pescatello, editor

AFRICANS AND SEMINOLES

FROM REMOVAL TO EMANCIPATION

Daniel F. Littlefield, Jr.

GREENWOOD PRESS

Westport, Connecticut • London, England

Contributions in Afro-American and African Studies, Number 32

Library of Congress Cataloging in Publication Data

Littlefield, Daniel F
    Africans and Seminoles from removal to Emancipation.

    (Contributions in Afro-American and African studies; no. 32)
    Bibliography: p.
    Includes index.
    1. Seminole Indians--Slaves, Ownership of. 2. Afro-Americans--Relations with
Indians. 3. Slavery in Indian Territory. 4. Indians of North America-- Indian
Territory--Slaves, Ownership of. I. Title. II. Series.
E99.S28L57   301.44'93'0973   77-86
ISBN 0-8371-9529-2

Library of Congress Catalog Card Number: 77-86
ISBN: 0-8371-9529-2
ISSN: 0069-9624

First published in 1977

Greenwood Press, Inc.
51 Riverside Avenue, Westport, Connecticut 06880

Printed in the United States of America

Contents

	Maps	vii
	Preface	ix
1	Backgrounds	3
2	Black Men and War Policy	15
3	The Emigrants	36
4	Fear of the Creeks	68
5	A Breakdown in Relations	98
6	Return to Bondage	119
7	Bolt for Freedom	138
8	The Last Slave Controversies	162
9	Civil War and Emancipation	180
10	Conclusion	197
	Appendix	205
	Bibliography	257
	Index	263

Maps

Western Lands of the Five Civilized Tribes, 1840   69

Western Lands of the Five Civilized Tribes, 1845   99

Western Lands of the Five Civilized Tribes, 1860 181

Seminole and Creek Lands Following the
Treaties of 1866   198

ABOUT THE AUTHOR

Daniel F. Littlefield, Jr., associate professor of English at the University of Arkansas at Little Rock, specializes in American literature and Indian affairs. He has written articles for such journals as the *Chronicals of Oklahoma, Negro Heritage, American Indian Quarterly,* and *The Journal of Ethnic Studies.* His previous book-length works include *Hamlin Garland's Observations on the American Indians.* Professor Littlefield is currently researching material for a book on the history of Cherokee freedmen from emancipation to American citizenship.

Preface

From the eighteenth century to the present, the African has played a significant role in the history of the Seminole Indians. Yet the relationship between the two racial groups has been explored in detail for only the years of the First and Second Seminole Wars. That exploration has been the work principally of two men, Kenneth Wiggins Porter and John K. Mahon.

The present work carries the study forward through the next major historical phase, removal to the West and the years leading up to the Civil War. These years deserve close attention, for during this period the Africans emerged as a strong shaping force in the political and social destiny of the Seminoles in the West, playing significant roles in the establishment of separate lands for the Seminoles and of a basis for Seminole action during the Civil War.

Studies of the Seminoles during this period by Grant Foreman and Edwin McReynolds have been useful in putting African matters in a broader perspective. However, my emphasis is upon the blacks themselves and the governmental and Indian policies regarding them.

I have tried, where possible, to attach names and dates to the blacks and to give something of their personal histories. It was my desire to present them as real people who had a certain self-concept and certain aspirations for themselves and their posterity. Above all, I did not want to treat them simply as members of a social class in whose ranks individual identities were lost.

Research for this project was done during my tenure as a fellow of the Institute of Southern History at The Johns Hopkins University. The research was supported by a Younger Humanist Award from the National Endowment for the Humanities. My thanks go to that organization for the award and to The Johns Hopkins University for supplying the physical setting for the work. My thanks also go to the archivists of the Natural Resources Branch of the National Archives and to Martha Blaine, archivist in the Indian Archives Division of the Oklahoma Historical Society. My apologies go to others who have influenced this work, but whose names I have failed to mention.

Daniel F. Littlefield, Jr.

AFRICANS AND SEMINOLES

1

Backgrounds

Seminole is a Muskogee word first used in the 1770s to refer to the Alachua band of Lower Creeks. However, by the second decade of the nineteenth century, the term was current for all Lower and Upper Creeks, as well as for remnants of other groups such as the Yuchis, who had left the settled Creek towns and migrated to Florida during the eighteenth and early nineteenth centuries, either voluntarily or as a result of political intrigue, warfare, or civil strife. Their prolonged isolation from the Creeks proper and their slow withdrawal from the Creek Confederation earned them the title of *Seminole,* meaning "wild" or "runaway."[1]

By the beginning of the eighteenth century, northern Florida contained hardly any native population, but during the century the void was filled by peoples destined to become known as Seminoles. Early in the century, to create a buffer against the English, the Spanish with some degree of success invited some of the Lower Creeks to settle at Apalachee. The War of Jenkins' Ear and King George's War, 1739-48, drove other Indians south. Cowkeeper's Oconee band, driven to the lower Chattahoochee by the Yamassee War of 1715, moved on to the Alachua region where they were well established by 1750. During the same time, other Lower Creeks moved into the Apalachee region. Because of English and Creek raids, some of the Apalachicolas moved south, as did the Chiahas, who with the Tamathlis were important in establishing the Mikasuki band, first referred to during the British Period, 1763-83. These groups were Hitchiti-speaking. After 1767, Muskogee-speaking people migrated to Florida. In that year Upper Creeks from Eufaula town settled at Chocachatti, northeast of Tampa Bay.

Other Upper Creeks, including the Tallahassees, settled in West Florida. In 1778, some people of Kolomi, Fushatchee, and Kan-tcati migrated. The last significant migration followed the Creek War of 1813-14. The warring faction, mainly Upper Creeks known as Red Sticks, were defeated by Andrew Jackson's forces at Horseshoe Bend on March 27, 1814. Dissatisfied with the treaty that ensued, many Red Sticks went to Florida, swelling the Indian population to about 5,000, at least twice what it had been before the war.[2]

These bands of Lower and Upper Creeks, along with small groups of Yuchis and others, comprised what was popularly known as the Seminole tribe by the second decade of the nineteenth century. Nearly all of the tribe, the Yuchis being a notable exception, were of the Muskogean family, speaking Muskogee or Hitchiti, and all were Creek in cultural background. For the most part left to themselves by both the Spanish and the British, the Indians firmly established themselves on Florida soil. Although generally British in sentiment, they managed to stay out of the American Revolution, isolated as they were from the Creek Confederation. However, during the British Period they had reached their Golden Age, and in the 1780s and 1790s they began to be drawn into conflicts with the Americans on the Alabama and Georgia frontier. It was during this latter period that the designation of *Seminole* gained currency. According to William C. Sturdevant, the Seminoles demonstrate the importance of ethnonymy: "the naming of sociopolitical ('tribal' or 'ethnic') groups by their own members and by outsiders." That naming, he says, was "in response to European pressures, for the tribe is an entirely post-European phenomenon, a replacement by Creek settlers of the Florida aborigines whom they eliminated in frontier military campaigns growing out of antagonisms between European powers."[3]

THE ESTELUSTI

It is interesting, and perhaps significant, that about the time the Seminoles were acquiring their name, another social group—the Africans—became involved in Seminole affairs. When the Seminoles were removed from Florida between 1838 and 1843, nearly five hundred persons of African descent accompanied them to the West. Some of the blacks, whom the Muskogee-speaking Indians called *estelusti*,[4] had only recently joined the Seminoles through purchase, theft, or escape from nearby plantations. Several families, however, had been among the Indians as slaves or free blacks for fifty years or more and were part of an alliance of Africans and Seminoles that began about the time the Seminoles were first being recognized as a tribe separate from the Creeks. The exact date that the alliance began is uncertain. In the late seventeenth century, Spain began granting asylum to runaway slaves from the Carolinas, and large numbers of blacks sought refuge in Florida during the eighteenth century. However, as late as 1774, blacks were apparently not living among the Seminoles. As slaves continued to escape from the American colonies, settlements of blacks sprang up in Florida, but their relations with the Indians were not always good.[5]

It was apparently during the last two decades of the eighteenth century that the Florida Indians adopted a system of African slavery. During the next several years their slaves and enclaves of free blacks, mainly runaways from the American states, brought the Indians into conflict not only with whites but with Creeks as well. Escape of blacks to Indian country irritated the whites, and there were accusations of slave stealing from all sides. However, the greatest source of irritation between Seminoles and Creeks came from the Creeks' insistence on authority over matters relating to slaves among the former, whom they considered a part of the Creek Confederation. In the Treaty of New York (1790) and Treaty of Colerain (1796), the Creeks agreed to return all runaways in their country, including those among the Florida Indians.[6]

In the absence of descriptions of the institution of slavery among the Seminoles during the early years, one can only speculate about its characteristics. One scholar has postulated that the Seminoles were at first impressed enough with the prestige attached to ownership of Africans to exchange livestock for them but, not subscribing to the system of economics of the whites, were at a loss as to what to do with them. The Indians therefore gave them tools with which to build houses of their own, and set them to work cultivating crops and raising livestock of their own, a small portion of which the master took as tribute. However, this assessment appears to have been based on descriptions of slavery written a generation after it began among the Seminoles.[7]

More important, perhaps, than why and how it began are the questions of why the Seminoles perpetuated the institution and why soon after its adoption it began to assume characteristics greatly different from slavery in the neighboring tribes. By century's end, for instance, several Creeks owned slaves, some taken during the Revolutionary War, some obtained

as gifts from the British, and some stolen. According to Creek Agent
Benjamin Hawkins, most Creeks did not use them to economic advantage;
they produced little and became an expense to their owners. At Eufaula,
however, the Creeks had begun to improve their farms by slave labor. As
time passed, slavery among the Creeks resembled more and more that
among the whites, although it always differed in some respects from the
latter. By 1824, the Creeks had a slave code much stricter than any regulations of blacks ever maintained by the Seminoles.[8] In nearly all studies
of slavery among the Indians, the Seminoles are cited as exceptions to the
generalizations.

As the work of Kenneth Wiggins Porter has shown, slavery among the
Seminoles took a different direction, in part, because of the exigencies
of political intrigue and war. However, in a recent study which attempts
to synthesize the evidence on African slavery among the Indians, William
G. McLoughlin finds that explanation incomplete. The blacks among the
Seminoles were, after all, still slaves and not equals, he says. McLoughlin
theorizes that the Indians made distinctions between themselves and
blacks on the basis of "racial prejudice or racism" acquired during the
Indians' struggle to maintain their identities, through adaptation in agricultural practices, and by the influence of slaveholding missionaries.[9]
However, McLoughlin presents little evidence relating to the Seminoles
and turns his attention to other tribes, particularly the Cherokees.

While McLoughlin's theory may be somewhat applicable to the Seminoles
at midnineteenth century, there is little evidence that it applies before removal. During that time, rather, the relationship between Seminoles and
blacks seems to have been based in great measure on political and military
expediency. Established among the Seminoles at the time they were emerg-
ing as a separate tribal entity, the institution of slavery was shaped by the
same international pressures which Sturdevant says established the tribe.
Historical circumstances forced blacks among the Seminoles to assume the
role of comrades-in-arms with their Indian masters. This role, in turn,
shaped the institution of slavery as it was practiced among that tribe.

THE FIRST SEMINOLE WAR AND ANNEXATION

The first significant military alliance of Seminoles and blacks occurred
during the so-called Patriot War of 1812, when American settlers in Spanish

East Florida revolted and attempted to annex the territory to the United States. Participation of Seminoles and their blacks in the resulting battles and skirmishes has been well documented.[10] The war made two points clear: The blacks were formidable warriors, and by 1812 there was a close alliance between some Seminole bands and numbers of blacks who lived near them in separate towns and fought when the Indians called them into service.

It also became apparent to southern slaveholders that the black settlements in the Seminole country and elsewhere in Florida represented a threat to slavery in the nearby states. American forces assisting the Patriots had penetrated the Alachua country early in 1813, destroying the settlements, including one black town. In 1814, they defeated the Red Sticks, who had been assisted in war by their blacks and who afterward fled to Florida. That same year, the British built a fort near the mouth of the Apalachicola and manned it with refugee Red Sticks, their blacks, and runaway slaves, whom they left with the fort and armaments when they withdrew from Florida. The Indians, too, moved eastward, leaving the post to the blacks. About a thousand runaways, seeking its protection, settled in the surrounding region. Slave owners demanded the destruction of the Negro Fort, and on July 27, 1816, American forces leveled it, killing 270 and capturing sixty-four of its inhabitants. Survivors fled eastward and joined the Seminoles on the Suwannee, where the latter had fled after the Alachua towns were destroyed in 1813. Early in 1817, blacks were reported six hundred strong in the Seminole country, armed and going through military drills. Later that year, border warfare broke out at Fowl Town, with Indians and blacks continuing to make raids until early 1818 when Andrew Jackson and his command of white and friendly Creek troops entered Spanish Florida and destroyed the Mikasuki settlements and those on the Suwannee. Known as the First Seminole War, this invasion resulted in a general movement of the Seminoles and their blacks to the east and south, where they were followed by many runaways.[11]

Jackson's invasion not only effectively pushed the Indians and enclaves of blacks farther from the borders of the United States but it also led to the annexation of Florida. A cession treaty was signed with Spain in 1819, and the transfer took place in 1821. Once inside the confines of the United States, the Seminoles and blacks, whose destinies by that time were inalterably intertwined, faced an uncertain future. Demoralized by Jackson's invasion, impoverished by the loss of stores, crops, and property, and faced with reestablishing their settlements, they watched helplessly as the Americans entered Florida, opening plantations and restricting the bounds of Seminole lands.

THE SEMINOLE VERSION OF SLAVERY

By the time of the "change of flags," as the Indians called it, slavery among the Seminoles was firmly established and had assumed character- istics which were alarming to white planters in the region. Travelers among the Seminoles in the early 1820s noted the kind, even indulgent, treat- ment of slaves by Seminole masters who required little labor from the blacks. According to one writer, "Though hunger and want be stronger than even the *sacra fumes auri,* the greatest pressure of these evils, never occasions them to impose onerous labours on the Negroes, or to dispose of them, though tempted by high offers, if the latter are unwilling to be sold."[12] The blacks lived in separate towns from the Indians and, like the Indians, planted and cultivated fields in common, apart from the Indian fields. They also owned large herds of livestock. The masters took only an annual share or tribute of the produce and livestock. As a result, the slaves never produced a surplus for trade for their masters and apparently barely supported them.[13]

For the most part, the Seminole blacks lived like their masters and allies. They dressed Seminole fashion and lived in houses built of timbers and shingles lashed to posts and rafters with strips of oak. The men owned guns and supplemented their diet with game. Described as "stout, and even gigantic" in comparison to the Indians, these blacks were more clever than their masters. Most spoke Spanish and English as well as the Indian languages. As a result, they were called upon more and more as interpreters and go-betweens when the Indians dealt with the whites. By 1822, for instance, Whan (or Juan), a former slave of King Payne, had already emerged as a principal interpreter, the Seminoles placing "the utmost confidence in him, when making use of his services, in their dealings with the whites."[14]

One estimate set at four hundred the number of blacks among the Seminoles at the end of the First Seminole War. How many of these be- longed to the Indians by legitimate purchase is uncertain; many were fugitives. The lax system of slavery and the Indians' kind treatment of the fugitive blacks among them were not compatible with the interests of

Florida planters, who viewed the system with alarm. Both Indians and blacks, who had been taught by the Spanish to distrust the Americans, began to fear the loss of their land and their freedom.[15]

As contact with the whites increased, the Seminoles grew more dependent on the blacks. Their common distrust of the Americans, the blacks' greater agricultural skill and the resulting economic advantage, and their ability to speak English contributed to the dependency as well as to a tendency by the Seminoles to view the blacks in many instances as allies, if not as equals.[16] This peculiar relationship, which became significant during the Second Seminole War, was no doubt fostered by the blacks, for the life they pursued among the Seminoles must have looked easy indeed in comparison to the slave's life on the white plantations.

THE SECOND SEMINOLE WAR AND THE INDIAN REMOVAL ACT

Events of the decade and a half following the Florida cession laid the groundwork for the outbreak of the Second Seminole War.[17] The Americans at once began to ponder the disposition of the Seminoles. There was some agitation to remove them. The obvious solution was to send them back to the Creeks, which, of course, the Seminoles would resist. They had broken completely with the Creeks, whom they distrusted and whom the Red Sticks particularly hated. The alternative was to confine them to a smaller area. A treaty council at Moultrie Creek in September 1823 resulted in a treaty which granted reservations on the Apalachicola to chiefs Neamathla, Blunt, Tuskihadjo, Mulatto King, Emathlochee, and Econchatta Micco and a reservation north of the Charlotte River to the remaining Seminoles. The Indians agreed, in part, to try to prevent runaway slaves from joining them.

The Indians were slow to remove to the reservation. Hunger forced them to range wide, preying on the herds belonging to whites. There were instances of violence and intrusion on Indian lands by whites, and runaway slaves among the Seminoles irritated the planters. Fearful of the influence of the Seminole blacks on slaves of white planters and on their own Indian masters, Florida Governor William P. DuVal unsuccessfully requested that whites be allowed to purchase blacks from the Indians. Gad Humphreys, appointed Seminole agent in 1822, emerged as champion of the Indians' cause. Under his supervision, the Seminoles returned many runaways, but the whites were not satisfied, and the Indians became convinced that the whites would not be satisfied until they had all of the blacks among the Seminoles. Humphreys was accused of being too slow in returning slave property and of profiteering in Indian slaves and cattle. When Jackson became President, he yielded to pressure from Floridians and removed Humphreys.

Under Jackson's administration, the Indian Removal Act was passed on May 28, 1830, and a commission was appointed to treat with the Seminoles. The treaty of Payne's Landing on May 9, 1832, provided for a delegation of seven Seminole chiefs to inspect Creek lands west of the Mississippi; if they found the land favorable and the Creeks willing for the Seminoles to reunite with them as one tribe, an agreement to remove within three years would be binding. It is amazing that the Seminoles would even consider reunion with the Creeks, who had marched against them in war and had raided their towns looking for slaves. There were charges that the black interpreter Abraham had misrepresented that part of the treaty to the Seminoles, for in return for their work during the negotiations, Abraham and Cudjo, Agent John Phagan's black interpreter, were guaranteed two hundred dollars each for the improvements they would have to abandon upon removal. Nevertheless, the seven chiefs, Agent Phagan, and Abraham went to the West. At Fort Gibson, about sixty miles west of Fort Smith, Arkansas, under rather vague circumstances the chiefs were induced to sign a treaty on March 28, 1833, in the name of all Seminoles, saying that they were satisfied with the land and were willing to remove. The Seminoles on the Apalachicola agreed under another treaty to remove, but the bands farther east repudiated the treaty of Fort Gibson.

The Seminole blacks became a major issue in the matter of removal. Whites attempted to seize the blacks among the Apalachicolas before they could be taken from Florida. The Seminoles began to fear that if they removed to the West, the Creeks would take their blacks by force, for the Creeks had asked the government to undertake new negotiations whereby the Seminoles would agree to settle, not as a body but scattered among the more numerous Creeks. When it appeared for a time that the removal would take place, the blacks began to exert their influence over the Indians, playing on the Seminole fear of the Creeks, urging their masters and allies not to emigrate, evidently suspecting that once they were assembled for emigration, they would be seized and sold to the whites.

When Seminole Agent Wiley Thompson called the chiefs together on October 21, 1834, they challenged the validity of both the Treaty of Payne's Landing and the Treaty of Fort Gibson, charging the government with trickery. The conference drove a wedge between the agent, who represented the government, and the Seminoles and between factions of the Seminoles themselves, some of whom favored removal. Thompson blamed opposition to removal on unscrupulous whites who allegedly encouraged the Seminoles to remain in Florida, so that once Florida laws were extended over the Indians, the whites could divest them of their slave property.

During 1835, relations deteriorated. Citizens of Florida claimed that about a hundred of their slaves had run away to the Seminoles since the Treaty of Moultrie Creek. Agitation increased to take the blacks from the Seminoles. There were plans to purchase the black leaders to remove their influence over the Indians and to eliminate a possible source of conflict between the Seminoles and Creeks in the West. During the spring, Thompson offended the Indians by striking the names of Micanopy, Jumper, Holata Mico, Sam Jones, and Coa Hadjo as head men and by imprisoning Osceola to force him to attest the validity of the Treaty of Payne's Landing. Sporadic violence occurred through the next few months, and on December 26-27, King Philip's Indian and black forces raided the St. Johns valley plantations. On the following day, the opening shots of the Second Seminole War were fired. At Fort King, Seminoles under Osceola killed Agent Thompson, among others, and fifty miles away, a relief column under the command of Major Francis L. Dade was annihilated by Indians and blacks under Micanopy, Alligator, and Jumper.

THE ROLE OF THE BLACKS

Despite Thompson's mistakes, he had seen clearly the role of the blacks in the opposition to removal and had suggested solutions which, if followed, might have averted the war. He knew that the blacks violently opposed removal because they lived in dread of being transferred from their state of ease and comparative liberty to one of bondage and hard work under overseers on sugar or cotton plantations. Since the blacks exerted such great influence over their masters, the Indians were susceptible to counsel against removal. Thompson wrote to the Secretary of War in 1835, "An

Indian would almost as soon sell his child as his slave, except when under
the influence of intoxicating liquors. The almost affection of the Indian
for his slaves, the slaves' fears of being placed in a worse condition, and
the influence which the Negroes have over the Indians, have all been made
to subserve the views of the Government." Thompson had tried to assure
the blacks that he would do all he could to prevent a change in their status,
promised the Indians the security of their property, and refused to allow
whites to buy the slaves. He urged the War Department to turn the influence of the blacks toward securing removal by allaying their fears about
enslavement and by making promises to them. He suggested that the department offer "a few hundred dollars" to such influential blacks as Abraham
to buy their influence in favor of the government's policy.[18] But the
government officials in Washington did not follow Thompson's suggestions,
and when the war broke out, they found the blacks were formidable warriors.

Throughout the long and costly war, blacks played significant and often
decisive roles not only as warriors but as advisers, spies, and interpreters
as well. Some entered the field as chiefs or captains of their own warriors,
while others served as lieutenants under the Seminole chiefs. Participation
of blacks in the major engagements of the war has been documented:
Withlacoochee campaign, March 1836; Wahoo Swamp, November 1836;
John Caesar's raid near St. Augustine, January 1837; Lake Okeechobee,
December 1837.[19]

As the war progressed, the ranks of blacks were swelled by refugees
from Florida plantations and others captured by the Indians. It is impossible
to say how many blacks were among the Seminoles during the war. One
early estimate set the number of black warriors at 250, with 150 of these
estimated to be runaways. Another estimate set the total number of blacks
at 1,400, of whom only an estimated two hundred were slaves of the
Indians.[20] Yet when the Seminoles were finally removed between 1838
and 1843, nearly five hundred blacks went west with them.

Removal of the Seminoles was apparently as much an attempt to solve
the "Negro problem" as it was to settle the "Indian problem" of Florida.
Removal of many blacks who were not the legitimate property of Seminoles,
although expedient as war policy, failed to solve the problem. Subsequent
events in the Indian Territory show that it was simply transferred to the
West, where once more the system of slavery practiced by the Seminoles
and their kind disposition toward free blacks among them came in conflict
with the practice of their neighbors. This time, the enclaves of blacks
threatened the Creeks and Cherokees, and to a lesser degree the Chickasaws

and Choctaws, whose systems of slavery, as time passed, became more like that of the white South.

As the following account will demonstrate, the history of the Seminole blacks between removal and the American Civil War is the story of a struggle by some to regain the degree of freedom they had enjoyed among the Indians in Florida and by others to establish a free status in the new lands. While the Seminoles, the Creeks, and the government of the United States considered them all legally slaves, with a few exceptions, many of the blacks felt that they were free because of promises made to them individually or as a people by military officials in Florida. The Seminoles tried for some years to maintain their peculiar system of slavery and to perpetuate their close relationship with the blacks, but because of pressure from the Creeks and proslavery officials of the War Department, they ultimately found it politically inexpedient to do so. Thus, the struggle by the blacks to acquire the freedom they had hoped to find in the West proved bitter, disastrous, and futile until it was ended by the Civil War.

NOTES

1. R. M. Loughridge, comp., *English and Muskokee Dictionary* (Reprint ed., n.p., 1964), 183; Frederick Webb Hodge, ed., *Handbook of American Indians North of Mexico* (Washington: Government Printing Office, 1907), Pt. 2, 500; John K. Mahon, *History of the Second Seminole War, 1835-1842* (Gainesville: University of Florida Press, 1967), 7.

2. Mahon, 2-7; John R. Swanton, *The Indians of the Southeastern United States* (Reprint ed., New York: Greenwood Press, 1969), 181; William C. Sturdevant, "Creek into Seminole," *North American Indians in Historical Perspective,* Eleanor Burke Leacock and Nancy Oesterich Lurie, eds. (New York: Ramdom House, 1971), 101-103; Swanton, *Early History of the Creek Indians and Their Neighbors* (Reprint ed., Johnson Reprint Corporation, 1970), 398-405.

3. Mahon, 7, 18-19; Sturdevant, 93.

4. Loughridge, 132.

5. For an authoritative account of blacks in Florida, 1670-1763, see Kenneth Wiggins Porter, *The Negro on the American Frontier* (New York: Arno Press and The New York Times, 1971), 155-181; see also, Mahon, 19, 20.

6. Mahon, 20; Benjamin Hawkins, *A Sketch of the Creek Country in the Years 1798 and 1799,* Collections of the Georgia Historical Society, vol. III, Pt. 1 (New York: William Van Norden Printer, 1848), Appendix.

7. Porter, 186-187.

8. Hawkins, 26, 29, 31, 39, 44, 49; Hawkins, *Letters of Benjamin Hawkins, 1796-1806,* Collections of the Georgia Historical Society, vol. IX (Savannah: The Morning News, 1916), 29, 41, 43, 48, 174-175. In 1824 the Creeks prescribed death to any black who killed an Indian or another slave, forbade inheritances by African children who had one Indian parent since it was "a disgrace to our Nation for our people to marry a Negro," prohibited slaves from owning property, provided for emancipation of slaves by owners, appointed a receiver of runaway slaves, and relieved masters of any obligation made by their slaves. Antonio J. Waring, ed., *Laws of the Creek Nation,* University of Georgia Libraries Miscellaneous Publications No. 1 (Athens: University of Georgia Press, 1960), 17-27.

9. William G. McLoughlin, "Red Indians, Black Slavery and White Racism: America's Slaveholding Indians," *American Quarterly,* 24 (October 1974), 370-379.

10. Authoritative treatment of the war appears in Porter, 183-203; see also, Charles H. Coe, *Red Patriots: The Story of the Seminoles* (Reprint ed.), Gainesville: University Presses of Florida, 1974), 11-13.

11. Authoritative treatment of Negro Fort and the First Seminole War appears in Porter, 211-234; see also, Coe, 16-23.

12. [William Hayne Simmons] *Notices of East Florida* (Reprint ed., Gainesville: University of Florida Press, 1973), 42, 50.

13. [Simmons] 76; Porter 46, 187, 189-190; Coe, 14-15.

14. [Simmons] 45, 76-77; Porter, 47.

15. [Simmons] 75, 42, 44.

16. Porter, 47.

17. The following brief survey of events leading to the outbreak of the war is based on accounts in Woodburne Potter, *The War in Florida* (Reprint ed., Ann Arbor: University Microfilms, Inc., 1966), 13-95; Coe, 43-65; and Mahon, 33-106.

18. Wiley Thompson to Elbert Herring, December 2, 1834, and Thompson to Secretary of War, April 27, 1835, National Archives Microfilm Publications, *Microcopy M234* (Records of the Office of Indian Affairs, Letters Received)-806, Frames 93 and 103; Thompson to C. A. Harris, *Microcopy M234*-800, Frame 359; Thompson to Lewis Cass, September 21, 1835, National Archives Record Group 75 (Records of the Bureau of Indian Affairs), *Records of the Commissary General of Subsistence,* Seminole.

19. Authoritative treatment of black participation in these and other engagements during the war appears in Porter, 244-261.

20. Porter, 46, 244.

2

Black men and war policy

Removal of the blacks with the Seminoles was the direct result of war policy begun by Brevet Major General Thomas S. Jesup, who assumed command of the army in Florida in December of 1836. When his orders came, Jesup was in command of troops who had been sent into the field in Alabama to contain certain elements of the Creek tribe and to prevent them from joining the Seminoles. Early in his command, it became apparent to Jesup that defeat of the Seminoles depended upon the defeat or surrender of the blacks, who represented some of their fiercest and most intelligent warriors and leaders. It became his policy, and that of his successors, to treat with and make promises to the blacks in order to get them to separate from the Indians. Those promises made to them by American commanders before, during, and after their surrender or capture profoundly affected the direction of Seminole history in the West, for the status of most of the blacks in the West was directly related to the means by which they came into the hands of the army and assembled for emigration from Florida.

JESUP'S CLASSIFICATION OF BLACKS

General Jesup divided them into six distinct groups: 1) those captured by a regiment of Creek warriors who were under contract to fight the Seminoles; 2) those protected by the convention of Fort Dade, March 6, 1837; 3) those captured by United States troops, including those who separated voluntarily from their Indian masters and came in; 4) those who came in with Alligator and his band in April 1838; 5) those brought in by their owners and sent west with them; 6) those really the property of white men but not claimed by or returned to their owners before emigration.[1] To these groups could be added a seventh: those blacks who later claimed freedom on the basis of partisan action on behalf of the United States.

FIRST GROUP–CREEK CAPTIVES

The first group consisted of blacks captured by a regiment of Creek warriors under Jesup's command during his first campaign in the winter of 1836-37, the principal battles of which took place on the Withlacoochee River, near Lake Apopka, and on Hatcheelustee Creek during January 1837. The Creeks had been recruited by Jesup during the summer of 1836. An agreement with Opothleyohola, Little Doctor, Tuckabatchee Micco, Mad Blue, Jim Boy, and Jelka Hajo provided for six hundred to a thousand warriors to go against the Seminoles. Besides $31,900 to be applied against the debts of their bands, the Creeks were to receive the pay and emoluments of soldiers in the army of the United States and, most important, "such plunder as they may take from the Seminoles." If the Creeks remained in service after the Seminoles had been subdued, they were to receive an additional $10,000. By the time Jesup assumed command, he was convinced that he was engaged in "a negro not an Indian War." He therefore expanded the term "plunder" to mean any Seminole property, including slaves. The Creeks were to have any Seminole black they captured as the spoils of war. But fugitive or captive blacks from white plantations were to be returned to their owners, and the Creeks were to receive a reward of twenty dollars for each one they captured.[2]

Shortly after the battle of Hatcheelustee Creek in January 1837, Jesup entered negotiations with the Indians and blacks at Fort Dade. The spring was spent trying to preserve a shaky peace and to persuade the Indians to come in and emigrate. On June 2, Jesup ordered about ninety blacks, most of them captured by the Creek warriors, to be sent to Fort Pike at New Orleans, and placed in the hands of Major Isaac Clark. The major was to imprison them and, if possible, hire them out for their own support. Seventeen other blacks remained at Tampa Bay. By this time, Jesup's troops had also captured about ninety blacks who belonged to citizens of the United States; most of those had been sent to St. Marks and St. Augustine.[3]

Among the blacks captured by the Creeks were a number of extremely important individuals. Ben, described as "one of the most important and influential characters among the Indian negroes," had never had a white master. Ben (a second by that name) and Jacob, the slaves of Holatoochee, were called "most intrepid and hostile warriors," as was Mundy, the slave of Miccopotokee. Murray, who was apparently the property of Colonel John Crowell, a white man, was claimed by the Seminole Nelly Factor. He was considered "the best guide in the nation." Toney and Toby, listed as the slaves of Miccopotokee, were described as "Hostile; either qualified to take the lead in an insurrection."[4]

Jesup mustered out part of the Creek volunteers in June and the rest that fall. As time drew near to settle accounts, Jesup realized that he could not allow the captured blacks to be sent to the West as slave property of the Creeks, for conflicts with the Seminoles would arise over them. Thus on September 6, 1837, he personally took the blacks on account of the government for $8,000 to be paid to the Creeks in proportion to the number of captives taken by each battalion. Of the slaves belonging to citizens of the United States, the Creeks had captured thirty-five, for whom they were to receive rewards. A few days later, Jesup sent the remaining Creek warriors to Pass Christian, Mississippi, to be discharged. Since Creek removal to the West was then under way, they were to be taken to New Orleans to be paid for the captives and to prepare for emigration, since the families of many of them had already removed. Captain John Page, superintendent of the Creek removal, then at New Orleans, was specifically instructed not to remove the blacks with the Creeks.[5]

Jesup hoped that the purchase would "end all difficulty." Regarding the ultimate disposition of the blacks, he wrote to Secretary of War Joel R. Poinsett: "It is highly important to the slave holding states that these negroes be sent out of the country; and I would strongly recommend that they be sent to one of our colonies in Africa. The sum paid to the Indians is entirely satisfactory to them though it is far less than the value of the negroes." However, the agreement on the purchase price was not as firm as Jesup had thought. When they reached Pass Christian, the Creeks refused the $8,000 but emigrated without the blacks, who remained at Fort Pike during the next several months. In February 1838, Jesup ordered

Major R. A. Zantzinger, the commander at Fort Pike, to move as many of them as he thought advisable to New Orleans Barracks and to employ them in earning their subsistence.[6] Several months more passed before they finally emigrated to the Indian Territory.

SECOND GROUP—THE FORT DADE AGREEMENT

The second group of black emigrants to the West were those protected by the convention of Fort Dade of March 6, 1837. That agreement grew out of negotiations which followed the battle of Hatcheelustee Creek on January 27, 1837. Among the twenty-three blacks captured during the battle were Ned and his family. Jesup sent Ned to the hostiles with an offer to negotiate. On January 31, Abraham came in. Well known as an interpreter and one of the most intrepid of the black leaders, Abraham had been at the battle of Hatcheelustee. Through his efforts, Jesup was able to arrange a council with chiefs Micanopy and Jumper on February 3.[7]

Abraham, about fifty, had great influence over the Indians because of his long association with them. He had been a slave in Pensacola when he was young. How he came to be among Micanopy's people is uncertain, but by 1825 he was firmly established. In that year and the next, he accompanied Micanopy and other chiefs to Washington as interpreter. Micanopy, who was the principal chief among the Seminoles during the war, had given Abraham his freedom because of his service. As interpreter he had signed the Treaty of Payne's Landing and had acted as interpreter for the delegation to the Indian Territory to inspect the land to which the government proposed to remove them. However, Abraham had counseled the Indians against removal to the West, for the blacks felt that once they were rounded up for emigration, they would be easy prey for any whites who might lay claims to them. When the war broke out, Abraham was one of the principal leaders of the black forces. Because of his close association with and influence over Micanopy, who from all evidence was not a very clever man, Abraham often assumed the important role of interpreter and negotiator.[8] Such was the case in the negotiations at Fort Dade.

The meeting of February 3, 1837, led to another with General Jesup at Fort Dade on March 6. Micanopy did not attend, but Jesup treated with Jumper, Holatoochee (Davy), Yaholoochee (Cloud), Cotsee Tustenugee (representing Halpatch Hajo), and the black war leader John Cowaya (or Cavallo). Claiming to represent Micanopy, the chiefs agreed to cease hostilities, bind the entire nation to immediate emigration, and leave hostages with the army, among them Micanopy and John Cavallo, to ensure compliance. They further agreed to withdraw immediately to the south of the Hillsborough before April 1. The Indians were to assemble for emigration before April 10, Cloud coming in at once with his people as an example for the other towns. In the name of the United States, Jesup agreed that the Seminoles and their black allies who came in and voluntarily emigrated would be secure in their lives and property and that the blacks and their bona fide property would accompany the Indians to the West, with expenses borne by the United States. Their cattle and ponies would be paid for, and the chiefs, warriors, and their families and blacks would be given subsistence from the time they assembled at Tampa Bay until twelve months after they arrived in the West. Finally, all of the advantages secured to the Indians by the Treaty of Payne's Landing were recognized and secured by the convention of Fort Dade.[9]

Jesup had granted the Indians liberal terms; severer terms might have led to a renewal of hostilities. As for the concessions made to the blacks, he later wrote, "Throughout my operations I found the negroes the most active and determined warriors; and during the conference with the Indian chiefs I ascertained that they exercised an almost controlling influence over them."[10] He knew that the slave question was at the root of the war and that the blacks had counseled the Indians against removal, and he hoped to answer their objections to removal by guaranteeing the free blacks safe passage to the West and guaranteeing the safety of the Seminoles' slave property.

A few days after the agreement was made, Micanopy surrendered and, on March 18, approved the convention and convinced Jesup that he could persuade others to surrender. For the first time, Jesup began to believe that the war was at an end. However, success of the peace depended to a great extent on the citizens of Florida: "The same errors . . . that renewed the war in Alabama would renew it here—I mean the imprudent violence of the citizens. Should they attempt to seize any of the Indians, either as criminals or as debtors, the scenes of the last year will be renewed."[11]

CONFLICT OVER THE FORT DADE CONVENTION

The most crucial point of matters as they stood concerned the blacks. For his policy to succeed, the agreement made at Fort Dade had to be carried out; on that point turned the entire matter of the war and emigration. As Jesup suspected, the agreement soon drew fire from the citizens of Florida. An influential group, including the former Seminole Agent Gad Humphreys, attacked the agreement for not providing for indemnity for property captured or destroyed by Indians or for restitution of stolen property, especially slaves. Jesup's peace terms were generally condemned by Floridians, and he was attacked by the press. The worst of Jesup's fears concerning slave hunters were confirmed in late March, when two or three citizens of Florida showed up at his camp on the Withlacoochee. Thirty or more of the black warriors were encamped nearby, but when the slave hunters came, they dispersed, causing Jesup to have grave doubts that they would come in again. Jesup further excited the blacks when, on April 8, he persuaded some of the chiefs to surrender the blacks belonging to white men, particularly those taken during the war.[12]

On May 5, Commissioner of Indian Affairs C. A. Harris approved the convention of Fort Dade and endorsed Jesup's attitude toward the blacks: "The importance of preventing the interference of the whites with the Indians, or with their negroes, is fully appreciated by this Department. It must not be permitted under any pretense. Arrest and detention of any of the Seminoles would be a violation of the articles of the convention and may be resisted by any proper and legal means at your disposal." The matter of emigration was turned over to Jesup.[13]

By this time, Micanopy, Jumper, Cloud, and Alligator and their people had assembled at Tampa Bay for removal. Others, including Osceola, Sam Jones, Coa Hadjo, Philip, his son Wild Cat, and Tuskinia had talked of surrendering but had not. The Indians were slow in coming in, but Jesup was hopeful until the night of June 2, when two hundred warriors under Osceola and Sam Jones, two of the most hostile leaders, raided the emigration camp near Tampa Bay and absconded with about seven hundred Indians and blacks, including Micanopy, John Cavallo, and the other chiefs.[14] With this event, the convention of Fort Dade, which had resulted in the surrender of several hundred persons, fell through. However, in subsequent years, both the Indians and the blacks made claims on the government as if the agreement had held.

That summer, Jesup claimed to have captured nearly all of the black leaders of influence during the previous winter's campaign. "The negro portion of the hostile force of the Seminole nation not taken is entirely without a head," he said.[15] It was true that the most important ones had come in under the convention of Fort Dade, but Jesup's statement is not entirely correct. John Cavallo had surrendered in April and was apparently satisfied, but he had been one of the ringleaders in the seizure of the Indians on June 2. Now he was out again, and other black leaders such as Long Bob and Charles were still out. However, several of the important black leaders and warriors were in custody. Abraham, the most important, was the principal black chief and was now supposedly friendly to the whites.[16] He had remained with the army when the rest of the Seminoles and blacks escaped in early June.

There was also Juan, aged forty-five, "the commander of the negro force on the Withlacoochee; the chief counsellor among the negroes, and the most important character." A well known interpreter and adviser as early as 1822, Juan was one of the principal leaders of the blacks and had possibly been a field commander under Abraham. Juan, his wife Eliza, and children Toby and Catherine, listed as slaves of Micanopy, had come to Fort Armstrong with Abraham in late May.[17]

Another black who had come in under the convention of Fort Dade and had remained with the whites was Toney Barnet, aged thirty-six, who was said to be "a good soldier, and an intrepid leader. He is the most cunning and intelligent negro we have here." Toney, his wife Polly, and children Beckey, Grace, Lydia, Mary Ann, and Martinas claimed to be free. Toney was claimed, however, by David Barnet, a half-blood Creek, whose uncle had apparently once owned Toney. About 1822, Toney had run away from Barnet's Flint River, Georgia, plantation, gone to Florida, and attached himself to the band of Jumper, who claimed him. In 1826, Agent Humphreys needed an interpreter and sent to the Creek Nation for James Hardridge, who on arrival at the Seminole agency recognized Toney. Hardridge later bought Toney, and Jumper gave him up. When Hardridge left Florida, Humphreys bought Toney, who stayed with him a number of years until Toney's wife, described as a mulatto and the widow of old Chief Bowlegs, bought and freed him.[18]

Murray, who had been captured in January, also remained in custody. Jesup had retained him because he would be an important guide if the army took the field in the fall. Jesup guaranteed Colonel John Crowell, Murray's owner, that the government would pay for Murray should he be killed in service and make payment to Crowell for his services as guide.[19]

While Jesup intended to use these and other blacks where he could, he did not trust them, believing that they would rally to the cause of the

Indians if the hostilities were renewed. To Secretary Poinsett he wrote: "The two races, the negro and the Indian, are rapidly approximating— they are identified in interests and feelings."[20] Thus, in early July, Jesup ordered the commander at Tampa Bay to watch Abraham, Toney, and Bob closely and to place them inside the pickets at the first sign of Indians in the neighborhood. Jesup believed that emigration was so unpopular with the Indians that the war council would prevail, in which event the blacks would take the first opportunity to escape.[21]

Lieutenant Colonel Samuel Miller at Tampa Bay disagreed and asked Jesup to reconsider his order. Abraham had told Miller that nothing short of Jesup's orders would induce him to go within reach of the hostile Seminoles, for fear that he would be singled out for revenge for having taken an active part in bringing about the agreement of Fort Dade. He offered to lead Jesup to all of the strongholds of the Indians should the war continue. By this time, Abraham had evidently committed himself to the idea of removal. In April, he had written to Jesup concerning Toney and himself. They had "done everything promised" by them and now wanted Jesup to keep his promises. Abraham sent Toney to Jesup: "We wish to get in writing from the General, the agreement made with us." They were ready to emigrate: "We do not live for ourselves only, but for our wives & children who are dear to us as those of any other men. When we reach our new home we hope we shall be permitted to remain while the woods remain green, and the water runs."[22] When the Indians had made their escape in early June, they had urged Abraham to go with them, but he had refused.[23]

Jesup had promised Abraham freedom for him and his family if he remained faithful and had threatened to hang him if he did not. Abraham admitted that he remained with the whites because it was in his interest to do so; deserting the army would forfeit the liberty of his family and his property, if not his life. He readily admitted his close friendship with Micanopy, who had sent word that he would like to see Abraham. The feeling was mutual, but Abraham would not go out, fearing for his life and saying that if anyone went to talk with Micanopy, it should be Bob. Acting Seminole Agent Lieutenant John Casey believed that if Abraham were confined as Jesup wished, his confidence in the whites would be broken, and it would no longer be in his interest to give them advice and information. On July 15, Abraham asked to be sent to the West at once because he had incurred the deadly enmity of some of the war party. Jesup revoked his order to confine Abraham and the other blacks.[24]

During the succeeding months of his command, Jesup found them indispensable as guides and interpreters, and the treachery he expected did not develop.

THIRD GROUP—PRISONERS OF WAR

The third major group of black emigrants to the West were those captured by the United States troops, including those who had separated from their Indian masters and had voluntarily come in. Most of those actually captured by the troops were taken during Jesup's command. His first campaign has already been discussed, except a raid his troops made during his march from the Creek country to assume command in early December 1836. At the head of Lake Eustis, his command overran and burned a village of Seminole blacks, taking about forty prisoners. These were the first prisoners, either black or Indian, taken in the war.[25] This event was signal, for at that point Jesup began to realize the extent of the involvement of blacks in the war, and the realization shaped his war policy throughout his command.

After Jesup's anger subsided following the collapse of the Fort Dade convention, he began to take stock of his achievements. Throughout the succeeding weeks, he returned to a theory that he had held when he assumed command: that this was "a negro war." He began to devote great effort to separating the blacks from the Seminoles and, where possible, securing their aid against their former allies and masters. During the summer of 1837, he revived the policy he had used with the Creek warriors. He issued orders to the militia as well as to the regular troops under his command that the army had no obligation to spare the property of the Indians. Their blacks and other property would become the possessions of the corps by which they were captured.[26]

Jesup tried to recruit a thousand northern Indians, intending to extend them the same offer. He let his plan be known to the black interpreters and to the Creek warriors still in Florida so that word would get out to the hostile camps; not only would he allow the recruits to keep Seminole property, including blacks, he said, but he would also allow them to take Seminole women and children as slaves. This latter was just a threat, no doubt, but he had set a precedent in his agreement with the Creeks. Jesup extended a similar offer to volunteers being recruited in Alabama and to the Choctaws, whom he never succeeded in recruiting.[27]

JESUP'S BREACHES OF THE RULES OF WAR

In early September, John Philip, the slave of Chief Philip (Emathla) and an important leader of the blacks, surrendered. With John Philip as guide, troops under General Joseph M. Hernandez marched about thirty miles south of St. Augustine where they succeeded in capturing Philip, Euchee Billy, and his brother Euchee Jack, some of the most hostile Indian leaders, who were in Jesup's estimation worth "fifty common Indians or negros." Hernandez captured forty-nine Indians and blacks. Chief Philip sent word to his son Wild Cat to come in. He did so with Blue Snake under a white flag on September 26. Then Jesup committed the first of his famous breaches of the rules of war; he had the Indians seized and made prisoners in spite of the flag of truce.[28]

After this event, Jesup wrote to Governor Richard Keith Call of Florida that the blacks were now "entirely without a leader, all their other chiefs having been secured in June last."[29] It is true that the black leadership had been greatly impaired. Perhaps that is why, in early October, seventeen blacks left the Indians and surrendered at Fort Peyton. Jesup also let Wild Cat go, using his father as hostage, to try to persuade other Indians to come in. Wild Cat returned October 17 with several chiefs and an additional seventy-nine blacks.[30]

Wild Cat reported that about one hundred Indians would be at Pellicer's Creek on the following day, including Osceola and Coa Hadjo, who wanted to talk. Jesup sent General Hernandez to the area, where he found several Indians and the black subchief John Cavallo, who conducted the talk for the Indians. He said that Osceola and Coa Hadjo were expected that night or the following morning. On October 20, Cavallo informed Hernandez that the Indians were camped near Fort Peyton. Jesup ordered Hernandez to find out why the Indians had not surrendered the blacks taken from the citizens of Florida as Coa Hadjo had promised to do at a council with Jesup at Fort King in late August. Hernandez was also to find out if Micanopy, Jumper, Cloud, and Alligator intended to surrender the blacks with them. Finally, he was to find out if the Indians themselves were going to surrender. If Hernandez did not get the answers Jesup wanted, he was to seize the Indians and bring them to St. Augustine. When the general met with them, the chiefs agreed to surrender all property taken from the whites, but showed no willingness to surrender themselves. Therefore, Hernandez seized the group, consisting of seventy-one warriors, six women, and four blacks, including John Cavallo.[31]

This capture was the second and most famous of Jesup's breaches of the rules of war. Jesup had long believed that the Mikasukis, whom Osceola led, and the Tallahassees, Hitchitis, and Yuchis, along with the blacks, stood in the way of peace. If they could be disposed of, he believed he would "have but little difficulty with the Seminoles proper." He blamed Osceola, Wild Cat, and John Cavallo for their having failed to fulfill the agreement of Fort Dade.[32] The propriety of Jesup's actions has been argued elsewhere, and is not to the point here.[33] He had got results. After two months of the fall campaign, he had most of the leading "war spirits" in custody, had taken about five hundred Indians and blacks, and had killed about thirty others.[34]

A few days after the seizure of Osceola, four other blacks and Osceola's family surrendered. In this latter party were his two wives, his two children, his sister, three warriors, and about forty blacks.[35]

In late October, Jesup prepared to mount another campaign. He placed Colonel Zachary Taylor in command of all troops and posts south of the Withlacoochee, north of Charlotte Harbor, and west of the Kissimmee. Jesup had learned that the Indians were near Lake Istokpoga, southeast of where the trail crossed Pease Creek; Taylor was to attack them there. Abraham, Murray, and William Factor were to be used as guides and interpreters. Jesup, still distrustful of the blacks, told Taylor to insure Abraham's loyalty by informing him that Jesup had learned from prisoners recently taken that twenty warriors had been appointed to kill Abraham for aiding the whites. He was to assure Murray that if he remained loyal, his wife and his cousin Katy would be free. Above all, Taylor was not to send Abraham or Murray with messages to the Indians, for they would surely be killed. That task was to go to Bob, who could travel safely among the Seminoles. While these preparations were being made, captives were being brought in elsewhere. Near the end of October, General Hernandez brought in thirty-five captive Indians and blacks. A major setback occurred, however, on the night of November 29, when Wild Cat, John Cavallo, sixteen warriors, and two women escaped from Fort Marion at St. Augustine and made their way south to join the hostiles.[36]

JESUP'S THIRD BREACH OF THE RULES OF WAR

Another major setback came in the form of a delegation of Cherokees who had been sent by the government to try to persuade the Seminoles to emigrate. Jesup resented their coming, but finally allowed them to enter hostile territory, led by Coa Hadjo. They returned to Fort Mellon on December 3 with Micanopy, Cloud, Tuskegee, and Nocose Yohola. Jesup met with them on December 5 and demanded the immediate surrender of their people and the rest of the Seminoles. The chiefs agreed, and Jesup sent messages to those who were still out, keeping the chiefs as hostages. The Cherokees also went back to do what they could to persuade the rest to come in, but this time they failed. They returned on January 14, and Jesup immediately made prisoners of the seventy-three he had held as hostages, among whom was one black. He loaded them on a steamer and sent them to St. Augustine.[37]

This was Jesup's third famous breach of the rules of war. The Cherokee delegation was outraged and felt that its honor had been violated. John Ross, the principal chief of the Cherokees, protested against "this unprecedented violation of that sacred rule which had ever been recognized by every nation." The Cherokees felt that the Seminole chiefs had come into Jesup's headquarters at Fort Mellon under a flag of truce. They blamed the ultimate failure of their negotiations on Wild Cat's escape from St. Augustine, which produced "A sudden distrust and change of mind of the chiefs and warriors still outside."[38]

JESUP'S PROCLAMATION

Those blacks who made up the third group of black emigrants had separated themselves from their Indian masters and come in voluntarily. Most of them did so after the battle of Lockahatchee on January 24, 1838. This battle led to a conference on February 8 between Jesup and the chiefs Tuskegee and Halleck Hadjo and to communications with the black chiefs August and John Cavallo. The chiefs agreed to assemble within ten days at Jesup's camp, south of Fort Jupiter, and to surrender all of the blacks among them, whether their own or those captured from United States citizens, and to await the decision of the President as to whether they must emigrate or might remain on lands assigned to them in Florida. Jesup promised to recommend a grant of a small tract in south-western Florida, but he made it clear that the blacks were to be separated from them at once and sent to the West, whether the Indians were permitted to remain in Florida or not. To the blacks it was stipulated that

they would be sent west as part of the Seminole nation and settled in a
separate village under the protection of the United States. This stipulation
was assented to by Tuskegee and Halleck Hadjo. To the black chiefs August
and John Cavallo, he sent promises of freedom and protection if they
separated from the Indians and surrendered.[39] These leaders and Jesup
himself later interpreted this promise as applying to all blacks, and they
responded as might be expected.

On February 11, Jesup wrote to Secretary of War Poinsett, asking that
the Seminoles be allowed to remain in Florida. While the chiefs awaited
an answer, they encamped nearby. The blacks began assembling in such
large numbers that Jesup put them and the Indians in the charge of Second
Lieutenant W. G. Freeman, who was ordered to enroll them for emigration.
In response to Jesup's offer of freedom, 154, including the black leader
July, were brought in by the blacks August and Latty. Taking advantage
of the fact that the Indians were dispersed in small bands over the territory,
Jesup ordered 118 of the blacks sent to Tampa Bay. Thirteen others were
retained because of illness, and Sam Bowlegs was retained to act as an
interpreter.[40]

By March 1838, Jesup had succeeded in separating most of the blacks
from the Indians and had sent them to Tampa for immediate removal.
In all, his troops had taken about 240 blacks in the present campaign,
including nearly all of the slaves belonging to United States citizens. These
latter had been restored to their owners. By March 15, officials estimated
that not more than fifty blacks of all ages remained with the Seminoles
and that not more than five or six of those were the property of whites.
Of the blacks surrendered to that point, between forty and fifty were
capable of bearing arms, and Jesup felt that their surrender would weaken
the Indians more than the loss of the same number of their own people.[41]

ORDERS TO EMIGRATE

About this time, word came that the War Department had refused to
establish a reservation for the Seminoles; they must emigrate. Jesup called
a council to inform them, but the Indians failed to appear. To prevent
hostilities from being resumed, he ordered Colonel David E. Twiggs to
disarm and take captive all of the Indians in the camp and to take immediately to Tampa Bay the blacks with Micanopy's and Cloud's families as

well as Tuskegee and his family. The rest of the Indians were to be sent
to St. Augustine as soon as possible. On the following day, he ordered
Zachary Taylor to send to Fort Pike all of the Indians and blacks with
him except Abraham's, Toney's, and Cudjo's families. That was the "only
means of securing them completely, and preventing improper intercourse
with them by white men."[42]

As far as the blacks were concerned, Jesup's promise of freedom in
exchange for voluntary separation from their Indian allies remained in
effect. Throughout the remainder of the war, blacks surrendering on
their own volition claimed freedom under "Jesup's proclamation," as they
called it, and had the various commanders write statements to that effect.
These "free papers" were often produced in the Indian Territory as evidence
of their status.

FOURTH GROUP–ALLIGATOR'S FOLLOWERS

The fourth group of black emigrants to the West consisted of those
who surrendered with Alligator. One of the most hostile Seminoles, having
been at Dade's massacre and at the battles at Withlacoochee and Okeechobee,
Alligator had sent word to Jesup in March 1838 that he desired peace, and
offered to surrender under certain conditions. Jesup had little faith in
him, but agreed that if he surrendered, he would be entitled to all of his
property, including his blacks who had not previously separated and surrendered. Jesup sent Abraham and Holatoochee to see Alligator; they
brought him and eighty-eight others, including John Cavallo and twenty-
seven other blacks, to Fort Bassinger where they surrendered in the first
week in April.[43]

FIFTH AND SIXTH GROUPS–BLACKS OF KNOWN OWNERSHIP

The fifth group of black emigrants to the West were those brought in
by their owners and emigrated with them. According to Jesup's policy
and the promises he made to the Indians, the status of these blacks did
not change when they arrived in the Indian Territory.

The sixth group of blacks were those who were really the property of
whites but were not claimed by or returned to their owners before emigration. Official government sanction of the emigration of such blacks came

in the spring of 1841. This group will be treated in detail in relation to Jesup's successors as commander of the army in Florida.

BLACK PARTISANS

A final class of black emigrants to the West might be added—those who claimed freedom because of partisan action on behalf of the United States. The promises made to the families of Abraham, Murray, and others have been treated. There were others who had lived among the Indians but who had not borne arms for them; they voluntarily gave their services to the United States. Foremost among them was Cudjo.

Cudjo had become the interpreter at the Seminole agency in 1827, a job he held until the Seminole war broke out. As interpreter, Cudjo signed the Treaty of Payne's Landing and, like Abraham, was granted the sum of two hundred dollars for his abandoned improvements upon removal. In 1836, it was suggested that the amount granted by the treaty to Abraham be added to that granted to Cudjo since Abraham had been engaged on the side of the Seminoles in the fighting. Cudjo, however, had been faithful and was described as "needy and a cripple" who was "advancing well in years."[44]

When the war broke out, Cudjo remained with the whites. As a result, he lost 150 cattle and fifteen horses to the hostile Seminoles, for which he asked remuneration in 1836. Those who knew him supported the claim. "Cudjo is really so worthy & deserving man; & has exerted himself so efficiently to advance the views of the government that I feel a great desire to see justice done him," said one officer. At the time, Cudjo had been hired by the government as interpreter for the officers in charge of emigration and was expected to travel with the emigrants to the West. One writer has suggested that Cudjo remained with the whites because of the partial paralysis from which he suffered. Whatever his reasons, Cudjo became a valuable aid to General Jesup with whom he lived.[45]

One of Cudjo's sons, Ned, was also in the American camp. In August 1837, a party of twenty Mikasukis arrived at Fort King and encamped about two miles out. Cudjo's eldest son was among them. He sent Ned out, and the other son came in. From him, Captain P. H. Galt, commander at Fort King, obtained information about the disposition of the Indians toward war. Jesup warned Galt to be vigilant and not to allow any hostile Indians or blacks within the pickets. He did not distrust Cudjo's honesty and loyalty, but felt that "both his sons require close looking after." For that reason, he wanted Galt to let Cudjo know the details of his plans to recruit a number of Indian troops for the second campaign, suspecting that word would get back to the hostiles through Cudjo's sons. Cudjo's loyalty was never in doubt. In September 1838, Acting Agent John C. Casey wrote that "though the Seminole negroes are generally very bad subjects, yet Cudjo is a faithful interpreter and has rendered real service during this war."[46]

Another noted black who never bore arms for the Seminoles but served the whites was William Factor, better known as Billy. He had lived among the Apalachicolas since childhood. His mother, Rose, was the wife of Sam Factor, an Indian who freed them. When the war broke out, the Factors were sympathetic to the American cause. In 1837, Captain Casey hired Billy as herdsman for the government, and he served as interpreter for the Creek warriors as well as for the army. He was used as a courier, sometimes having to perform his duties under dangerous circumstances.[47] He was one of the interpreters assigned to Colonel Taylor during his campaign in the winter of 1837-38 and served the army until he emigrated in 1841.

SHIPMENT OF BLACKS FROM TAMPA

Many of the black emigrants were assembled with the Indians at Tampa Bay during the spring of 1838. On April 6, Jesup ordered his officers to retain all Indians and blacks who could be trusted to remain faithful and who could be of any use as guides and interpreters in the war effort. The rest were to be sent immediately by sea to New Orleans for subsequent shipment by steamboat to Fort Gibson. An emigration party of eighty-seven blacks and three Indians arrived at New Orleans on April 9, another group of forty-seven blacks arrived on May 11, and a group of twenty-six Indians and seventy-four blacks arrived on May 14.[48]

Shipping the blacks from Tampa was the last significant official act Jesup performed as commander in Florida. At his request, he was relieved of command on May 15. That day, Jesup signed a statement which said that Abraham, "interpreter of the Seminole nation," was engaged in the service of the United States on the condition that if he should prove faithful, he and his family were to be free. Jesup signed a second statement which said that when Murray was captured at the Panasaufka Swamp, he gave

Jesup important information relative to the positions of the Indians and the disposition of the several chiefs. As a result, Jesup had contracted with him on the part of the United States to secure his freedom if he proved faithful.[49] Thus, Jesup's last acts as commander were aimed at fulfilling the promises he had made to some of the Seminole blacks.

During his command, Jesup had obtained immediate results through his policy regarding the blacks. Most significant was the great reduction in the Indians' fighting force and destruction of the Seminole economy by removing large numbers of their farming class. He had made it impossible for the Indians to resume the war on a large scale. His promises to many of the Indians and blacks, however, were not written down, and they sometimes conflicted with each other. Nevertheless, he had pledged his word as an official of the United States, and the Seminoles and the blacks expected the government to honor it.

Jesup's policy indicates that removal of the blacks was as much an attempt to solve Florida's "Negro problem" as it was an attempt to solve the "Indian problem." But instead of solving problems, it simply transferred them to a new setting. The seven groups of black emigrants to the West, as described above, were defined according to the terms of their surrender or the circumstances of their capture, which formed the bases on which they tried to define their status during the first decade after removal. Many had legitimate claims to freedom on the basis of Jesup's promises. Others who had no such claims later made nebulous claims to freedom by virtue of the vague terms "Jesup's proclamation" or "Jesup's promises of freedom."

Jesup's failure to put the agreements in writing was perhaps his greatest mistake regarding the blacks. All of their claims to freedom, valid or not, depended upon whether the government would support the agreements he had made with the various groups and individuals. The War Department had overtly sanctioned the Fort Dade agreement and, by its silence, sanctioned all others. By failing to put them in writing, however, Jesup simply contributed to the anomalous position in which many of the black emigrants found themselves in the West.

NOTES

1. *Official Opinions of the Attorneys General of the United States* (Washington, 1852), 4:725.

2. John K. Mahon, *History of the Second Seminole War, 1835-1842*
(Gainesville: University of Florida Press, 1967), 195, 196; 25 Cong., 2
Sess., *House Executive Document 381,* 1-2; C. A. Harris to Captain Samuel
Cooper, May 2, 1838, 25 Cong., 3 Sess., *House Document 225* (hereafter
cited as *Document 225*), 44.

3. Lieutenant T. B. Linnard to Major Isaac Clark, June 2, 1837;
Linnard to Lieutenant G. H. Terrett, June 2, 1837; General Thomas S.
Jesup to Colonel J. Gadsden, June 14, 1837; and Jesup to Roger Jones,
July 20, 1837, National Archives Record Group 94 (Records of the
Office of the Adjutant General), *General Jesup's Papers,* Letters Sent
(hereafter cited as *JPLS*).

4. Registry of Negro Prisoners, *Document 225,* 67-69; the registry
is reproduced as List A in the Appendix.

5. List of Creek Volunteers, June 13, 1837, *General Jesup's Papers,*
Letters Received (hereafter cited as *JPLR*), Box 12; Orders No. 175,
September 6, 1837, and Jesup to Lieutenant W. G. Freeman, Septem-
ber 9, 1837, *Document 225,* 4, 72; Jesup to Lieutenant Frederick Searle,
September 9, 1837, and Linnard to Captain John Page, September 22,
1837, *JPLS*.

6. Jesup to Joel R. Poinsett, September 23, 1837, *JPLS*; Lieutenant
T. T. Sloan to Harris, May 6, 1838, and Lieutenant James A. Chambers
to Major R. A. Zantzinger, February 18, 1838, *Document 225,* 43, 24;
Zantzinger to Chambers, February 1, 1838, *JPLR,* Box 12.

7. Kenneth Wiggins Porter, *The Negro on the American Frontier*
(New York: Arno Press and The New York Times, 1971), 316-317;
Mahon, 197-199.

8. Porter, 296, 305-307, 313-314.

9. Capitulation of the Seminole Nation of Indians and Their Allies,
March 6, 1837, *Document 225,* 52; Mahon, 200; Jesup to Major T. Cross,
November 17, 1837, 25 Cong., 2 Sess., *House Document 327* (hereafter
cited as *Document 327*), 10.

10. Jesup to Jones, March 6, 1837, *Document 225,* 51; Jesup to William
L. Marcy, April 3, 1848, National Archives Microfilm Publications, *Microcopy M574* (Special Files of the Office of Indian Affairs, 1807-1904)-13,
Special File 96: Seminole Claims to Certain Negroes, 1841-1849 (hereafter
cited as *File 96*).

11. Jesup to Jones, March 18, 1837, *Document 225,* 54.

12. Mahon, 201; Gad Humphreys, et al., to Poinsett, March 18, 1837,
Jesup to R. K. Call, April 18, 1837, and Jesup to Colonel W. S. Harney,
April 8, 1837, *Document 225,* 11, 10, 55.

13. Harris to Jesup, May 5, 1837, *Document 225,* 39.

14. Mahon, 203-204.

15. Jesup to Jones, July 20, 1837, *JPLS.*

16. Porter, 250, 333; Jesup to Lieutenant John C. Casey, July 18, 1837, *JPLS*; Registry of Negro Prisoners, *Document 225,* 69.

17. Porter, 318; Registry of Negro Prisoners, *Document 225,* 68.

18. Registry of Negro Prisoners, *Document 225,* 69; Humphreys to Colonel R. B. Mason, December 5, 1845, National Archives Record Group 393 (Records of the United States Army Continental Commands, 1821-1920), *Fort Gibson,* Volume "Indian Affairs," 15; Statement of David Barnet, February 2, 1842, National Archives Microfilm Publications, *Microcopy M234* (Records of the Office of Indian Affairs, Letters Received)-226, H1047-42. *Microcopy M234* is hereafter cited as *M234,* followed by the roll number.

19. Jesup to John Crowell, June 17, 1837, *JPLS* and *Document 225,* 18. Murray was, in fact, killed. While on a march with the army near Fort King, he was killed by a soldier. J. W. Washbourne to George W. Manypenny, May 27, 1856, *M234*-802, W68-56.

20. Jesup to Poinsett, June 16, 1837, *JPLS.*

21. Jesup to Colonel Samuel Miller, July 8, 1837, *JPLS.*

22. Miller to Jesup, July 13, 1837, *JPLR,* Box 12; Abraham to Jesup, April 25, 1838, reprinted in Porter, 332.

23. Jesup to Brigadier General W. K. Armistead, June 6, 1837, *JPLS.*

24. Jesup to Harris, September 24, 1837, and Linnard to Miller, July 16, 1837, *JPLS;* Casey to Jesup, July 14, 1837, and Miller to Jesup, July 16, 1837, *JPLR,* Box 12.

25. Jesup, years later, put the number of captives at forty-three; Jesup to Marcy, April 3, 1848, *File 96.* Mahon (190, 196), however, lists forty-one. More details appear in Jesup to Lieutenant Colonel D. Caulfield, May 20, 1837, *JPLS.*

26. Jesup to Colonel John Warren, July 7, 1837, *JPLS;* Jesup to Lieutenant Colonel W. J. Mills, July 24, 1837, and Orders No. 160, August 3, 1837, *Document 225,* 19, 4.

27. Jesup to Captain P. H. Galt, August 13, 1837, Jesup to Captain David S. Walker, September 7, 1837, and Jesup to William Armstrong, September 17, 1837, *JPLS;* Jesup to Captain B. L. E. Bonneville, September 17, 1837, *Document 225,* 21.

28. Jesup to Major Stewart, September 15, 1837, Jesup to Poinsett, September 25, 1837, Jesup to Casey, September 25, 1837, and Jesup to Call, September 27, 1837, *JPLS;* Mahon, 211-212, 214. John Philip became an interpreter for the army, claiming freedom under Jesup's promise of freedom to the blacks who surrendered. In 1839, he was sent out with a message to Wild Cat, who took him prisoner. In 1841, John escaped and came to Sarasota. He again became a guide and interpreter, staying with

the army until 1845. That year, Wild Cat made a claim for him, but the army officers felt that John was free and refused to send him to the West. After John left the army, he went to work at the T. P. Kennedy trading house at Charlotte Harbor. Marcellus Duval to Commissioner, December 6, 1845, and Captain J. T. Sprague to William Medill, May 18, 1846, *M234-*801, D1046-46 and S4006-46.

29. Jesup to Call, September 27, 1837, *JPLS.*

30. Jesup to Poinsett, October 8, 1837; Jesup to Jones, October 19, 1837; and Jesup to Call, October 22, 1837, *JPLS.*

31. General Joseph M. Hernandez to Jesup, October 22, 1837, Jesup to Lieutenant R. H. Peyton, October 20, 1837, and Notes of a Talk Between Brigadier General Hernandez and the Indian Chiefs, . . . on the 21st October, 1837, *Document 327;* Jesup to Hernandez (two memoranda), October 21, 1837, *JPLS;* Mahon, 214-215.

32. Jesup to Major General Alexander Macomb, July 11, 1837; Jesup to Captain J. A. d'Lagnel, July 14, 1837; Jesup to Charles J. Nourse, August 13, 1837; Jesup to Poinsett, October 10, 1837; and Jesup to Jones, October 21, 1837, *JPLS.*

33. Mahon, 216-217.

34. Jesup to Jones, October 21, 1837, *JPLS;* Jesup to Poinsett, October 22, 1837, *Document 327,* 3. Osceola was imprisoned at St. Augustine and then transferred to Fort Moultrie at Charleston, where he died in late January 1838. See Mahon, 217-218.

35. Jesup to Mills, October 23, 1837, *JPLS;* Mahon, 217.

36. Jesup to Colonel Zachary Taylor, October 27, 1837, *JPLS;* Captain Harvey Brown to Chambers, November 2, 1837, *JPLR,* Box 15; Mahon, 223-224; Porter, 253.

37. Jesup to Poinsett, December 6, 1837, and Jesup to Jones, December 14, 1837, *Document 327,* 8-9; Mahon, 222-223.

38. John Ross to Poinsett, January 2, 1838, *Document 327,* 12.

39. Jesup to Marcy, April 3 and July 1, 1848, *File 96.*

40. Mahon, 235-236; Orders No. 62, February 25, 1838, in Jesup to Marcy, July 1, 1848, *File 96* and *Document 225,* 5; Negroes brought in by August and Latty at Fort Jupiter, *JPLR,* Box 12 (the list of blacks is reproduced as List B in the Appendix); Porter, 255; Orders No. 63, February 27, 1838, and Jesup to Jones, February 28, 1838, *File 96* and *Document 225,* 6; List of Seminole Indians and Negroes sent from Fort Jupiter . . . , and List of Indians and Indian negroes enrolled for emigration . . . , *Document 225,* 74-79. These lists are reproduced as Lists C and D in the Appendix. July later became a guide for the army, was killed by hostile Indians, and was buried by the troops. Washbourne to Manypenny, May 27, 1856, *M234-*802, W68-56.

41. Jesup to G. R. Gilmer, March 5, 1838, Jesup to Armistead, March 6, 1838, and Freeman to Harris, March 15, 1838, *Document 225*, 25; Jesup to Call, March 15, 1838, Jesup to Lieutenant D. H. Vinton, March 17, 1838, and Jesup to Poinsett, March 18, 1838, *File 96*.

42. Mahon, 237; Orders No. 77 and Orders No. 78, March 21 and March 22, 1838, and Jesup to Taylor, March 22, 1838, *Document 225*, 6, 25.

43. Jesup to Marcy, July 1, 1848, Jesup to Poinsett, March 14, 1838, and Jesup to William Wilkins, May 22, 1844, *File 96;* Mahon, 238.

44. Joseph W. Harris to Commissary General of Subsistence, October 5, 1836, National Archives Record Group 75 (Records of the Bureau of Indian Affairs), *Records of the Commissary General of Subsistence*, Letters Received (hereafter cited as *CGSLR*), Seminole, and *Copies of Records, ca. 1823-1860*, Seminole Emigration; Wiley Thompson to Elbert Herring, March 3, 1835, and August 1, 1835, *M234*-800, Frames 336 and 421; Estimate of the Probable Loss of Property Accruing to the Friendly Seminole Indians, July 27, 1836, *Copies of Records, ca. 1823-1860*, Seminole Emigration.

45. Joseph W. Harris to C. A. Harris, September 13, 1836, and Joseph W. Harris to Commissary General of Subsistence, September 14, 1836, *CGSLR*; Kenneth W. Porter, "Negro Guides and Interpreters in the Early Stages of the Seminole War, December 28, 1835-March 6, 1837," *Journal of Negro History*, 35 (April 1950), 177; Casey to C. A. Harris, September 22, 1838, *M234*-289, C824-38.

46. Galt to Jesup, August 11, 1837, *JPLR*, Box 12; Jesup to Galt, August 13, 1837, *JPLS;* Porter, "Negro Guides and Interpreters," 178; Casey to C. A. Harris, September 22, 1838, *M234*-289, C824-38.

47. W. K. Sebastian to Commissioner, May 1, 1852, *M234*-801, S90-52; M. Thompson to Jacob Thompson, December 6, 1858, *M234*-802, T346-58; Chambers to Galt, October 15, 1837, *JPLS*.

48. Freeman to C. A. Harris, March 24 and March 30, 1838; Jesup to Taylor, March 30 and March 31, 1838; Jesup to Armistead, April 1, 1838; Chambers to Casey, April 1, 1838; Orders No. 88, April 6, 1838; Freeman to Lieutenant John G. Reynolds, April 7, 1838; and Chambers to Reynolds, April 29, 1838, *Document 225*, 81, 82, 7, 26-27, 101; List of Negroes as turned over by Lieut. Terrett, 9th April 1838, List of Negroes as turned over by Lieut. Mack, U.S.A., 11th May 1838, and List of Negroes received at Tampa Bay, National Archives Record Group 75, *Miscellaneous Muster Rolls, 1836-46*. These lists of blacks appear as Lists E, F, and G in the Appendix.

49. Mahon, 239, 240; Statements of Jesup, May 15, 1838, *File 96*.

3

The emigrants

Jesup had reasons other than military ones for ordering the immediate shipment of all blacks, except interpreters and guides, to New Orleans. Whites were making claims to some of them, and Jesup knew that if the matter was tied up in Florida, emigration would be delayed, increasing chances of a new outbreak of the war. A number captured by the Creek warriors had been returned to their white owners, and during Jesup's last campaign a few more had been taken and restored to their owners. But a number of blacks who had surrendered or were captured were claimed under what Jesup called "pretended purchases" from the Indians. Some had once been in the possession of the white claimants but had run away to join the hostiles or had been captured by them. Some had never left the Indians after the "pretended purchases" by whites. For the most part, the Indians viewed these claims as unjust or fraudulent, asserting that many times the sales were made by Indians who were not the real owners, or that the agreed price had never been paid.[1] Some of these claims followed the emigrants to their new home. The blacks had long known that they would be vulnerable to claims once they were assembled for removal, and in the spring of 1838, it appeared that their fears would prove correct and that many of them would never reach the West.

GAD HUMPHREYS' CLAIM

The principal white claimant was Gad Humphreys, the former Seminole agent, who had championed the Seminoles' cause during the 1820s. Humphreys had tried without success to retrieve his slaves in the spring of 1837. Jesup did not believe Humphreys' claim was valid. He believed that there was no legal authority under the Intercourse Act of 1834 to sanction the purchase of slaves from Indians. Second, since agents were forbidden to trade with the Indians, any purchase Humphreys made while Seminole agent was invalid. Finally, after he left the post of agent, Humphreys could not trade with the Indians unless he was a licensed trader, and he was not. When Humphreys presented his claim again in the spring of 1838, Jesup claimed he had neither the time nor means to investigate the claims nor the legal authority to decide them. Since he considered the matter to involve questions of personal and national honor as well as of constitutional law, he decided to send the blacks west.[2]

There was no doubt that Humphreys had lost some slaves, whether or not he held them legally. After he left office as agent, he had settled on a plantation in Alachua County near the Indian country. In 1830, a number of his plantation slaves absconded and remained with the Indians until 1833, when they were restored by the chiefs. Shortly thereafter, twenty-five absconded and rejoined the Indians. Humphreys failed in 1835 to have them returned, and in the summer of 1836, the Indians captured thirty-four more. Humphreys was among the Floridians who protested Jesup's right to treat with the blacks at Fort Dade and to remove them to the West without giving white claimants a chance to recover their slaves. To prevent delays in amassing the Indians and blacks for removal, Jesup had issued Orders No. 79 on April 5, 1837, prohibiting any white not in the service of the United States to enter any part of the territory between the St. Johns River and the Gulf of Mexico, south of Fort Drane about twenty miles south of present-day Gainesville. This action was to stop the "interference of unprincipled white men with the negro property of the Seminoles." The same order provided for the return of all slaves at Tampa Bay who were the property of United States citizens. They were to be sent to St. Marks and their owners notified to come and take them immediately.[3]

Humphreys and others who had slave claims against the Seminoles objected to Jesup's order. They protested "against allowing the Indians to convert the slave of the white man into the servant and feudatory of the savage," and against the "quasi independence he feels under Indian dominance." Humphreys applied personally to Jesup for the return of his slaves, some of whom he suspected were among those captured by Jesup's forces or received under the convention of Fort Dade. He sent Jesup a list of forty-seven blacks whom he claimed were among the Indians, but he received no satisfaction. By May 1838, he was convinced that his slaves were being protected "with sinister privity and connivance of those whose duty it is to demand their surrender." He asked Secretary Joel Poinsett to prevent any of his blacks from being sent out of Florida.[4]

Some blacks Humphreys claimed were among those captured by the Creek warriors and had been at Fort Pike for months. He wanted them returned until he could prove his claim. Among them were Katy and her daughter Fanny. Katy, who had belonged to a Seminole woman Colkeechowa, had married Mungo by whom she had four children—Sally, Nancy, Jim, and Grace. During a time of great scarcity among the Indians, while Florida still belonged to the Spanish, Mungo went to the trading house of Horatio Dexter at Volusia to obtain subsistence. Later, Mungo sent for Katy and the children, and while they were at Volusia, the brother and sister of Colkeechowa sold them to Dexter. Colkeechowa, who received no part of the purchase price, called on Humphreys to get her slaves back. Dexter advertised them for sale at St. Augustine, where Humphreys went and rescued them by buying them. By this time Katy had had another son, Israel. When he and Jim grew up and became acquainted with their history, they ran away and joined their Indian owner. Katy, two of her daughters, and their children remained with Humphreys. Katy was among Humphreys' slaves who were captured by the Seminoles in the summer of 1836, and she and Fanny were captured by Jesup's troops and sent to Fort Pike in June 1837. Katy was a cousin of Murray, the black who served as guide after his capture. To keep him loyal, General Jesup promised to secure Katy's freedom.[5]

Humphreys wanted his claim and all others like it submitted to a judicial tribunal in Florida's jurisdiction, for it was difficult and expensive to wage a legal battle in a "foreign court," he said. The War Department was deaf to Humphreys' pleas. Officials felt that the department's action in the matter had concluded when, in April, the Creek delegation had been told to dispose of the blacks.[6]

THE CREEKS' CLAIM

The Creeks complicated Humphreys' claim and others by selling their interest in the blacks whom they had captured. In April 1838, their delegation to Washington asked for a settlement of their claim. Upon failing to purchase the blacks from the Creeks in 1837, Jesup had suggested that their value be charged against the Seminole annuity. Commissioner C. A.

Harris felt, however, that to do so would deprive the friendly Seminoles as well as those who had been hostile. In another way, it would be paying the Creeks with their own money, for the Treaty of Payne's Landing had provided for the reunion of the Creeks and Seminoles and for their sharing annuities. Jesup had also suggested that Congress appropriate the money to pay for the blacks and for their transportation to Africa, but Commissioner Harris felt that the government could not do that since public opinion at the time was sensitive toward the subject of slavery. The alternative was to turn them over to the Creeks. Taking the blacks from their Seminole owners, with whom they were being held at New Orleans, would be a delicate matter, and Harris felt that the transfer should take place before the blacks were taken to the western country, for seizure of the slaves there would likely result in conflict between the two tribes.[7]

Following this latter suggestion, the War Department ordered the blacks placed at the Creek delegation's disposal. By this time, there were about eighty-five blacks claimed by the Creeks. The Creeks would have to identify those they had captured and to eliminate those that whites claimed as stolen or runaway property. For these latter, the Creeks would be paid twenty dollars each under Jesup's original agreement with them. Commissioner Harris directed the Creeks to divest themselves of the slaves before they moved west, assuring them that any arrangement they made respecting the sale of the blacks would be approved by the Department of War.[8]

The Creek delegation immediately sold the blacks for $14,600 to James C. Watson of Columbus, Georgia. The sale was approved, and General Jesup and Major R. A. Zantzinger, commander at Fort Pike, were ordered to turn the blacks over to Nathaniel F. Collins, Watson's brother-in-law, who was to hold the slaves, subject to the lawful claims of all white persons. Abraham and his family were excluded from the sale because of Jesup's promises to him. Officials were cautioned to deliver only those blacks captured by the Creeks. The problem handed Collins was a difficult one. Commissioner Harris gave him a list of blacks believed to be included in the sale. All of those Collins sought were supposedly at Fort Pike, but it was for Collins to find them, without expense of any kind to the United States.[9]

THE LOVE CLAIM

Meanwhile, because of the sickly condition of the Seminoles and blacks at Fort Pike, General Edmund P. Gaines, commander of the Western

Military Division, had ordered Major Isaac Clark, the quartermaster at
New Orleans, to prepare to move the prisoners to Fort Gibson as soon as
possible.[10] But Clark was unable to carry out the order because the heirs
of Hugh Love of Georgia filed claims for sixty-seven of the blacks, whom
they claimed Love had purchased from Creek individuals in 1835.

Love, a licensed trader among the Creeks in the West, had supposedly
bought the blacks from a Creek woman named Gray whose relatives had
left the eastern Creek Nation many years earlier and joined the Seminoles.
About 1795, they returned from Florida and stole her slaves, consisting
of Pompy and Dolly and their children, and took them to Florida where
they had remained until removal. About 1815, the Seminole chief Hicks
informed Mrs. Gray of their whereabouts, and she sent her son and a
company of men to recover them. The blacks fought with and defeated
the company, killing some and seriously wounding her son. Mrs. Gray
never tried to recover them again. After his purchase, Hugh Love started
to Florida to capture the blacks, but he was thwarted by the Seminole
agent. He died shortly thereafter. John Love, his brother, took up the
claim. In May 1838, he obtained a writ of sequestration from the local
courts in New Orleans to keep the army from removing the slaves from
the jurisdiction of the court. The Seminoles then at New Orleans, including
Micanopy and other chiefs, were nearly in a state of mutiny. They believed
that, as they had suspected before the war, removal was aimed at taking
their blacks from them; the government had brought them to New Orleans
to rob them. Commissioner Harris directed U.S. District Attorney Thomas
Slidell of New Orleans to advise the Indians and assist them in retaining
their legitimate property. Above all, Slidell was to prevent, if possible,
impediments from being thrown in the way of their speedy removal to
Fort Gibson.[11]

John Love named General Gaines as defendant in a suit for recovery
of the slaves or damages of $67,000, and the blacks were taken from Fort
Pike and put in the local jail. On May 9, Gaines asked the court to set
aside the order on two basic grounds: that the slaves were prisoners of
war, taken in combat, over whom the army had exclusive custody and
that there was no proper defendant in the case. Gaines denied that he had
control over the prisoners since the boundary of his jurisdiction was the
Mississippi River and the barracks were on the east side, which was under
Jesup's jurisdiction. The judge held, however, that Gaines did have control
over the prisoners. He aptly pointed out that only a few days earlier the

general had ordered the prisoners transported up river. No witness could be found to swear that any of the blacks were carrying arms when they were captured; therefore, the slaves were not prisoners of war but the property of the Indian prisoners. It was useless to argue, the judge said, that once the prisoners reached their destination and were released from military control, the plaintiffs could prosecute their claim. It would be too difficult to get the Seminoles to give up the property. Therefore, he upheld the jurisdiction of the court.[12]

INTERFERENCE BY LIEUTENANT JOHN G. REYNOLDS

At this point Lieutenant John G. Reynolds, who was in charge of removing the Seminoles, returned from Tampa Bay. During the preceding few weeks he had failed to get the first contingent of Seminoles and blacks sent up the river to Fort Gibson. He had arrived at New Orleans in March with a contingent including Micanopy, Coa Hadjo, and Philip, planning to pick up the blacks who had been captured by the Creeks, move them from Fort Pike to New Orleans Barracks, and prepare them for the trip upstream. However, Major Zantzinger refused to let the blacks go because Reynolds' instructions did not specifically name the blacks for emigration and therefore thwarted plans to move the first large party of black emigrants upstream. Correct orders were issued by General Gaines, and Reynolds once more made arrangements to depart. He left the blacks at Fort Pike until he was ready to leave, for he was convinced that "many individuals with fraudulent claims" waited for the blacks to arrive in New Orleans to make their claims.[13] However, Reynolds was ordered back to Florida before he could depart.

On his return to New Orleans, Reynolds made immediate arrangements to send all of the Indian and black prisoners, now totaling 1,160, to Fort Gibson, except those blacks for whom claims had been made. Like Gaines, he felt that the Love claims were fraudulent, but he decided to leave the sixty-seven blacks, their Indian owners, and witnesses in the case.[14]

Meanwhile, Love's heirs dropped their suit against Gaines and filed another, claiming only thirty-two of the original group of blacks, because John Love had not been able to identify all of them. Upon his arrival at New Orleans, he had found Pompy, Dolly, about thirty of their descendants, and others in one camp and had them secured. The rest were in another camp, and when word reached there that Love was on his way, all of the blacks in the camp painted themselves so that none could be identified.[15]

Pompy subsequently died, leaving thirty-two in custody. Most were the descendants of Pompy and his two wives, Melinda and Dolly, who was about seventy-five at the time. The old Mikasuki chief Kinhijah (also known as Capichee Micco) had bought Melinda and Dolly near St. Augustine during the English reign in Florida. The women, not related, were purchased from different men; both became wives of Pompy. From them came most of the slaves of whom Miccopotokee was guardian. He inherited them from his maternal uncle Kinhijah according to Indian custom. At first, Miccopotokee refused to take them and left them with Tuskeneehau and his sisters, the children of Kinhijah. Tuskeneehau killed himself, and his sisters died. Then Miccopotokee took charge of the slaves by virtue of his double claim of the will and of relationship. Later, it was claimed that he held them as guardian for Tuskeneehau's daughters. He had the matter investigated by Seminole Agent Wiley Thompson in April 1835, and received a certificate of title. The following captives at New Orleans were descendants of Pompy and Melinda: Long Toney; Molly, his sister; Teena, their aunt; Mary and Nancy, her daughters; and Mary's five children. And the following were descendants of Pompy and Dolly: Prince; Peggy, Scilla, Fanny, and Eliza, daughters of Dolly; Hagar, daughter of Peggy; Hagar's baby; Bella, daughter of Scilla; Charles, Margaret, and Silvia or Silba, the children of Fanny.[16]

Several of the others claimed by Love were considered the property of Harriet Bowlegs, who had come to Jesup's camp during the peace at Fort Dade and had remained with the Americans. Described as an intelligent woman who spoke English fluently, she had had repeated assurances from Jesup and from Agent John C. Casey that all of her slaves would be secured to her in compliance with the Fort Dade agreement. Among her slaves detained by Love were Flora, who was very old, her daughter Juba, and Juba's daughter, Abbey or Cumba. Fai or Fy, the mother of Flora, had been owned by Cow Keeper, who bequeathed her to one of his female relatives, a sister of Echo Fixico. From her, King Bowlegs (Eneha Micco) purchased Flora. When King Bowlegs died, he left Flora and her offspring to his daughter Harriet. Love also claimed Noble, the son of Beck, who had been bought by Bowlegs during the English time at St. Augustine, before the birth of her first child Polly. Polly became the mistress of old Bowlegs, and he freed her and her children. After Bowlegs' death, Polly married

Toney Barnet. The other children of Beck, including Noble, were bequeathed to Harriet. Love likewise claimed Jacob and Daily, brothers, who were the grandsons of Rose, whom Bowlegs had bought. Rose and her offspring were willed to Harriet's sister, who had died in 1837, when the property passed to Harriet.[17]

Among the others detained was Louis, described as a good-looking, intelligent man about forty, who could read and write and could speak Spanish and English as well as the Indian language. Louis had been, in turn, the property of General George Brooke and Major James McIntosh. About 1830, he was bought by Don Antonio Pacheco of Sarasota. Louis, who was apparently in collusion with the Indians, had been the guide for the ill-fated command of Major Francis Dade, massacred on December 28, 1835. Finally, there were Katy and her daughter Fanny, who were claimed by Gad Humphreys.[18]

Leaving these thirty-two blacks in New Orleans, Reynolds started up-stream with the other blacks and Indians. On May nineteenth, 453 Indians embarked on the steamer *Renown,* and three days later, 674 prisoners, including 249 slaves, embarked on the *South Alabama.* There were also six free blacks. Indians in this party included the chiefs Micanopy, Coa Hadjo, and Philip.[19]

WATSON'S CLAIM ONCE MORE

Among the emigrants were some of the blacks purchased from the Creeks by J. C. Watson. His agent Nathaniel F. Collins had arrived at New Orleans on the day after Reynolds had left but overtook him at Vicksburg, where he demanded Watson's blacks. Reynolds was apprehensive because the Love claim had caused great excitement among the Seminoles in New Orleans, and not wanting to lose any time during the emigration, he persuaded Collins to travel with him as far as Little Rock, Arkansas, feeling that before they arrived there, he could prevail upon the Seminoles to give the blacks up voluntarily.[20]

Reynolds called a meeting of the chiefs and others owning slaves, read the department orders directing relinquishment of the slaves to Collins, and told the Seminoles that the Creeks would take the slaves forcibly upon their arrival at Fort Gibson, if the Seminoles did not give them up. Micanopy led the Seminoles in their refusal, saying that the department's action was contrary to the promise made them by General Jesup concerning the security of their property if they agreed to emigrate. Reynolds did not again broach the subject until they reached Little Rock, where the party was held up by low water. On the night of their arrival, he assembled the Seminoles and again they refused, this time becoming more vexed than before. Exasperated, Reynolds concluded that only force could gain Collins the slaves.[21]

He called on the governor of Arkansas for aid in taking them. Sam C. Roane, the acting governor, refused and asked that Reynolds not try to turn the blacks over within the state, especially near Little Rock, urging Reynolds to be on his way as soon as possible so that Arkansans might "be relieved from the annoyance of a hostile band of Indians and *savage negroes*." The citizens of Arkansas had been concerned about Indian hostilities ever since the government had begun to settle Indian tribes on lands west of the state. There had been much agitation among the settlers along the western border for the establishment of a fort near the line. Roane felt that the government was inviting the massacre of citizens by bringing the Indians to the West, provoking them, and then turning them loose. So he visited the chiefs and assured them that their blacks would not be taken from them; the chiefs, in turn, promised to go to their country peaceably.[22] The fact that the department had hoped to avoid removing the blacks in question was of little consequence to Roane.

After such an unfriendly reception from Roane, Reynolds went on immediately to Fort Gibson, arriving there on June 12. He asked General Matthew Arbuckle, commander of the Second Department of the Western Military Division, to use force to obtain the blacks for Collins. Arbuckle declined because it would be difficult to identify those claimed with certainty, since they were in company with such a large number of other Seminole blacks and since there was no one at Fort Gibson at the time who could point them out. The Seminole chiefs also remained adamant in their belief that the slaves claimed by the Creek warriors came under Jesup's promise that they would retain their slave property if they emigrated. Arbuckle called a council with the chiefs, and each one voluntarily promised to give up the blacks if the President of the United States decided that they must. Action of the President was not likely, for the department considered itself rid of the problem of Watson's claim. And in regard to other blacks captured by the United States troops and removed to the West, Commissioner Harris felt it "inexpedient" for the government to interpose.[23]

ARRIVALS AT FORT GIBSON

Meanwhile, blacks continued to arrive at Fort Gibson. One contingent, arriving on June 19, consisted of 117 Indians and two blacks, Samuel and Davey. Samuel, interpreter for the group, had been hired as an interpreter in March and had accompanied Lieutenant Colonel W. S. Harney on an expedition to the Jupiter River east of Lake Okeechobee, where he had remained until he was sent west. Another group of 305 Indians and thirty blacks arrived on June 28.[24]

Thwarted in his efforts to recover the slaves for Collins, Reynolds had returned with Collins to New Orleans where the Love claim remained to be settled. On June 17, the United States district attorney obtained an order to show cause why the thirty-two blacks in question should not be delivered to Gaines and Reynolds and the suit dropped. Ten days were allowed for the heirs of Love to file an appeal, but they did not. On June 27, the blacks were turned over to Reynolds, and the Love claim was dropped. For some reason, Collins, who also claimed the blacks for Watson, had left New Orleans on the preceding day. Since neither Collins nor any agent authorized by him was present, Reynolds sent the blacks immediately on their way to Fort Gibson.[25]

Reynolds himself embarked on July 11 with sixty-six Seminoles, including Alligator, and one black. There was as well a slave belonging to Micanopy who served as an interpreter. When the party reached Little Rock, Reynolds learned that the contingent of blacks who had left ahead of him had been detained there for several days because of low water and a consequent absence of boats. They had finally left with a party of emigrating Cherokees and had reached Lewisburg some seventy miles upstream near present-day Morrilton, where they were again forced to stop because of low water. They stayed there several days until their conductor had procured ox teams and wagons and started overland with them.[26]

When Reynolds and his party reached Clarksville, he learned that the blacks were encamped nearby. He rode out and brought them on board the steamer, only to be stopped again two days later by low water. Reynolds disembarked his party two miles below Fort Coffee on the north side of the river, procured the necessary wagons for the sick, baggage, and provisions, and made the last leg of the journey overland. The weather was extremely hot and the people complained considerably, but they reached Fort Gibson in good health on August 5.[27]

That done, Reynolds left for New Orleans. Little did he know that a furore awaited him there. Upon learning that he had shipped out the blacks Love claimed, Commissioner Harris had written him an urgent letter condemning the action. The department had wanted to prevent the blacks from being carried west to avoid contentions and difficulties over them between the Creeks and Seminoles. Harris felt that the Creeks would not be satisfied with the Seminoles' keeping the blacks and that the Seminoles could not live in the same country with the Creeks and see their slaves in the hands of the latter. The Secretary of War feared that the blacks would "form a dangerous population" in the new country as they had in Florida. Thus, Harris ordered Reynolds to do all he could to recover the blacks and deliver them to the Creek agent.[28]

But it was too late. Harris' letter arrived after Reynolds had gone upstream with Alligator's party. Had it arrived earlier, he could have sent the blacks back when he overtook them in Arkansas. When Reynolds answered Harris in early September, he expressed doubt whether the Creeks would have obtained the slaves, anyway, since there were many persons such as Collins ready with claims similar to Love's. He had sent the blacks on to prevent further difficulties. But Collins had not been in New Orleans when the blacks were released from custody, nor had anyone else with authority to receive them. And since he had been ordered to incur no expense in regard to the Creek claims, Reynolds had sent them on.[29]

Reynolds' problem had been aggravated by Collins, who had complained to Harris about his failure to obtain the blacks he sought from the first contingent. He charged duplicity on Reynolds' part regarding the second group. Collins claimed he was still in New Orleans when the blacks were turned over to Reynolds, and that Reynolds had set about secretly chartering a boat. Collins charged that he had demanded the slaves, but that Reynolds had claimed the sheriff would not give them up. With the sickly season coming on, Collins had left New Orleans. He felt that the release of the slaves on the day following his departure and their immediate shipment from the city smacked of a plot to deprive him of his property.[30]

Commissioner Harris was convinced that there had been "a great disregard, if not violation" of the orders of the department and asked Reynolds to explain. This attack surprised Reynolds because he had done all he could to aid Collins. What object, Reynolds asked, could he have had in clandestinely sending the blacks to Indian Territory? Reynolds' action was defended and his statements corroborated by Sheriff Fred Buisson of New Orleans, George Whitman, and John Love's attorney, Tod Robinson. Major Clark laid blame for the whole affair on the courts. He had told Collins that if the blacks were given to him in New Orleans, they would be seized on immediately by other claimants and would give the army more trouble; therefore, it would be better if they were shipped to the West where the matter could be settled.[31]

GENERAL ARBUCKLE AND THE SLAVE CLAIMS

At any rate, Reynolds was finally rid of the matter, which now lay in the hands of General Arbuckle. The matter was further complicated when J. C. Watson paid the agreed sale price to William Armstrong, the western superintendent of Indian affairs, who paid it to the Creeks on July 4. Unaware that the money had been paid, the Secretary of War directed Arbuckle to do the job which Reynolds had failed to do. But the prospects of obtaining the blacks seemed slight to Arbuckle. Now that the Creeks had been paid, they would not likely concern themselves with delivering the slaves to Watson's agent, and in spite of their promise, the Seminole chiefs would not give them up, knowing that they would be taken from the country and sold to whites. The Seminoles, still greatly under the influence of the blacks as they had been in Florida, were not likely to surrender the blacks without force. Even then, success was doubtful, for the Seminoles and the other Seminole and Creek blacks would probably come to their aid, or they would bolt and leave the country. If they were taken, it would be difficult to keep them under proper guard. Arbuckle felt that it would be best to persuade the Seminoles to refund the sale price from their annuity and settle the matter. Yet he had his orders.[32]

On September 26, 1838, when Jim Boy and several of the Creek warriors were at Fort Gibson, Arbuckle asked for their aid in turning the blacks over to Watson's agent, but having been paid, they wanted nothing further to do with the matter. Arbuckle also appealed without success to Micanopy, now recognized as the principal chief of the Seminoles, who told Arbuckle to consult the individuals who owned them. Since the owners and all of the blacks in the Seminole camp were opposed to the claim, Micanopy probably did not have the power to turn them over. Arbuckle viewed the influence of the blacks as an insidious one. In his opinion, the great number of "bad negroes" brought to the Creek country by the Seminoles would ultimately prove an injury to the tribe and to the states of Missouri and Arkansas by "furnishing a harbor for runaway negroes and horse-thieves." The only resort was force.[33]

Collins doubted that Arbuckle could obtain the blacks, so he asked Secretary of War Poinsett to seek government payment for them upon Arbuckle's failure. The suggestion was welcomed by the Secretary, who was afraid that use of military force in taking the blacks would result in disruption of Indian policy. Therefore, Superintendent William Armstrong and Arbuckle were directed to open negotiations with the Creeks to adjust all claims against the citizens or the government of the United States. If they found Watson's claim just, they were to insert a provision in any agreement they reached to allow the matter to be handled as the President might determine.[34]

The new commissioner, T. Hartley Crawford, however, agreed with Arbuckle that nothing could be gained by calling the Creek chiefs together regarding the blacks, since the chiefs had so far refused to interfere. Arbuckle maintained that the best solution was the government's paying Watson for his loss, with interest and a reasonable allowance for his time and expense in trying to recover the blacks. The matter was taken up in the House of Representatives, and a resolution was passed on January 28, 1839, calling for a complete report by the department on the disposition of all slave property captured during the Seminole War.[35] There the matter rested for the time being.

Watson had been encouraged to purchase the blacks by Secretary Joel Poinsett, and he and Commissioner Harris had done their best to prevent the slaves from reaching the West. A contemporary antislavery critic charged that they consciously attempted to return the blacks to a state of servitude, and a historian of the Seminoles has charged that Harris "emerges in the role of a public official working to obtain property for men of political influence at the expense of the Indians and to the detriment of the slaves."[36] Whatever their personal motives may have been, Harris officially justified their action by saying that turning the blacks over to the Creeks was the alternative to shipping them to Africa, an action which would have proved unwise for the government to take "when the public mind here and elsewhere is so sensitive upon the subject of slavery."[37]

GENERAL ZACHARY TAYLOR AND THE WAR IN FLORIDA

While these events transpired in the West, the war had continued in
Florida. Brevet Brigadier General Zachary Taylor, who succeeded General
Jesup as commander of the army in Florida, was faced immediately with
some of the problems left over from Jesup's policy, but he dealt with them
in short order. One of the first matters to come to his attention was Collins'
difficulty in obtaining the blacks claimed by Watson. On June 2, 1838,
only a few days after he assumed command, Taylor made his policy plain.
He would do the utmost in his power to get the Indians and their blacks
out of Florida and to their new homes west of the Mississippi. He refused
to meddle for the benefit of Collins, the Creeks, or anyone else, "or to
interfere, in any way, between the Indians and their negroes which may
have a tendency to deprive the former of their property, and reduce the
latter from a comparative state of freedom to that of slavery." Yet he
would do what he could to restore to their lawful owners any slaves who
had absconded to the Indians or had been captured by them.[38]

During the next few months, the Indians in Florida committed depredations upon the whites and engaged the soldiers in minor skirmishes. Taylor
estimated that there were four or five hundred Mikasukis and Tallahassees
and a few renegade Creeks left in Florida. Over the months, a few continued
to straggle in, and Taylor negotiated with them when he could. On June 5,
Taylor had sent west the first Indians and blacks removed under his command—a contingent of 305 Indians and thirty blacks.[39]

The few Apalachicolas remaining agreed to emigrate in the fall of 1838.
Some of the chiefs, including Blunt and Davy, had agreed in 1832 to emi-
grate to Texas. When they left Florida in 1834, about six hundred others
remained on the Apalachicola River, where they fell victim to both their
Indian and white neighbors. Some of them under John Walker and
Econchatta Micco took to the field against the Seminoles in late 1835.
In March 1836, some of Econchatta Micco's white neighbors, who he
thought were his friends, stole twenty-two of his slaves and took them to
New Orleans. The same men later entered his town by night and took away
all of the firearms, telling the Indians that the militia had been called out
and was on its way to kill them all. The people of Econchatta Micco's
town and those of John Walker's fled into the brush. In spite of their trouble,
they did not want to emigrate and be massacred by the "savage Creeks

and Seminoles" who had often tried to persuade them to take sides in
their wars.[40]

However, by 1838 they were willing to go, leaving Pensacola on October
29. A treaty with some of the chiefs on June 18, 1833, had provided for
the relinquishment of their Florida lands and for their settlement on lands
of the Creeks and Seminoles if they decided to emigrate to the West. By
1838, there were only about three hundred left. Whether they took any
blacks with them is uncertain. A census of 1833 showed that in Blunt's
town there were nine blacks: one slave owned by Toney Hadjo and eight
by Blunt. In Mulatto King's town (later Walker's town), there were five:
a slave of Walker Pachassee and four free blacks. These latter were the
family of Rose Sena Factor, of whom more will be said subsequently. In
Econchatta Micco's town there were his twenty-four slaves. By 1838, twenty-
two of those had been stolen, and Blunt's had presumably gone to Texas
with him, leaving only a few in the Apalachicola towns.[41]

In November 1838, thirty-one Indians and two slaves emigrated. Mostly
remnants of Blunt's tribe who had joined the other Apalachicolas after
Blunt's removal, they reached Fort Gibson on February 13, 1839. Another
party of 205, including sixty-two blacks, was shipped from Florida on
April 13. One slave belonged to Coa Hadjo, three to Holatoochee, sixteen
to Harriet Bowlegs, two to Abraham, the interpreter for the group, twelve
to Micanopy, five to Polly, one to Nocose Yohola, and eight to Miccopotokee.
The rest were free blacks: Tom, Cudjo, Toney Barnet, John Bull, Martinus,
Kitty, Polly, Becky, Judith, Margaret, Grace, Ludy, and Mary Ann. This
was the last emigration during Taylor's command. He was relieved on May 5,
1840, by Brevet Brigadier General Walker K. Armistead.[42]

ARMISTEAD'S POLICY

Armistead's policy was to keep the Indians unsettled by destroying
their crops and by constantly sending out scouting parties. He also made
a practice of offering bribes to the chiefs to surrender their bands. While
several came in to talk, only Coosa Tustenuggee surrendered for $5,000
in the spring of 1841. The policy of bribery, however, was adopted with
more success by Armistead's successor.[43]

Armistead sent no emigration party to the West until the spring of 1841.
By that time, he had several hundred captives awaiting removal at Tampa
Bay. Like his predecessors, he was harassed by whites who claimed to have

runaway slaves among the captives. On March 12, Secretary of War John C. Spencer directed him to surrender all slaves to which the Indians had gained possession since the Treaty of Payne's Landing unless the effect would be to prevent the Indians from coming in and removing. It would be better, he was told, for the blacks to which whites had a valid claim to be removed with the Indians than to jeopardize removal with a slave claim. If necessary, such slaves could be brought back later or paid for by the government.[44] The directive was most significant. In effect, it gave official sanction to policy which Jesup and Taylor had pursued without that sanction. For the first time, a commander in Florida had clear orders regarding slave claims by whites.

Under his new orders, Armistead sent a contingent of emigrants to the West in late March: Le Grand G. Capers, the disbursing agent of Indian affairs, accompanied the 205 Indians and seven blacks, including a slave of Parhose Fixico, five persons in the party of Dennis (a free black), and Friday or Jim, listed as a slave but not assigned to an owner. On April 19, the party landed on the south bank of the Arkansas below Fort Gibson, where they were loaded into wagons and taken to the western part of the Creek country to join Micanopy's people, who had settled on the Deep Fork or northern-most branch of the Canadian River.[45]

The people in Dennis' party were his wife Mary, her two-year-old child, and her mother Hannah. Hannah and Mary were claimed by Matteo Solano and Miguel Papy. Don Filipe Solano had bought Hannah and her son Joe at St. Augustine in 1820. The bill of sale was signed by the Indians Sofaly, Estomastque, Fapjara, and Fais Torque of Alachua Town and the interpreter, Antoin Huertas. Solano took the blacks to his plantation about thirty miles from St. Augustine, and a few months later, Hannah married a black named Dick, who also belonged to Solano. She had a daughter named Maria Gracia. During the first year of hostilities, Hannah, Joe, and Maria ran away and joined the Indians.[46]

In 1839, Hannah, Joe, and Mary (Maria) were recognized at Tampa Bay. Matteo Solano, son of the late Filipe, with a power of attorney from Papy, sent an agent to Tampa in February 1841 to take Hannah and her family to Key West. But he was too late. Hannah, Mary, her husband Dennis, who was owned by Harriet Bowlegs, and Mary's child emigrated on March 20. Joe, Hannah's son, had surrendered to General Taylor under the promise of freedom and had emigrated in 1839. Friday, the other black in the contingent, was the property of General D. L. Clinch and had been appraised at a value of $1,000. There was no doubt concerning his ownership, but Armistead removed him under the department's directive of March 12.[47]

Another party prepared to leave Tampa Bay in early May 1841. Among the blacks in this group was the slave Sophia, said to belong to Coosa Tustenuggee but claimed by Gad Humphreys. In 1836, Sophia was at work on Humphreys' plantation in Alachua County, when she and thirty-three other slaves were captured by Indians. She and three others were recaptured by troops. Free blacks in the contingent included Teena, Nanny and child, Susan and child, Sampson, Nelly, Christopher, Jenny, Nareta, and Poor Gal. The party, numbering 206, arrived at New Orleans on May 13. General Armistead had given the Indians permission to visit the city for several days before being sent up the river. However, Major Isaac Clark sent them on immediately. Clark justified his action by saying that he had "discovered a lot of loafers from Georgia looking out for negroes," pretending to claim blacks to whom they had no legal right. To have detained the Indians would have caused trouble. Clark gave strict orders that no white man was to be allowed on board the steamer on the way to Fort Gibson. He undoubtedly exaggerated the situation, but for what reason is uncertain. Le Grand Capers, the emigration agent, gave a more logical account of the immediate departure: The river was high, there were unusual numbers of steamers in the city, and transportation could be obtained economically. The group arrived at the Choctaw agency on June 13, and went overland the rest of the way.[48]

General Armistead was relieved of his command on May 31, 1841, at which time he had 236 Indians and blacks on hand awaiting removal.[49] He was succeeded by Colonel William Jenkins Worth.

WORTH'S COMMAND

The first significant event during Worth's command was the capture of Wild Cat on June 4. The Indian had come to Fort Pierce on May 1 for a council, at which time he was given thirty days to prepare his people for removal. When it became apparent that he did not intend to do so, he and fifteen of his tribesmen were seized and sent immediately to New Orleans. Colonel Worth, who wanted to use Wild Cat to bring other Indians in, ordered his return. Wild Cat apparently accepted his defeat and for a consideration of about $8,000 set about trying to induce others to surrender. He sent messages to his people, and on August 8, nearly all of them came in. Wild Cat later induced old Hospitake to come aboard a vessel for a conference, and he was seized.[50]

Worth, in his turn as commander, was besieged by whites who claimed to have slaves among the captives. By late summer, he was convinced that it was unwise to allow any of the blacks to remain in Florida in the hands of whites, for it would anger the Indians and impair removal efforts. His views were upheld by Secretary Spencer, who reaffirmed the orders to General Armistead on March 12 past: Worth was not to permit any black to be taken by white claimants if it proved injurious in any way to the removal effort.[51]

By October, Wild Cat felt that he had done all he could to persuade the Indians to come in, and he asked that he and those at Tampa Bay be removed at once. In November a party numbering two hundred, including Wild Cat, arrived at Fort Gibson. Among this group were fifteen blacks, including Charles Payne, Micanopy's slave who had surrendered to General Jesup, Payne's wife Jane, who was owned by Payne, and his son Simon. Billy Factor was the interpreter for the party. In Factor's group were his wife Nancy, their children Portia and July, and his mother, Rose Sena Factor. Sam, another member of the party, was owned by Wild Cat. In his party was one female Indian, presumably his wife. There was one male slave of Ah-halac Hadjoche. Finally, there were Jenny, a free black, and her four children.[52]

Rose Sena Factor and her family were claimed by Matteo Solano and Miguel Papy, who had bought her at St. Augustine in 1821. She stayed with Solano about a year and then escaped. He pursued her until he came to an Indian camp on the west side of the St. Johns River about five miles from Volusia. The Indians told him that they had given Rose a horse and that she had gone into Indian country. Later she was captured with a child near Tampa Bay by Captain William Miller, a half-blood Creek, who took them to the Creek Nation and sold them to Chilly McIntosh. Rose then became the property of a Creek named Black Factor, who belonged to Walker Pachassee's band on the Apalachicola River. Black Factor gave Rose to his son Sam Factor for a wife. But at the death of Black Factor, his property, including all of his slaves, was claimed by Nelly Factor, under the Indian law which gave property to the children of the brother or sister of the deceased, rather than to his own children. Sam Factor claimed that he had bought his wife and her two children, William (Billy) and Sarah, from Nelly.[53]

Nevertheless, a conflict subsequently arose between Nelly and Sam Factor over the ownership of Rose. Nelly's claim was by virtue of her right of inheritance. However, in 1827, the chiefs of the Apalachicola towns judged that Rose was the property of Black Factor who had given her to his son Samuel. Nelly persisted in her claim. In September 1828, Governor William P. DuVal called a meeting of the chiefs to settle the matter. They decided that Nelly was the heir of Black Factor and therefore entitled to his property except for Rose, who was given to Sam by Black Factor during his lifetime.[54]

In 1832, Sam Factor manumitted his wife Rose, "to enjoy all the freedom and privileges of the tribe." He also freed her daughter Sarah, her son Billy, and Sarah's sons Daniel and Paladore. The manumission was sanctioned by the chiefs, and Sam reaffirmed the manumission in February 1835 before Seminole Agent Wiley Thompson.[55]

In July 1834, a white man named Isaac Brown from near Columbus, Georgia, and a man named Douglas and his "company of negro stealers" made a raid on Emathlachee's town on the Apalachicola. Douglas, who hunted slaves for a livelihood, was from Mobile, and he came with two large trained dogs to take Billy Factor. Finding resistance on the part of the Indians, Douglas left to recruit some help. Whites in the area knew of similar activities of Douglas in the Creek Nation and believed he would return with a large company to take Billy, Rose, Jim, and other blacks. Through Jim, his interpreter, Chief John Walker asked Wiley Thompson for protection by the civil authorities.[56]

Billy was claimed by Levin Brown, Isaac's brother, who lived on the Chattahoochee in Jackson County, Florida. Governor DuVal had rendered a verbal decision against Brown's claim. It was that decision which had sparked the raid. Agent Thompson asked the U.S. attorney for the Western District of Florida to prosecute Isaac Brown. However, the Indians were too far away from the seats of civil authority to receive much protection.[57]

Sometime later, another raid was made with Sam Factor's family as its object. Ezekiel Robertson came from near Columbus and claimed Rose. He gathered a force of fifteen or twenty men. They made a raid, taking Rose and her family captives. Rose and Billy Factor escaped and made their way back to the Indians, but Sarah and her two children were taken up river to Stewart County, Georgia. Whether the latter were recovered is uncertain. In 1837, Billy called on Governor Call of Florida to try to recover his sister and her children.[58] Emigration rolls, however, do not indicate that they emigrated with Rose and Billy in 1841.

When hostilities broke out, the Factors were sympathetic to the American cause. At the time, Rose, Billy, and his wife Nancy were owners of a great deal of personal property in herds and crops. In 1837 Billy was hired as army herdsman by Captain John C. Casey; he later served as interpreter in the Creek regiment and waited upon General Jesup. Under General Taylor's orders, he served as interpreter for the navy on board a steamer between Florida Point and St. Augustine and was a go-between in the negotiation of Wild Cat's surrender. Rose went to Tampa Bay where General Jesup promised her that he would find her children and grandchildren. She served as an interpreter and allegedly saved the lives of some whites during the war. The Factors lost their property, partly to the Seminoles and partly to the American volunteer troops who wanted to keep it out of the hands of the hostiles.[59]

In order to prevent difficulties with the Indians, Colonel Worth decided to send Rose and her family to the West. On October 11, 1841, a military board assessed their value. From the evidence obtained, the board decided that the bill of sale to Papy and Solano established their right to Rose. They valued her at four hundred dollars and Billy, who had an injured limb, at five hundred dollars. Rose, Billy, his wife and two children emigrated on October 11.[60]

THE FORRESTER CLAIM

Colonel Worth constantly faced the problem of slave claims such as Solano's and Papy's. The orders of the spring and fall of 1841 to Armistead and to Worth had evidently signaled the white claimants that it was useless to pursue the matter on the Florida front. Therefore, in the spring of 1842, some of them took their claims to Washington. One such claimant was A. J. Forrester, who in 1841 had sought the return of his slave John, who had been captured by the Seminoles with a number of other blacks at Forrester's Spring Garden plantation in December 1835 and had surrendered with Wild Cat's band. Colonel Worth easily identified him and promised to hold him in Florida, but when Forrester sent for him, John had been valued by a military board and shipped west. In March 1842, Forrester asked the Secretary of War to return the slave since the valuation was too low and since Forrester held the rest of John's family as slaves. While the board had valued John at three hundred dollars, slave brokers and auctioneers valued him at five hundred dollars. The discrepancy in price resulted from the instructions to the appraising officers "to consider the difficulty and expense which would have attended the recovery of the slave, and to make a correspondent deduction from his intrinsic value." Authority for John's removal to the West under those circumstances was clear.[61]

Commissioner T. Hartley Crawford considered Forrester's claim an important one because whatever measure of compensation was granted to one claimant would be expected by all. It was impossible to estimate the amount of claims which would result from the blacks having emigrated with the Seminoles as a result of government policy. Crawford therefore recommended that some general rule or tribunal be established for adjudication of such claims. On April 12, 1842, Secretary John C. Spencer issued a most significant directive. It seemed to him that the Executive, having determined to allow the Indians "to take with them these persons with whom they had formed strong attachments" for the sake of expediency, must pay the expense of such an agreement. In no other way could justice be done to the citizens whose property had been taken for public use. The blacks taken to the West could not be reclaimed without a breach of public faith, nor could it be done without the risk of new hostilities in the West. Colonel Worth was therefore instructed to find the names and value of all slaves who had been allowed to be taken west by the Seminoles after March 12, 1841. When amounts that should be allowed claimants were found, he was to pay them out of funds on hand for the removal of the Indians. In making future arrangements with any of the Seminoles for their surrender, Worth was instructed to avoid, when possible, any stipulation that would allow the Indians to take to the West any captured slaves. If such stipulations could not be avoided, he was to determine the owner and the value of the slave and pay the owner out of the funds on hand.[62]

Forrester renewed his claim, but Spencer steadfastly refused to recognize it. The public faith had been pledged to Wild Cat that he might keep John when he emigrated, and the department could interfere in no way other than to pay for him. Slaves who had been with the Seminoles as long as John had taken up Indian ways and would no longer be suited for domestic labor. If they remained in Florida, they would incite the plantation slaves to rebel and would probably seek the safety of the Everglades, from which they could carry on a predatory warfare more devastating than that of the Seminoles. Spencer's final word, then, was indemnity for those slaves carried away after March 12, 1841. Thus, in the summer of 1842, Forrester was allowed four hundred dollars for his claim.[63]

Here ended perhaps the single most important claim arising out of the emigration of the Seminoles. Forrester's claim had forced officials of the War Department to define and adhere to an established policy in regard to the slaves belonging to citizens but allowed to emigrate with the Indians after March 12, 1841. It had the effect of eliminating future demands upon the Indians for those blacks and gave the officials of the War Department a way to deal with subsequent claims of the same type.

FINAL EMIGRATION PARTIES

The directive was drafted about the time another emigration party left Tampa Bay. In the party were three blacks: Sampson, a free black who had surrendered to Jesup, and Jenny, who had one other female slave in her party. As the party neared their destination, orders came to land them on the south side of the Arkansas River a few miles above or opposite the mouth of the Grand, if possible. Above all, they were not to land at Fort Gibson, within the Cherokee Nation, where some parties had landed and had remained in spite of the objections of the Cherokees. General Taylor was in the West as commander of the Second Department of the Western Division and, understanding Indian affairs, was anxious to keep these and future emigrants within the lands claimed by the Creeks in order to avoid difficulties. The party disembarked on June 1, 1842, to march overland to the Deep Fork; they refused to go. Instead, they wanted to go to Fort Gibson and join the Seminoles under Alligator. Troops had to be sent from the fort to force the Indians to go on to the western Creek country.[64]

On July 21, another party of Indians and blacks reached New Orleans. Blacks in the party included Isaac, who had come in with Coosa Tustenuggee in April of 1841, and who was claimed by Eneah Micco. In Isaac's party were Clanda, Affrey, Scipio, Bob, Jim, and Milley. Also in the party were Toney, Rebecca, and Cyrus. But the most important emigrant among the blacks was John Cavallo or Gopher John, aged thirty-five, who had been well known as a chief of the blacks during the war. Variously known as John Cohia, John Cowaya, and John Horse, Gopher John had been the property of Charles Cohia, then dead, and was claimed by Cohia's widow who had already emigrated. Gopher John, however, who had acted as an interpreter after his surrender, claimed freedom for his wife and children for having complied with the promise made by General Jesup at Fort Dade. He had in his possession some papers to that effect, signed by General Taylor, as well as a statement from Worth, which read: "The bearer John Cohia, commonly called Gopher John has rendered honest and faithful service, has proved an intelligent guide and trailer, and full of courage; his attachment and fidelity to the whites and hatred of the Indian, has secured him the hostility of the latter, and gives him a strong claim to protection." John's party was held up by low water and had to march overland from Little Rock to the Creek council ground by way of the Choctaw agency. They arrived in the Creek country on September 6.[65]

This was the last removal until January 1843, when a party of ninety-nine arrived at New Orleans. Tyra was the only black listed. John Crews was the interpreter who traveled with the group. In June 1843, he had purchased himself at St. Augustine and had then become an interpreter for the navy at Indian Key. Crews returned to Florida with Le Grand Capers and then removed himself, with a party which reached New Orleans in early March. Besides Crews, the party included Joe and Toney Barnet, who had returned to Florida in 1840 as part of a Seminole delegation sent to persuade others to emigrate. The party consisted mainly of Pascofar's band. They were put ashore on the south bank of the Arkansas on April 26 and were marched overland to Fort Gibson.[66] The arrival of this group marked the end of removals for over a decade.

According to the source of title, the slaves who had emigrated with the Seminoles fell into five groups. First were the descendants of blacks who had been taken by the Seminoles in earlier wars from the citizens of Georgia, who had been indemnified by earlier treaties. Second were the blacks whom the Indians had purchased from the Spanish authorities and from individuals who had settled in Florida and become Spanish subjects. Many of the latter had engaged in the so-called Patriot War against the Spanish and had had their property confiscated, including their slaves, some of whom the Seminoles then purchased. Third were blacks who had been taken from the Florida plantations before the Treaty of Payne's Landing, which had provided for indemnity for them. Fourth were blacks who had been purchased, legally or illegally, from the Indians. Some had been in the possession of the purchasers but had run away and rejoined the Indians, some had been recaptured by the Indians, and some had remained with their Indian masters after the purchases had taken place. Finally, there were those who were really the property of whites but who were not claimed by their owners before being sent west to avoid difficulties with the Indians.[67] During the first two or three years after the Seminoles emigrated to the

West, numerous claims arose for blacks in the last two groups. Many were simply continuations of claims which had begun before removal; others, especially in regard to the last group, were a direct result of the emigration policy. Fortunately for the Seminoles and the blacks among them, the government dealt with the claims, for the most part, in such a way as to prevent white claimants from following the Indians to the West and making raids upon their communities as had often been the practice in Florida.

Nearly all of the bureaucratic machinations which attended the old claims of Humphreys, Solano, and the others took place in the East. The Indians and the blacks among them in the West had to be little concerned for the first few years about such claimants coming among them to attempt execution of their claims. But removal had been a policy of expediency regarding the blacks. While it prevented controversies in Florida, it created them in the West. As indicated by some of the cases presented above, titles to many of the black emigrants were hopelessly confused. Frequent theft, sale, resale, marriage, manumission, and decrees of chiefs simply contributed to the confusion of war and removal in obscuring the details surrounding property ownership. To have decided all cases before removal would have put off removal indefinitely.

Once removal became inevitable, many blacks hid behind the vagueness of the titles in order to get out of Florida, hoping to find more freedom among the Indians in the West. But the confusion which permitted their removal from Florida placed them in an anomalous position in the West. They were not long in attracting the attention of slave hunters from the Creek and Cherokee Nations as well as from Arkansas. Once more, the Africans among the Seminoles became a source of controversy. Indeed, no sooner had the first emigrants arrived than they became a point of conflict between the Seminoles and the Creeks.

NOTES

1. For example, Lieutenant James A. Chambers to Lieutenant F. E. Hunt, March 4, 1838, and Chambers to Lieutenant Colonel J. B. Crane, March 4, 1838, 25 Cong., 3 Sess., *House Document 225* (hereafter cited as *Document 225*), 24-25; Brevet Brigadier General Thomas S. Jesup to J. C. Spencer, December 28, 1841, 27 Cong., 2 Sess., *House Document 55* (hereafter cited as *Document 55*), 2.
2. Jesup to Spencer, December 28, 1841, *Document 55, 2.*

3. Jesup to William L. Marcy, April 3, 1848, National Archives Microfilm Publications, *Microcopy M574* (Special Files of the Office of Indian Affairs, 1807-1904)-13, Special File 96: Seminole Claims to Certain Negroes, 1841-1849 (hereafter cited as *File 96*); Gad Humphreys to Joel Poinsett, May 10, 1838, and Humphreys to Charles Downing, May 30, 1838, *Document 225,* 93; Wiley Thompson to Lewis Cass, July 19, 1835, National Archives Microfilm Publications, *Microcopy M234* (Records of the Office of Indian Affairs, Letters Received)-800, Frame 411; Orders No. 79, April 5, 1837, National Archives Record Group 94 (Records of the Office of the Adjutant General), *General Jesup's Papers,* Orders, 20. *Microcopy M234* is hereafter cited as *M234,* followed by the roll number.

4. Archibald Smith, Jr., et al., to Jesup, April 18, 1837; Humphreys to Downing, May 30, 1838; A List and Descriptive Roll . . . ; and Jesup to Poinsett, May 10, 1838, *Document 225,* 104, 99, 108, 93. Humphreys' list is reproduced as List H in the Appendix.

5. Humphreys to Downing, May 30, 1838, and Registry of Negro Prisoners, *Document 225,* 104, 68; Thompson to Cass, July 19, 1835, and Thompson to C. A. Harris, September 8, 1835, *M234*-800, Frames 411, 428; Jesup to Colonel Zachary Taylor, October 27, 1837, *General Jesup's Papers,* Letters Sent (hereafter cited as *JPLS*).

6. Humphreys to Poinsett, May 10, 1838; Harris to Captain Samuel Cooper, May 25, 1838; and Humphreys to Downing, May 30, 1838, *Document 225,* 48, 104, 93.

7. William Armstrong to Commissioner, April 23, 1838, *Document 225,* 90; Harris to Cooper, May 1, 1838, National Archives Record Group 393 (Records of the United States Army Continental Commands, 1821-1920), *Second and Seventh Military Departments,* Letters Received (hereafter cited as *2nd and 7th LR*), Box 2, and *Document 225,* 43.

8. Harris to Armstrong, May 5, 1838, *Document 225,* 44.

9. Opothleyohola, et al., to Harris, May 8, 1838, *2nd and 7th LR,* Box 2, and *Document 225,* 92; Report of House Committee on Indian Affairs, April 12, 1842, 30 Cong., 1 Sess., *House Report 724,* 2; Harris to Cooper, May 9, 1838, Harris to Major General Alexander Macomb, May 9, 1838, Harris to Zantzinger, May 10, 1838, and Harris to Nathaniel Collins, May 9, 1838, *Document 225,* 28, 45, 46.

10. Special Orders No. 8, April 29, 1838, and Harris to Lieutenant John G. Reynolds, May 11, 1838, *Document 225,* 90.

11. John H. Love to James Logan, July 3, 1840, *M234*-923, A899-40; Heirs of Love vs. E. P. Gaines, n. d., Major Isaac Clark to Harris, May 3, 1838, Harris to Clark, May 11, 1838, and Harris to Thomas Slidell, May 12, 1838, *Document 225,* 31, 47.

12. Heirs of Love vs. E. P. Gaines, n. d., *Document 225,* 31.

13. Reynolds to Jesup, April 4, 1838, Harris to Reynolds, March 22, 1838, Reynolds to Zantzinger, March 25, 1838, and Zantzinger to Chambers, March 28, 1838, *General Jesup's Papers,* Letters Received (hereafter cited as *JPLR*), Box 12; Grant Foreman, *Indian Removal* (Norman: University of Oklahoma Press, 1932), 357; Special Orders No. 4, March 21, 1838, Reynolds to Harris, March 22, 1838, Harris to Lieutenant W. G. Freeman, March 22, 1838, and Reynolds to Harris, March 26, 1838, *Document 225,* 81, 42, 82. A list of the blacks appears as List I in the Appendix.

14. Reynolds to Harris, May 15, 1838, *Document 225,* 92; Foreman, 364-365.

15. Tod Robinson to Reynolds, October 2, 1838, Gaines to Roger Jones, May 18, 1838, and Reynolds to Harris, May 21, 1838, *Document 225,* 30, 124, 97; Love to Logan, July 3, 1840, *M234-*923, A899-40.

16. Lieutenant John C. Casey to Clark, July 11, 1838, *Document 225,* 119-120; List of Seminole Negroe Prisoners turned over at Fort Pike, March 21, 1838, National Archives Record Group 75 (Records of the Bureau of Indian Affairs), *Miscellaneous Muster Rolls, 1832-1846;* List of Slaves owned by Miccopotokee or Copiah Yahola, April 29, 1835, *M234-*802, D153-56. This last list appears as List J in the Appendix.

17. Casey to Clark, July 11, 1838, *Document 225,* 119-120.

18. *Ibid.;* John K. Mahon, *History of the Second Seminole War, 1835-1842* (Gainesville: University of Florida Press, 1967), 104, 106; Joshua R. Giddings, *The Exiles of Florida* (Columbus, Ohio: Follet, Foster and Company, 1858), 106-107, 114. Louis returned to Florida in 1892 and died there in 1895. The account of his life by Giddings conflicts with that of Kenneth W. Porter in his "Three Fighters for Freedom," *Journal of Negro History,* 28 (January 1943), 65-72; the latter is the more reliable.

19. Reynolds to Harris, May 26, 1838, and Muster Roll, 1838, *Document 225,* 97, 99; Foreman, 365.

20. Reynolds to Harris, May 26, 1838, *2nd and 7th LR,* Box 2; Collins to Harris, July 29, 1838, *Document 225,* 97; Foreman, 366.

21. Reynolds to Harris, June 2, 1838, *2nd and 7th LR,* Box 2, and *Document 225,* 100; Foreman, 366.

22. Reynolds to Governor of Arkansas, June 3, 1838, and Sam C. Roane to Reynolds, June 4, 1838, *Document 225,* 102; Foreman, 366.

23. Reynolds to General Matthew Arbuckle, June 12, 1838, and Reynolds to Harris, June 18, 1838, *Document 225,* 101, 103; Muster Roll of Seminoles emigrated June, 1838, conducted by Lieutenant J. G. Reynolds, *Miscellaneous Muster Rolls, 1832-1846;* Arbuckle to Reynolds, June 13, 1838, National Archives Record Group 393, *Second Military Department,* Letters Sent

(hereafter cited as *2nd LS*); Harris to Cooper, May 25, 1838, and Collins to Harris, July 29, 1838, *Document 225,* 48, 124.

24. Arbuckle to Jesup, July 4, 1838, *2nd LS*; Harris to Clark, June 26, 1838, *Document 225,* 49; Foreman, 367-368; *Arkansas Gazette,* June 13, 1838, and June 27, 1838; Muster Roll of Emigrant Seminoles who arrived upon their lands west of the Mississippi . . . 19th day of June, 1838, *Miscellaneous Muster Rolls, 1832-1846.*

25. Collins to Harris, July 29, 1838, Tod Robinson to Reynolds, October 2, 1838, and Reynolds to Harris, June 28, 1838, *Document 225,* 124, 104; Collins to Reynolds, June 25, 1838, *2nd and 7th LR,* Box 2.

26. Reynolds' Journal, in *M234*-291, R415-39.

27. *Ibid.;* Muster Roll of Seminole Indians who arrived west on 5th August, 1838, *M234*-924, S1114-38. One of the blacks, Bella, died on July 22.

28. Harris to Reynolds, July 6, 1838, *M234*-291, R415-39, and *Document 225,* 49.

29. Reynolds to Harris, September 7, 1838, *M234*-291, R415-39; Edwin C. McReynolds, *The Seminoles* (Norman: University of Oklahoma Press, 1957), 213.

30. Collins to Harris, July 29, and August 8, 1838, *Document 225,* 111, 112.

31. Harris to Reynolds, August 27, 1838, Statement of Fred Buisson, September 1838, George Whitman to Reynolds, September 12, 1838, Clark to Reynolds, September 13, 1838, and Robinson to Reynolds, October 2, 1838, *Document 225,* 50, 116, 118, 124; Reynolds to Harris, September 20, 1838, *M234*-291, R415-39.

32. Report of House Committee on Indian Affairs, April 12, 1842, 30 Cong., 1 Sess., *House Report 724,* 2; Arbuckle to William Armstrong, August 27, 1838, and Arbuckle to Poinsett, August 27, 1838, *2nd LS,* and *Document 225,* 114.

33. Arbuckle to Poinsett, September 28, 1838, *2nd LS,* and *Document 225,* 126.

34. Collins to Poinsett, October 18, 1838; T. Hartley Crawford to Armstrong and Arbuckle, November 15, 1838; and Crawford to Collins, November 14, 1838, *Document 225,* 126, 51.

35. Arbuckle to Crawford, January 12, 1839, *2nd LS;* Resolution, *Document 225,* 1.

36. Giddings, 194-213; McReynolds, 212.

37. Harris to Cooper, May 1, 1838, *2nd and 7th LR,* Box 2, and *Document 225,* 43.

38. Taylor to Jones, June 2, 1838, *Document 225,* 30.

39. Mahon, 248-251; Orders No. 13, June 5, 1838, and Captain Pitcairn Morrison to Harris, June 14, 1838, *Document 225,* 7, 100.

40. Mahon, 80-81; Smith to General Gibson, July 12, 1836, and Smith to Gibson, July 25, 1836, National Archives Record Group 75, *Copies of Records, ca. 1823-1860,* Seminole Emigration.

41. Charles J. Kappler, comp., *Indian Affairs, Laws and Treaties* (2nd ed., Washington: Government Printing Office, 1904), 2: 293-294; A Statement Showing the Number of Chiefs, etc. . . . , May 23, 1833, *Miscellaneous Muster Rolls, 1832-1846,* Apalachicola; Foreman, 368; McReynolds, 214-215. Econchatta Micco began a suit against Isaac Brown for payment for his slaves, but he received no satisfaction. The case was pursued in the War Department for a number of years. Smith to Gibson, September 1, 1836, *Copies of Records, ca. 1823-1860,* Seminole; Downing to Poinsett, January 27, 1838, Crawford to Poinsett, February 25, 1839, Daniel Boyd to Daniel Kuntz, April 27, 1838, and Downing to Crawford, February 10, 1840, *M234*-289, D467-38, W817-39, B728-39, and D424-40; Crawford to Downing, March 13, 1840, National Archives Microfilm Publications, *Microcopy M21* (Records of the Office of Indian Affairs, Letters Sent)-28, 183; Crawford to David Levy, March 9, 1842, *M21*-32, 23. *Microcopy M21* is hereafter cited as *M21,* followed by the roll number.

42. Orders No. 74, November 27, 1838, *Document 225,* 7; Muster Roll of Thirty-Three Indians, Blunt's Tribe, emigrated under Daniel Boyd, November, 1838, *Miscellaneous Muster Rolls, 1832-1846,* Apalachicola; Captain J. R. Stephenson to Crawford, February 13, 1839, *M234*-291, S1383-39; Morrison to Crawford, January 26, 1839, Morrison to Crawford, March 7, 1839, and Morrison to Crawford, April 16, 1839, *M234*-291, M616-39, M674-39, and M705-39; Mahon, 254-255; Foreman, 370; McReynolds, 218; List of slaves and free negroes, *Document 55,* 5. Polly was formerly the wife of the Seminole chief Bowlegs, who in 1819 manumitted her and her two children Margaret (or Margarita) and Martiness. Grace, Ludy (or Lydia), and Mary Ann were the children of Margaret, as were Nancy and Cuny, not listed and presumably born later. In 1854, all of Polly's descendants were considered free by virtue of Bowlegs' act. Polly was the wife of Toney Barnet. Statement of J. W. Washbourne, October 14, 1854, *M234*-801, D709-54. For a detailed treatment of events during Taylor's command, see Mahon, 243-273.

43. For details of events during Armistead's command, see Mahon, 274-293.

44. Spencer to Colonel W. J. Worth, April 12, 1842, *M21*-32, 100. J. C. Spencer (1788-1855), a native of New York, was confirmed Secretary of War on December 30, 1841.

45. LeGrand Capers to Commissioner, April 4, 1841, and William Belknap to Commissioner, April 19, 1841, *M234*-291, C1381-41 and B1175-41; *Document 55*, 6; Foreman, 378.

46. Deposition of Andreas Papy, n. d., *M234*-289, S3398-43.

47. Statement of Joseph Sanchez, February 27, 1841, Deposition of Sanchez, n. d., Major S. Cooper to T. S. Brown, July 21, 1842, Statements of Papy and Solano, February 10 and 27, 1841, in *M234*-289, S3398-43; Crawford to Josiah Vose, September 16, 1842, *M21*-32, 463; Adjutant General to Commissioner, August 25, 1842, and Thomas Butler King to Secretary of War, July 12, 1841, *M234*-291, A1282-42 and K361-41; Crawford to John Bell, August 21, 1841, National Archives Microfilm Publications, *Microcopy M348* (Records of the Office of Indian Affairs Report Books)-2, 490; List of slaves, *Document 55*, 6. *Microcopy M348* is hereafter cited as *M348*, followed by the roll number.

48. The three captured with Sophia were identified as Humphreys', and wages were paid to him for their service while they were in Tampa. It was on the basis of that that Humphreys sought payment for Sophia. In 1842, he made another claim for her, but Commissioner Crawford did not want to set a precedent that might force the government to pay for all of the blacks allowed to emigrate with the Indians as a part of government policy. If Humphreys' claim was paid, the door would be opened, the precedent would be set. Therefore, the claim was rejected. Adjutant General to Commissioner, August 25, 1842, *M234*-291, A1282-42; Smith and Dorman to Spencer, February 26, 1842, *M234*-289, S3113-42; Crawford to Smith and Dorman, April 20, 1842, *M21*-32, 111. Humphreys was more fortunate in some other instances. One of his slaves, Sampson, had surrendered to General Taylor. A board of officers on December 30, 1841, valued Sampson at $1,200. Sampson purchased himself and was free. Another of Humphreys' blacks, Morris, was valued at five hundred dollars by a board of officers on May 4, 1842. Morris purchased himself and remained in Florida as an interpreter at Fort King. Adjutant General to Commissioner, August 25, 1842, *M234*-291, A1282-42. Many of Humphreys' slaves, however, had been sent west. In 1846, he applied for payment for them, but again the government refused to honor the claim. In 1851, Seminole Agent Marcellus Duval made a list of twenty-three slaves belonging to Humphreys in the western country. Then in 1856, the commissioner asked Agent J. W. Washbourne for a count of blacks in the West who belonged to citizens of Florida. Washbourne reported that of Humphreys' twenty-three blacks none remained in the West. Some had died, Duval had sold one, and the rest had run off to Mexico. Worth to Marcy, March 27, 1846, *M234*-801, W2880-46; Washbourne to George W.

Manypenny, July 31, 1856, *M234*-802, W135-56; Adjutant General to
Commissioner, August 25, 1842, and Clark to Crawford, May 16, 1841,
M234-291, A1282-42 and C1413-41; Capers to Commissioner, May 18,
1841, and List of Slaves, *Document 55,* 7; Foreman, 378; McReynolds,
220.

49. Mahon, 287.

50. Mahon, 298-299, 301-302.

51. Spencer to Worth, April 12, 1842, *M21*-32, 100.

52. Mahon, 302; Capers to Crawford, July 27, August 9, August 14,
October 11, and November 6, 1841, and Adjutant General to Commissioner,
August 25, 1842, *M234*-291, C1495-41, C1503-41, C1509-41, C1557-41,
and A1282-42; Roll of Florida Indians . . . , 12 November, 1841, *M234*-806,
A1141-41; List of slaves, *Document 55,* 8; Foreman, 379, McReynolds, 232.

53. T. S. Brown to Crawford, April 28, 1842, Bill of Sale and Affidavit
of Toney Proctor, April 26, 1841, Statement of Arbuckle, n. d., and
William P. DuVal to Worth, December 22, 1842, *M234*-289, B1773-43
and S3398-43; Crawford to Vose, September 16, 1842, *M21*-32, 463.

54. Decision of the Chiefs, June 15, 1827, DuVal to Worth, December 22,
1842, Statement of Nelly Factor, September 4, 1828, and Statement of
DuVal, September 10, 1828, in *M234*-289, S3398-43.

55. Manumission papers, May 27, 1832, and Factor's Statement, February
14, 1835, in *M234*-289, S3398-43.

56. Walker to Thompson, July 31, 1834, *M234*-800, Frame 429; Woodburne
Potter, *The War in Florida* (Reprint ed., Ann Arbor: University Microfilms,
Inc., 1966), 16.

57. Thompson to Elbert Herring, September 23, 1835, *M234*-800, Frame
429.

58. Boyd to Harris, August 29, 1838, *M234*-289, B576-38; Jesup to
R. K. Call, October 14, 1837, *JPLS*; Potter, 15-16.

59. W. K. Sebastian to Commissioner, May 1, 1852, *M234*-801, S90-52;
M. Thompson to Jacob Thompson, December 6, 1858, *M234*-802, T346-58.

60. Captain J. T. Sprague to Commissioner, April 30, 1843, *M234*-289,
S3398-43; Worth to Commissioner, August 1, 1842, and Adjutant General
to Commissioner, August 25, 1842, *M234*-291, A1282-42.

About the time Rose emigrated, Matteo Solano revived his claim for the
restoration of Rose, Hannah, Joe, Maria Gracia, and Maria's two children.
However, only Rose and her family had emigrated during Worth's command,
there were discrepancies between the names of Maria and Mary, there was
no appraisement of Hannah and her family, and there were some doubts
about ownership. Thus, Worth had the matter forwarded to the commissioner.
During the next two months, attorney T. S. Brown took the claim to Com-

missioner Crawford himself. Brown to Worth, July 25, 1842, and Cooper to Brown, July 27, 1842, in *M234*-289, S3398-43; Worth to Commissioner, August 1, 1842, and Brown to Crawford, August 8 and September 12, 1842, *M234*-291, W1873-42, B1556-42, and B1578-42.

Crawford felt that title to the blacks apparently rested in Solano and Papy, although all of the documents submitted in evidence were copies, and the bill of sale for Rose was not signed by the assignee but by the interpreter. Nevertheless, if the state of Florida would accept the instrument, it was good if the Indian Istejacho had had the right to sell her. He finally decided that the government would recognize the claim if Solano and Papy could substantiate their possession of the blacks and if possession was not refuted by adverse claimants. Crawford to Vose, September 16, 1842, Crawford to Levy, September 17, 1842, Crawford to Vose, September 22, 1842, and Crawford to Brown, September 28, 1842, *M21*-32, 463, 468, 481, 491; Levy to Crawford, September 18, 1842, and Vose to Crawford, October 7, 1842, *M234*-291, L1748-42 and V192-42.

When General Worth finally undertook an inquiry, he was convinced that the claim to Hannah and Joe was valid but that there was some question concerning Mary. He believed she was born before the sale and did not, therefore, come within the claim. He also doubted the right of Istejacho to sell Rose and recommended that the claimants show proof of that right before indemnity was made. Solano and Papy obtained testimony to support their claim. Peter Masters testified that at the time of the sale he was in charge of the plantation of the late Filipe Solano about eight miles from the head of the North River in St. Johns County. He was there when Hannah and her son Joe were brought to the plantation. Masters' wife later acted as midwife when Hannah bore a daughter named Maria Gracia, commonly called Mary. Similar depositions were made by Andreas Papy and Sanchez regarding Hannah and her children. Worth to Brown, December 19, 1842; Affidavit of Sanchez, December 28, 1842, in *M234*-289, S3398-43.

On the other hand, William P. DuVal testified that in the spring of 1826 he had met with the Indians to receive surrendered runaway slaves belonging to the citizens of Florida. Many slaves were given up and delivered to their owners. Among the claimants at the agency was Solano, who claimed a slave who was delivered, but Solano did not at that time claim Rose. DuVal had thought at the time that she was the property of Sam Factor and believed that Solano purchased Rose from an Indian who had no right to sell her. In April 1843, after reviewing the new testimony in the case, Worth decided that the claim to Mary had been established and instructed the emigrating agent to pay $450 for Hannah and fifty dollars for Mary. However, he remained unconvinced that Istejacho had a right

to sell Rose. DuVal to Worth, December 22, 1842; Sprague to Brown,
April 24, 1843; and Worth to Brown, April 26, 1843, in *M234*-289, S3398-43.

Solano's lawyer believed that Worth had been listening to the blacks at
Tampa Bay. Even if they did assert, truthfully, that Istejacho had no right
to sell Rose, he said, admit "that Negroes may appear as evidence against
the rights of slave owners and you pose a grand emancipation act." He took
the claim for indemnity for Rose back to the commissioner, arguing that
Istejacho's right to sell her had gone unchallenged for twenty-two years.
As far as the burden of proof went concerning that right, he argued that
in the Southern tier of states, thousands of slaves daily changed hands
whose original titles were with Indians. He posed the following situation:
"Suppose any owner was required to show right of the Indian to sell twenty
years ago." The case wore on until October 1843, when the commissioner
decided that since Rose was in the hands of the Indians before the Treaty
of Payne's Landing, she should have been paid for under that treaty. The
funds appropriated under that treaty had been depleted. Therefore, there
was no way to pay the claim. Brown to Crawford, April 28, 1843, and
Worth to Crawford, June 17, 1843, *M234*-289, B1773-43 and W2160-43;
Crawford to Brown, June 7, 1843, *M21*-34, 42; Crawford to Levy, May 4,
1844, and May 20, 1844, *M21*-35, 179, 216.

61. Levy to Spencer, March 18, 1842, *M234*-291, L1575-42; Crawford
to Spencer, April 1, 1842, *M348*-3, 129.

62. Crawford to Spencer, September 1, 1842, *M348*-3, 129; Spencer to
Worth, April 12, 1842, *M21*-32, 100.

63. Levy to Spencer, April 17, 1842, Worth to Spencer, April 25, 1842,
and Worth to Commissioner, August 1, 1842, *M234*-291, L1605-42, W1789-42,
and W1873-42; Spencer to Levy, April 21, 1842, *M21*-32, 113.

64. Capers to Crawford, April 16, 1842, and Adjutant General to Com-
missioner, August 25, 1842, *M234*-291, C1700-42 and A1282-42; Lieutenant
W. W. J. Bliss to Colonel S. W. Kearny, May 13, 1842, National Archives
Record Group 393, *Fort Gibson,* Letters Received, Box 1; Captain Thomas
Alexander to Seminole Subagent, June 1, 1842, *M234*-806, M1663-42;
Foreman, 380; McReynolds, 233.

65. Capers to Crawford, July 21, 1842, *M234*-806, C1767-42; Adjutant
General to Commissioner, August 25, 1842, *M234*-291, A1282-42; Statement
of Taylor, April 30, 1840, and Statement of Worth, July 14, 1842, *Fort
Gibson,* Volume "Indian Affairs," 2; Foreman, 380; McReynolds, 233-234.

66. Capers to Crawford, January 7, 1843, and Capers to Crawford,
March 4, 1843, *M234*-806, C1873-43 and C1923-43; Adjutant General to
Commissioner, August 25, 1842, *M234*-291, A1282-42; Foreman, 381, 384.

67. Jesup to Marcy, April 3, 1848, *File 96; Official Opinions of the
Attorneys General of the United States* (Washington, 1852), 4: 725.

4

Fear of the Creeks

The Treaty of Payne's Landing had provided for settlement of the Seminoles on the lands of the Creeks in the West, and the Treaty of Fort Gibson of March 28, 1833, had designated, as land for the Seminoles, a tract lying between the Canadian and North Fork, west to a line running north and south between the two streams and striking the forks of the Little River, provided the western line did not extend more than twenty-five miles west of the mouth of the latter. This area embraced all of present-day Hughes County, Oklahoma, as well as the western half of McIntosh County and parts of Okfuskee and Seminole counties. When Opothleyohola and his Creek followers emigrated in 1837, they settled in the eastern part of this tract near the confluence of the North Fork with the Canadian. Fear of Creek dominance had been a major cause of Seminole resistance to removal. This fear persisted after removal, and upon reaching the West, most of the Seminole emigrants refused to settle among the Creeks and settled instead on Cherokee lands in the vicinity of Fort Gibson. Alligator's and Holatoochee's bands settled north of the post, Wild Cat's band settled south of it, and Concharte Micco's band settled south of them. Only Micanopy and Black Dirt and their bands went to the western part of the Creek Nation and settled on the Deep Fork and Little River, respectively.[1]

The Seminoles feared that union with the Creeks would result in loss of their tribal existence and interests; because of their numbers, the Creeks would control all internal regulations and tribal police and would make and execute laws partial to themselves. In short, the Seminoles were afraid of becoming a powerless and oppressed minority. They were particularly

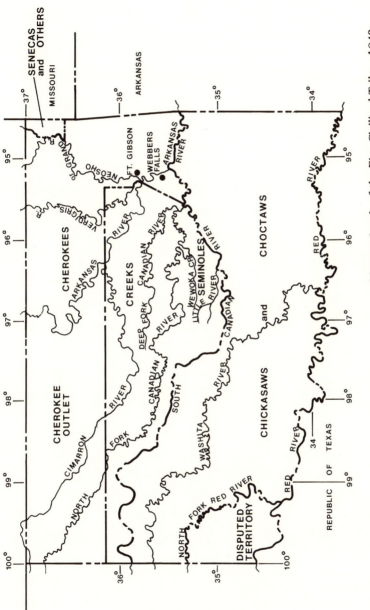

Western Lands of the Five Civilized Tribes, 1840

concerned about their blacks. Many were claimed by the Creeks, who charged that they had been Creek slaves who had absconded and taken refuge among the Seminoles while they were still in the East. Others they claimed had been captured by the Seminoles or had surrendered under Jesup's Proclamation and had emigrated with the Seminoles. Over the years, the Creeks charged, the Seminoles had come to look upon the blacks as their own property.[2] The Seminoles believed that once they united with the Creeks, the blacks would be taken from them by force or by laws enacted by the Creeks in their national council, which the Seminoles would be powerless to resist.

However, fear of the Creeks was not the only reason why the Seminoles remained scattered. As the groups had neared Fort Gibson, individual chiefs attempted to solidify their power by keeping their parties together. Micanopy and other leaders tried unsuccessfully to persuade them to join the Seminoles on the Deep Fork. The dissension pleased the Creeks, who did not want the Seminoles to unite, ostensibly because they felt that the Seminoles were not ready to settle in a body and become quiet and orderly neighbors, that among them were too many blacks who had participated in the war and who would now "exercise an improper influence" over the Indians.[3]

SEMINOLES ON CHEROKEE LANDS

By early 1839, there were about 2,000 Seminoles on Cherokee lands. With permission of the Cherokees and the consent of General Taylor, commanding the Second Military Department, they were allowed to plant crops upon the assumption that after harvest, they would remove to the Creek country. But time passed, and they remained near the fort, evidently content to take government rations, and showed little desire to farm.[4]

In the fall of 1838, the Seminole chiefs had written General Jesup that they liked the land which had been set aside for them but that the Creeks had it and they would not live among the Creeks, who looked upon them "as runaways" and would treat them "just as they would so many dogs."[5] Commissioner T. Hartley Crawford became convinced that forcing a union of the tribes would be fatal to the Seminoles, the weaker of the two. The Seminole annuities would soon run out, and they lacked farming tools. These facts and the determination not to unite with the Creeks made

Crawford recommend assigning the Seminoles another tract with which they would be satisfied. At President Van Buren's request, on February 13, 1839, Congress passed a bill designating the country to be set apart "between the Deep Fork or Little Fork and the North Fork of the Canadian so as to embrace a country equal in extent to the one the Seminoles were to have had in the Creek Nation between the main and the North Fork of the Canadian." Many of the Seminoles removed in the spring of 1839, but Alligator objected and persuaded others not to go, but to remain in the Cherokee Nation.[6]

The government tried to induce those who removed to cultivate corn and support themselves. Officials hired laborers to help the Indians break ground and plant, but they were late getting the crop in and as a result failed to make enough corn to support them during the winter of 1839-1840. Crawford wrote of them in his annual report for 1839: "They are indisposed to labor; their negroes are equally so, who, unfortunately, have great control over them. It is to be deeply regretted that their slaves were ever permitted to enter the Indian country."[7]

During 1840, the Seminoles on the Deep Fork made progress and raised some corn; Superintendent William Armstrong still found them lazy and much under the influence of the blacks, concerning whom they had "many difficulties." He wrote, "It is to be regretted that they were ever permitted to bring a negro with them; they exercise an improper influence over them, and show a bad example to other slaves."[8]

REVIVAL OF THE LOVE CLAIM

Armstrong probably referred to difficulties which had resulted from revival of the Love claim. During the summer of 1840, John Love tried to enlist the aid of the Creeks in acquiring the blacks he claimed, but General Arbuckle, who doubted the validity of the title, asked Chief Roley McIntosh not to interfere unless he was sure that the title was sound and that a fair price had been paid. Love had persuaded Coa Hadjo and Nocose Yohola to support his claim, but Arbuckle, still unconvinced, suggested that the Seminole chiefs meet in council to decide the case. On July 3, Arbuckle met with the Creek and Seminole chiefs, who unanimously agreed that Love's claim was good. Later that month, however, Micanopy, Cloud, and Nocose Yohola came to Arbuckle at Fort Gibson. In their opinion, the blacks in question were the property of Mah-pah-yist-chee and Mah-kah-tist-chee, the daughters of Tuskeneehau. Nevertheless, Love asked Creek Agent James Logan to turn the blacks over to him. Arbuckle urged Logan to prevent Creek interference until Love's claim was acknowledged by the Seminoles or until it was supported by unquestionable proof. Knowing that slavery was a touchy issue between the Creeks and Seminoles, he suggested that Logan bring the Seminole chiefs together for a full and fair investigation of the case.[9]

According to the chiefs, some of the blacks had been with them for over fifty years. The Seminoles had purchased Pompy and Dolly, the father and mother of the blacks, and had never agreed to sell them. It was an element among the Creeks, they claimed, who wanted the blacks taken from the Seminoles. In October 1840, William Armstrong referred the matter to Commissioner Crawford: "There is a great deal of dissatisfaction," he wrote, "about negro property. White men so often are setting up old claims that it is time a stop was made."[10]

When Love presented his claim in Washington the following May, Crawford concluded that the government should encourage such claims only from "an imperative sense of duty." The Love claim and others would cause "heartburning" among the Indians, who derived little advantage from slave property but held on to it stubbornly. Attempts to take it from them simply irritated them, which, in light of the government's relations with the tribe, east and west, it was important to avoid. Crawford concluded that departmental interference should be withheld.[11]

To General Jesup, the Love case called up "important questions of public law and national policy," which, however just Love's claim might be, should put the blacks beyond his reach. Jesup argued that in war, captured movable property rested absolutely under the law of the captor. In the case of the blacks, Jesup was the captor, who held them as trustee for the country. He had promised that they would be protected from capture by, or sale to, any United States citizen. The promise, he said in retrospect, was not made so much by an indisposition of the Indians to emigrate as by attempts by whites, under the sanction of officers of the government, to obtain their slaves. If the government failed to fulfill its promise, Jesup said, no matter how many troops were on the frontier, "no one can answer for the peace of the frontier." In the face of these adverse reports, Secretary John Bell took no action.[12]

REVIVAL OF THE WATSON CLAIM

In January 1841, J. C. Watson revived his claim, as he had tried unsuccessfully to do in the fall of 1839. This time, Watson's son, John H. Watson, forwarded a statement of James L. Hill, a trader who claimed that the Seminoles considered the blacks "Government negroes" and exercised no control over them whatever. Secretary Joel Poinsett admitted privately that he was willing to order their delivery if the order could be carried out without a conflict with the Indians. Crawford, however, had some reservations. Some of the Seminole owners were absent in Florida, where they had gone to try to induce the remaining members of their tribe to emigrate. Crawford wanted the order held up until the Seminoles returned so there could be no complaint about action taken during their absence. He would sanction the order only if it could be executed peaceably, for he felt that coercion, military or otherwise, was too dangerous.[13]

Watson's agents wanted a positive order, making clear that the Indians must comply, sent to William Armstrong and not to General Arbuckle, who they felt was prejudiced against the claim and would not trouble himself to execute the order or would, in fact, "most probably seize any excuse to disobey it." But just before he left office, Poinsett sent the order to Arbuckle the proper authority, instructing him to deliver the blacks to Watson's agent if it could be done without coercion and without endangering the peaceful relations between the frontier tribes and the United States. However, he was not to do so until the delegation in Florida returned home.[14]

John Bell, the new Secretary of War, issued similar orders to Armstrong. If the blacks could be identified with certainty as those captured and sold by the Creeks and if it could be ascertained that they were slaves of the Seminoles at the time of their capture, Armstrong was to deliver them to Watson's agent. Bell wrote, "It is highly important to the peace of the frontier, and especially in regard to this tribe of Indians, connected as they are with the Indians in arms in Florida, that the utmost circumspection should be exercised in the discharge of the delicate duty confided to you."[15]

Watson, though ill, went immediately to Fort Smith, Arkansas, only to be disappointed. Secretary Bell had become convinced that there was great danger of disturbing the peace and quiet of the Indians who had already emigrated and perhaps of frustrating further removals and a speedy end to the war which was still going on in Florida. Therefore, on April 29,

1841, he had issued an order countermanding the earlier one. That was Watson's last attempt to have the blacks taken from the Seminoles.[16]

CREEK SLAVE CODES AND SLAVE CLAIMS

While the Watson and Love claims were being pursued, the Seminoles were having more immediate problems concerning their blacks. The Creeks had passed a law taking horses, guns, and other property from their own slaves, and Micanopy and the other chiefs became concerned that the Creeks would try to apply their law to the Seminole blacks, who were allowed to own such property. They called on General Arbuckle at Fort Gibson in the spring of 1840 to prevent any interference and recieved assurances that the Creeks would not interfere as long as the Seminoles did not encourage or permit their blacks to harbor runaways.[17]

By this time, too, the Creeks had begun to press their own claims for some of the Seminole blacks. The case of Toney Barnet is a good example. Toney had emigrated in 1839, joining Micanopy's settlement on the Deep Fork, where he remained until David Barnet, a Creek, seized him as a slave. The Barnets claimed that sales in Florida which led to Toney's claim to freedom were invalid, and the Creek council backed them. When Barnet seized him, Toney's wife sought help at Fort Gibson, and upon General Arbuckle's request, Barnet freed Toney, who went back to the Seminoles. A short time later, Captain John Page began to organize a delegation of chiefs to go to Florida to try to persuade the remaining Seminoles to emigrate. Page first engaged Abraham as interpreter, but since Abraham's services to the United States had created hard feelings among some of the Indians, Nocose Yohola and Holatoochee asked that they be allowed to choose their own interpreters. Holatoochee chose Toney. During the selection process, David Barnet had made no mention of Toney, who Page assumed was free. Only later did Barnet object.[18] Over these objections in October 1840, Toney accompanied the delegation to Florida.

Regarding such cases, the Seminoles, of course, argued that when they removed, they were assured by the government that they would not be deprived of their blacks by the Creeks or by anyone else. In the fall of 1841, General Taylor took a firm stand to see that the promise was honored until he received different orders from the War Department. He told Creek Agent James Logan not to allow them to be deprived of a single slave without their consent and to put a stop, if possible, "even to the discussion of this subject as no good can result from the same."[19]

FOUR CLASSES OF BLACKS

Still concerned with slave claims made by whites, the government had sought to clarify the status of the blacks who had been captured or who had surrendered during the war. In response to a House resolution, on December 28, 1841, General Jesup reviewed his war policy. He divided the blacks into four classes, according to the means by which the Seminoles had acquired them: descendants of blacks taken from the citizens of Georgia by the Creek Confederacy in former wars, for which the citizens had been indemnified; blacks purchased by Indians from the Spanish authorities and from other individuals; blacks taken from plantations before the Treaty of Payne's Landing; and blacks claimed under pretended purchases from the Indians. The Indians considered many of these latter purchases fraudulent. Jesup pointed out that there could be no just claim to blacks in the first two classes. The Treaty of Payne's Landing had provided indemnification for those in the third class. As to the fourth, he argued that he could find no authority for the purchase of slaves from Indians under the intercourse laws, and none of the whites who had slave claims against the Seminoles were licensed traders. Those arguments and his belief that the matter involved questions "of the utmost importance as well in regard to personal rights as to national policy and constitutional law" had caused him to order all of the blacks who were not required as guides to be sent west to await the orders of the government or action of the claimants. Congress took no action in the matter because inadequate records prevented the Indian Office from finding how many of the blacks had been captured or what, if anything, had been paid for those captured.[20]

TROUBLE WITH THE CHEROKEES

As if troubles with the Creeks were not enough, the Seminoles began to have difficulties with their Cherokee neighbors. Those Seminoles who had stopped in the Cherokee country had at first been welcomed as temporary guests. In the fall of 1839, and again in the spring of 1841, Chief

John Ross of the Cherokees had tried to secure relief for Alligator, who complained that the government had not fulfilled the promise of a new rifle for him and tools and equipment for his people. In the latter instance, Secretary Bell sought the advice of Jesup, who substantiated Alligator's claim. The battle of Lockahatchee in January 1838 had led to a conference with chiefs Tuskegee and Halleck Hadjo, who surrendered their blacks and conditionally surrendered their bands. Many of the blacks had been sent off to the West and the rest were preparing to follow them when it became known that the President had not approved the conditions of the chief's surrender. They decided to go with their blacks, but several bands, including Alligator's, had not surrendered. He subsequently yielded and consented to emigrate. In their retreat before Jesup's army, his band had lost their tools and utensils, which Alligator wanted to collect before he surrendered. Fearing that the chief was trying to gain time, and considering the cost of transporting the property, Jesup sent word that new equipment would be given to Alligator and his band in the West.[21]

Upon Jesup's advice, Secretary Bell granted the request for equipment, but he wanted to use it to coerce Alligator's band to remove from Cherokee lands to the Deep Fork. Only on that condition would the articles be delivered. Superintendent Armstrong put pressure on Alligator and the other Seminoles to go to the Deep Fork, and he hoped to have them removed by the fall of 1841. But his plans were disrupted when Alligator and a delegation left the West for Florida to try to induce the remaining Seminoles to emigrate. His absence prevented his party from moving. Armstrong successfully advised that a subagent be sent to the Seminoles, since they distrusted the Creeks so much that they did not want to use the same agent. Such an officer might be able to adjust the differences between the factions and bring the Seminoles together.[22]

When Wild Cat emigrated in the fall of 1841, he settled his band of 230 on Cherokee lands in the river bottom just below the garrison. Efforts failed to remove them immediately to the Deep Fork, and his people were added to the ranks of those in the Cherokee Nation who were destitute because of a lack of building and farming tools. In March 1842, George W. Clarke, the disbursing agent at Fort Gibson, reported that the following Seminoles in the Cherokee Nation were not making corn because they lacked the tools: Tustenuggee Micco's town of 160, Cotsa Tustenucoochee's town of twenty, Hotalka Emathla's town of thirteen, Echo Emathla's town of 133, and Kitler Harjo's town of seventy. Immediately issuing tools meant that they would suffer only until fall; otherwise, they would suffer during the fall and winter, too. Alligator's town, numbering between 175 and two hundred, said Clarke, was also destitute of farming tools and had lived for the preceding twelve months by stealing from the Cherokees. The peace and quiet of the Indian country depended on the government's doing something for those people.[23]

Cherokee Agent Pierce M. Butler complained of depredations on Cherokee property which the Cherokees blamed on the Seminoles. The season was favorable, Butler said, for their removal to their own country so that they could plant crops. A new Seminole subagent was on his way to Fort Gibson, and upon his arrival he and James Logan were to accompany some of the principal Creeks and Seminoles on a visit to the bands, to point out to them the limits of their own country, and to inform them that the Cherokee agent had requested their removal. They were to move by May 1, or they would be moved by force. General Taylor ordered future emigration parties to land in the Creek country and not to enter the Cherokee Nation.[24]

Butler defended the Cherokee request for removal of the Seminoles, first, on the grounds that if the Cherokees chose to submit claims against the Seminoles for the destruction of stock, the claims would consume the present Seminole annuities when deducted from the payments. Second, the numbers of the Seminoles constantly increased, and removal would become more difficult. Yet Butler knew that removal was inevitable.[25]

KEEPING THE SEMINOLES DISUNITED

Meanwhile, however, a movement was afoot among the Creeks to keep the Seminoles from uniting as a group. In January 1842, Chief Roley McIntosh, Harlock Harjo, Sam Miller, and others sent a memorial protesting the designation of a separate part of the Creek lands for Seminole use, insisting that they would share what they had with the Seminoles, scattered as they were throughout the region. The Creeks maintained that it had been understood by both the Creeks and the United States commissioners who negotiated the treaty of February 14, 1833, that the Seminoles would not be established as a separate and independent nation but would merge with the Creeks and lose their national identity.[26]

General Taylor ceased all attempts to remove the Seminoles to the Deep Fork, and parties of emigrant Seminoles and blacks arriving in the territory were landed in Creek country south of the Arkansas to avoid adding numbers to the hundreds already on Cherokee lands.[27] Official momentum was lost, and the Seminoles remained another year in the Cherokee Nation.

Destruction of Cherokee property was ostensibly the reason for the Cherokees' change in attitude toward the presence of the Seminoles in their country. However, evidence external to that situation indicates that the change related to a growing fear of the presence of large numbers of blacks among the Seminoles. They represented a threat to the institution of slavery among the Cherokees, who by 1842 held large numbers of slaves. Their slave code more resembled the codes in the white South than did the codes of any of the other Indian nations, and it was severe in comparison to the easy relationship between the Seminoles and their blacks.

CHEROKEE SLAVE CODES

The Cherokees adopted their slave code for the western Nation between 1839 and 1842. A survey of it reveals that they were concerned about outside influence on their blacks. The earliest laws simply prescribed different punishments for Cherokees and blacks who violated the laws. An 1839 law stated that Indians convicted of rape were given one hundred lashes, while blacks convicted of the "offence against any free female, not of negro blood" were hanged. Another was a version of an earlier law, which prescribed up to fifty lashes for any free male or female citizen who married "any slave or person of color not entitled to the rights of citizenship," and one hundred lashes for "any colored male" convicted under the act. The council also passed an act that prescribed a fine of five to twenty dollars for an Indian convicted of disrupting a church service, and thirty-nine lashes for "any negro slave" convicted of the offense.[28]

The council in 1840 began reinstating a slave code similar to that which had existed before removal. It passed a law forbidding "any free negro or mulatto, not of Cherokee blood" to hold improvements in the Cherokee Nation, and made it unlawful for slaves to own horses, cattle, hogs, or firearms. All such property still held on June 1, 1841, was to be seized by the district sheriffs and sold at auction. The law also prescribed thirty-nine lashes for slaves, free blacks or mulattoes, "not of Cherokee blood," who introduced into and sold spirituous liquors in the Nation. The council of

1841 established patrol companies in the various neighborhoods, authorizing them to "take up and bring to punishment any negro or negroes, that may be strolling about, not on their owner's or owners' premises, without a pass from their owner or owners." The patrolers could also give up to thirty-nine lashes to "any negro not entitled to Cherokee privileges" found carrying a weapon of any kind. The same council passed an act prescribing a fine of one to five hundred dollars for teaching free blacks "not of Cherokee blood" or slaves to read and write.[29]

It is significant that those laws were aimed as much at free blacks and mulattoes "not of Cherokee blood" or not entitled to Cherokee privileges as they were aimed at the slaves of Cherokee citizens. Those "foreign" blacks were forbidden to hold improvements, sell spirituous liquors, or carry weapons. It was unlawful to teach them to read or write, and they were subject to punishment by the patrolers. The important question, then, arises of who were those free blacks, "not of Cherokee blood," in the Nation in such numbers that they had to be legislated against, if they were not the blacks who had accompanied the Seminoles to the West between 1838 and 1842.

THE INFLUENCE OF THE SEMINOLE BLACKS

From the start, officials of the Indian Office had feared the influence of the Seminole blacks upon slaves of the surrounding regions. How much influence they had on Cherokee slaves between Fort Gibson and Webbers Falls is uncertain, but for several reasons, the likelihood is great that there was intercourse between them, especially before Cherokee legislation limited the movement of slaves. Because of the rapids on the Arkansas River, in periods of low water Webbers Falls served as the disembarkation point for many of the Seminole and black emigrants who came from New Orleans aboard steamboats. Movement of emigrants offered local blacks a chance to observe them. Several of the free blacks, including Abraham, Gopher John, and Toney Barnet, were interpreters and as such had free access to the military post at Fort Gibson, the hub of activity in the Indian country and the clearinghouse for information in the territory.[30] Finally, Cherokees had bought a number of former Seminole slaves.

The result of the easy relationship between Seminole slaves and masters, the large numbers of blacks to whom the titles were contested, and the great numbers who claimed to be free was a sizable group of black people who lived with little or no control on their activities in a slave territory with a strict code, setting an example which slave owners in the surrounding regions feared. There is little doubt that legislation passed by the Cherokee National Council was directed at those blacks, the only large group of blacks without Cherokee privileges, who, according to official records, resided in the Cherokee Nation.

THE CHEROKEE SLAVE REVOLT

Any fears of bad influence the Cherokees may have had were undoubtedly fulfilled in their estimation in the early morning of November 15, 1842, when more than a score of slaves left the plantations of their Cherokee masters near Webbers Falls and traveled southwest across the prairies, presumably toward Mexican territory. Joined by a few Creek slaves during their flight, they fought off a group of pursuers and met with and murdered two travelers on the plains. They were finally captured by a party of Cherokees nearly three hundred miles southwest of Fort Gibson, and most of them were returned to their masters. Two were sent to Arkansas where they stood trial for murder. The event became known as the Cherokee slave revolt of 1842.[31]

Most of the blacks involved in the attempted escape were slaves of Joseph Vann of Webbers Falls and would have had an unusually good opportunity to observe the Seminole blacks. Vann owned a large plantation, on which he kept many slaves. Most of them farmed cotton and other crops, but some worked at the landing where the steamboats docked and where Vann operated a public ferry. As the Seminole emigrants disembarked at Webbers Falls, how Vann's slaves must have been impressed with the blacks, dressed Seminole fashion and carrying rifles and knives! Some of the Seminoles settled in the Illinois River bottoms not far from Webbers Falls. Since nearly all of the Seminoics had blacks, it is likely that the Cherokee slaves had opportunity to observe the Seminole blacks on a more routine basis.[32]

How much influence, direct or indirect, the Seminole blacks had had on the Vann slaves may never be known. However, Cherokee reaction to the slave "revolt" indicates that they regarded the influence of "foreign" free blacks as instrumental in the insurrection. On December 2, only a few days after the revolt, the Cherokee National Council passed "An Act in regard to Free Negroes." It directed the sheriffs of the several districts to notify all free blacks, except those who had been freed by Cherokee citizens, that they were to leave the limits of the Cherokee Nation by January 1, 1843, or as soon thereafter as practicable. Those who refused were to be reported to the agent for expulsion from the Nation.[33]

The concern of the Cherokees regarding "foreign" free blacks in their midst stands in striking contrast to the Seminoles, who had welcomed blacks among them for decades. It indicates the great difference between the Seminole and Cherokee attitudes toward blacks. As indicated above, the Creeks, too, had begun to restrict the movement and property rights of their blacks. During the next few years, these differences in attitude would prove to be a greater source of conflict between the Seminoles and their Indian neighbors.

FEAR OF CREEK DOMINATION

In his annual report for 1842, William Armstrong laid the blame for the Seminoles' refusal to leave the Cherokee country on fear of Creek domination. Although he believed that the Creeks should rightly fear the influence of the blacks over the Seminoles, he also granted that the Seminoles should fear oppression by the Creeks, especially whenever difficulty arose over the right to property. Most disputes of property rights had arisen over the blacks. Armstrong felt that the title to the blacks in question should be settled as soon as possible, for it was a problem "calculated to produce and keep up a bad state of feeling." Armstrong was now more kindly disposed to the blacks than he had been in earlier reports. The Seminoles on the Deep Fork had raised a surplus of corn, beans, pumpkins, and melons, and a few had raised small patches of rice that year. "The labor, however," he said, "is principally performed by the Seminole negroes, who have thus far conducted themselves with great propriety."[34]

In February 1843, another movement began to induce the Seminoles to remove from the Cherokee country. By this time, Thomas L. Judge, the Seminole subagent, had begun to have insight into the people of whom he had taken charge. The Cherokees had had some livestock killed and had made claims against the Seminoles. Judge thought that the Seminoles were being made scapegoats. He persuaded the Creeks to meet with the Seminoles to try to get them to remove. Washington officials hoped that the proposed council would remove any further obstacles in peaceably relocating the Seminoles.[35] For a time, it appeared that their hopes might be fulfilled.

However, officials realized in the summer of 1843 that the slave issue was the major barrier to Seminole unification in the western part of the Creek Nation. The outstanding case involved Toney Barnet. In early 1842, David Barnet had applied for Toney's return to the Indian Territory and payment for his services as interpreter in Florida since October of 1840. Captain Page believed that Toney was free and felt that Toney would have a "poor chance" if his status were decided by the Indians.[36]

At the time, Toney was at Cedar Keys, Florida, acting as interpreter for Colonel Worth. Page had promised him he could return to the Indian Territory when Holatoochee returned, but Colonel Worth could not spare him. Consequently, he was detained against his wishes. About this time, Worth offered Toney a reward of five hundred dollars if he would persuade the warriors of Octiarche's band to come in and emigrate and if Toney would be faithful at all times. But Worth soon found that Toney was up to "his old tricks of duplicity and double dealing" and as an example to the other interpreters ordered him whipped in their presence. Toney was sent west with a contingent of Octiarche's band and reached the Indian country on April 26, 1843.[37]

About forty miles below Fort Gibson, the Seminoles threatened to kill Toney, who fled to Fort Gibson for safety. They evidently blamed him for their having been taken to the West, for at Webbers Falls they murdered another black interpreter, as they had evidently secretly agreed to do when they reached the Indian country. He was lying down to take a nap when one of the Seminoles observed that it had been a year since he had decoyed them into Worth's hands. At that, the Seminoles jumped on him, stabbing him several times.[38]

Toney remained at Fort Gibson until June, when Chief McIntosh demanded that Colonel William Davenport, commander at the post, turn him over to David Barnet. But General Taylor was convinced that the sale of Toney in Florida had been a valid one, that he was therefore free, and that the Creek court decision giving title to David Barnet was invalid. Taylor also believed that Toney came under either Jesup's Proclamation or Jesup's promise to the Seminoles that their property would be secure in the West. Therefore, he directed Davenport not to give Toney to the Creeks. He was supported by statements by James and William Barnet, the sons of Toney's original owner in the East, who substantiated Toney's version of the events that led to his freedom.[39]

THE CREEK APPEAL

Angered at the army's interference in what they considered an internal affair and one which they assumed had been settled by their court, the Creeks appealed to the Secretary of War for a ruling in the case. When the Creek agent forwarded the complaint, he stated his concern about the slave question arising between the Creeks and Seminoles, blaming it on Jesup's war policy. He asked for a ruling on whether the blacks' claim to freedom, growing out of Jesup's orders, would be regarded as valid and sufficient in all cases arising under them.[40]

At first, Subagent Thomas L. Judge had felt that while the slave question had generated some excitement, no serious consequences would result from it. He had spoken of it with the Creek chiefs, who said that the Nation had no claims against the Seminoles but that some of their people had. They insisted, however, that they would take no measures except legal ones. Judge was inclined to believe them. For that reason, he had little patience with the Seminoles who remained in the Cherokee Nation. Wild Cat and Alligator were being deserted by some of their followers, who went to the Deep Fork, but generally they were stubborn in their position. Judge believed that the government should cut off all annuities to them until they gave in. Judge was obviously under the influence of the Creeks' opinion, which clouded his view of the situation. William Armstrong saw more of a problem than Judge did. If the matter of slave property remained unsettled, it might and probably would lead to "unpleasant collisions between the parties." He felt that the matter of settling the Seminoles among the Creeks needed revision in order to resolve the differences between the two.[41]

Judge subsequently decided that the slave issue was more serious than he had originally thought. In October 1843, the Seminoles and Creeks met in council, and those in the Cherokee Nation agreed to remove if a parcel of land could be found for them on the North Fork. The slave question, among others, came up. Judge now found that the question "was like to be attended with more serious consequences" than he had first thought. To ward off trouble, he took a firm stand for the Seminoles, guaranteeing the security of their property if they removed. Judge felt that the Seminoles would never submit to the Creek laws, especially those concerning blacks' rights to carry weapons and own property. And the Creek slave code was becoming increasingly more rigid. At a recent council, the Creeks had passed another law which forbade preaching to or by blacks.[42]

Commissioner T. Hartley Crawford, too, became convinced that the security of the Seminoles in their slave property was necessary for the peace and security of the country. Thus, in November, he recommended that a commission be appointed to meet with the Creeks and Seminoles to settle the dispute concerning the blacks and the occupancy of the land, and that in the meantime there be no removal of those on Cherokee lands. Secretary J. M. Porter approved the recommendation;[43] however, no instructions were forthcoming until the spring of 1844.

In January 1844, Crawford ruled in the case of Toney Barnet, whose status had been pending since he had fled to Fort Gibson. Crawford said that the government must be sustained against all who would interfere and disturb what it had guaranteed through its officers. The preponderance of evidence was in favor of Toney's freedom. This ruling and a statement by Casena Barnet, brother of the original owner, resulted in the issuing of "free papers" to Toney.[44] Crawford's decision meant that the Creeks would have to take matters into their own hands. Thus, trouble erupted between the Creeks and Seminoles over slave titles, and the first of a long series of raids by slave hunters on the Seminole blacks began.

RAIDS BY SLAVE HUNTERS

In this instance, a Creek named Siah Hardridge claimed some thirty blacks held by Sally Factor, a Creek who lived with the Seminoles. Hardridge had purchased a claim which predated emigration, agreeing to pay Sally $2,000 for the blacks. However, the blacks themselves opposed the sale and prevailed upon the Seminole chiefs, who induced Judge and Chief McIntosh to have Hardridge relinquish the bill of sale. Hardridge, of course, denied McIntosh's right to do so and brought Sally Factor before the chief to repeat the terms of the sale. She testified that she had sold the blacks to Hardridge but that the Seminole chiefs had said that she got too little for them and induced her to apply to McIntosh to cancel the sale. Sally had an absolute title to only ten of the blacks; the rest belonged to the children of her deceased sister, whose guardian she was. It was her desire, she said, for Hardridge to have her slaves and those of her sister's children if the Creek and Seminole chiefs decided she had the right to sell them.[45]

Creek Agent James L. Dawson and McIntosh directed Hardridge not
to touch the slaves until the Creek and Seminole chiefs reached a decision.
Although Hardridge said that he would not, he stole one of the blacks
named Dembo Factor. Micanopy sent Wild Cat to the commander at
Fort Gibson to enlist the army's aid in recovering Dembo. The Seminoles
suspected that he had been taken to the mouth of the Canadian where
he would be shipped downstream and sold. They wanted General Taylor
to search all boats passing Fort Smith. According to Wild Cat, the Seminoles
were much enraged over the incident and feared an outbreak of difficulties
between them and the Creeks if Hardridge and others like him were not
punished for kidnapping slaves.[46]

Agent Dawson pledged that if Dembo were not returned to the Seminoles,
the property of Hardridge would be held liable. The Creeks apparently
wanted to avoid a clash with the Seminoles and, disavowing any national
claim against the slaves of the Seminoles, declared themselves perfectly
willing for the United States to decide between their people and the individual
claimants. Micanopy, too, was conciliatory, asking the military officials to
write Chief McIntosh concerning Dembo's return, stressing that it was his
wish to live "brotherly" with the Creeks.[47]

When word of Dembo's abduction reached General Taylor, he reacted
as might have been predicted. To him, the faith of the government had
been pledged by General Jesup in Florida, and the emigrating Seminoles,
therefore, should not be harassed by claims for their blacks. On two previous
occasions, he had told the Creeks that he would tolerate no "forcible irregular
prosecution of such claims." He reaffirmed that stand, issuing a warning
to Hardridge: If he tried to gain possession of Seminole blacks, except by
regular application to the chiefs, Taylor would have him placed in irons
at Fort Gibson to await the pleasure of the government. Taylor was determined not to allow the harmony between the Seminoles and Creeks to
be jeopardized by kidnapping attempts by people such as Hardridge.[48]
Pressure from the military and from the Creeks finally resulted in Dembo's
release.

THE GOVERNMENT COMMISSION

It became apparent in Washington that strong pressure from the government was necessary in resolving the unsettled condition of the Seminoles,
stopping their depredations on the property of other tribes, settling their

difficulties with the Creeks, and removing the obstacles to their settlement on the land which was assured them by treaty. Only then could the
tribe make progress toward civilization. Thus, on April 10, 1844, Commissioner Crawford established a commission composed of William
Armstrong, the Chickasaw, Cherokee, and Creek agents, and the Neosho
and Seminole subagents to treat with the two tribes. The commission's
greatest challenge was to prevail on the Seminoles in the Cherokee country
to remove to the Creek Nation, for in light of recent events, they feared
Creek domination more than ever. However, Thomas Judge believed they
would settle on the North Fork of the Canadian if they were guaranteed
the safety of their property.[49]

In giving instructions to the commissioners, T. Hartley Crawford insisted
on certain concessions from both tribes. First, the Creeks, by virtue of their
larger numbers, should take the lead and their government and laws be
extended over both Nations, to be altered or repealed as the two tribes
saw fit. Second, the Creeks should agree that property brought with the
Seminoles from Florida or from the Cherokee Nation into the Creek country,
or any property acquired after the treaty, should not be liable to attachment or be taken from the Seminoles on any claim which predated emigration to the Creek country, unless the action was sanctioned by the President.
This concession would guarantee assurances given to the Seminoles in
Florida that they would retain the blacks sent west with them. Third, the
Seminoles should be urged to come to terms with the Creeks, for they would
ultimately have to go into the Creek country anyway. Finally, the Creeks
should be reminded that their treaty obligation carried no condition concerning the property brought with them or the ownership of that property based
on title acquired before their emigration.[50]

ALLIGATOR'S DELEGATION

About the time these instructions were issued, Wild Cat, Alligator, and
two subchiefs went to Washington. Micanopy and other head men, through
their interpreter Abraham, protested that the Seminoles were not bound
by the acts of the delegation, who did not have their sanction. Nevertheless, the delegation went to General Jesup, then serving as quartermaster
general, in the name of Micanopy to obtain fulfillment of treaty obligations
and of promises made during the war by the several commanders in Florida.

Jesup appealed in their behalf to Secretary William Wilkins. During the war, he had required the Indians' faithful fulfillment of the treaties and had guaranteed the same by the United States. He had assured them that the separate land guaranteed by the treaty of 1833 was set apart and waiting for them, and to some chiefs, such as Alligator, he had promised that property left in Florida would be replaced in the West. But the promises had not been kept.[51]

Jesup appealed, too, on behalf of the Seminole blacks, only an estimated one tenth of whom, he said, had been brought in during the war by their Seminole masters under the convention of Fort Dade and over whom the Indians had all the rights of slave owners. The rest either surrendered voluntarily or were captured by the army. To those used as guides, spies, or messengers, Jesup had pledged the government's faith that they would not be sold but would be allowed to settle on lands assigned to the Seminoles in the West, where they could live under the protection of the army. Jesup had evidently been told by Wild Cat and Alligator that Creeks, Cherokees, and citizens of the United States and Texas had been trying to gain possession of some of the blacks under pretended purchases from their former Indian owners. In view of the promises he had made to the blacks, Jesup could not "remain passive and witness the illegal interference with the rights of those people; every consideration as well of personal honor as of public obligation forbids it." He asked protection for all who had surrendered under his promise of freedom.[52]

Conferences with Alligator's delegation resulted in an extension of the authority of the treaty commissioners to negotiate an agreement, if possible, whereby the land designated for the Seminoles by the act of Congress on February 13, 1839, would be set apart exclusively for their use. Crawford felt that such a concession by the Creeks might result in the reunification of the Seminoles and ease tensions on the frontier, but the Creeks refused to yield. They disapproved of the departmental sympathy for the Seminole position and called it a "one sided business." They wanted the tribes to become one people and vowed they would never consent to a separate country for the Seminoles. They returned to their old line: The Creek people as a nation had no claims against the Seminoles for any of their blacks, but some individual Creeks had claims of purchase which would be "impartially investigated." Crawford and William Armstrong knew that the first and greatest obstacle to overcome in obtaining a separate land for the Seminoles would be inducing the Creeks to agree to it. They were

decidedly hostile to the idea, yet Crawford asked for the impossible: He
wanted Armstrong to obtain the concession without any cost to the government or to the Seminoles. As a last resort, Armstrong could allow the
Creeks something out of the $15,400 due the Seminoles under the Treaty
of Payne's Landing, if the Seminoles agreed to it. In deference to General
Jesup's request, he could allow the Seminoles $5,000 for the property
they had abandoned in Florida. And finally, he could allow a small amount
for the removal of the Seminoles from the Cherokee Nation to their
new homes.[53]

The Creek protest had put their opinions on the controversy about
slave property in a "more favorable position" with Crawford than before.
His view, however, was not shared by Subagent Judge, who by this time
was fully convinced that the Seminoles could not and should not ever be
a constituent part of the Creek Nation, for the two peoples had "no community of interest or feeling," and never could have. The farther apart
they were, the better, he said.[54]

TROUBLED TIMES

Alligator's delegation to Washington had been unpopular among some
of the Seminoles and resulted in the outright enmity of others for Gopher
John, who had acted as their interpreter. On his return to the Indian country
in July 1844, a Seminole shot at him and killed his horse. Word went out
that he was to be killed. His friends on the Deep Fork, where his home was,
sent him word to stay at Fort Gibson, for feeling against him was high in
the Creek country. Colonel Richard B. Mason, the commander at the post,
believed the attempt on John's life was a result of his services as guide and
interpreter for the army in Florida, but it seems strange that his enemies
had waited until 1844 to try to kill him. The reason was more nearly as
General Jesup said about the incident: Seminoles were hostile toward John
and other interpreters because the government had not fulfilled all promises
to the Indians, who began to suspect that the interpreters had deceived
them during negotiations and to hold them responsible for the government's
breach of faith.[55]

On the Deep Fork, John had over fifty head of livestock and a wagon.
If he did not get back, that property would be lost. Colonel Mason, however,
told him to stay at the post, where he and three other members of his

family would receive rations until Mason received instructions from Washington. When news of John's plight reached Jesup, he suggested that John be allowed to settle on the military reserve and that the Seminoles be held responsible for his property. Secretary William Wilkins agreed. In August, the Seminoles met in council and discussed the outrage on Gopher John. Micanopy, Wild Cat, Young Alligator, Yohola Harjo, Jim Jumper, and Tom sent an apology for the event and a statement that they were willing to pay for the horse. But there were no funds on hand, and John went unpaid.[56]

Gopher John was not the only one who returned from Washington to trouble. When Wild Cat and Alligator reached Fort Gibson, they found their people camped on the prairies near the post, starving. The Arkansas and Grand rivers had risen and driven them from the bottoms, destroying the crops they had planted and washing away all the corn they had stored in their cribs. Two hundred thirty-five Seminoles and blacks were completely destitute. Colonel Mason issued them half rations for eighteen days as temporary relief. Their situation was a marked contrast to that of the Seminoles on the Deep Fork, Elk Creek, and Little River, who had large crops of corn, potatoes, and rice on hand, had a fair crop in the ground, and maintained increasing numbers of cattle, horses, and hogs.[57]

In his annual report of August 1844, Thomas L. Judge again insisted that the recent stress on the relations between the Creeks and Seminoles made it "highly impolitic and improper" for the Seminoles to move among the Creeks or for the government to make them become a part of the Creek Nation. William Armstrong agreed that it would be difficult to induce the most refractory Seminoles to incorporate with the Creeks, but he believed it could be done. He relied on their destitution as a result of the spring floods to make them more willing to go to the Deep Fork than they might otherwise have been.[58] He was apparently right.

CREEK-SEMINOLE TREATY

When the United States commission entered negotiations with the Creeks and Seminoles, the blacks were of foremost concern to the latter. The chiefs drafted a memorial in which they submitted "propositions to avoid unpleasant feelings in the part of the Creeks." In view of the excitement between the Seminoles and some Creeks over slave claims, they asked the

Creeks to prevent their citizens from interfering with any of the Seminole blacks, who they maintained were placed under their protection by the government and could not be taken away without governmental consent. They wanted any case arising over title settled by the President. Finally, they wanted a separate country of their own, subsistence upon settlement in their country, and an agent of their own.[59]

While the Seminoles insisted that they would not submit to Creek laws on any terms, the Creeks at first would not have it any other way. Then Seminole resolve crumbled. The commission—consisting of Armstrong, Cherokee Agent Pierce M. Butler, and James Logan—held out monetary inducements and found a compromise. The annuity guaranteed by the Treaty of Payne's Landing was increased from $3,000 to $5,000, the increase to be paid in goods. The Creeks were given an additional $3,000 for educational purposes, and their present annuity was extended for thirteen years. The treaty, agreed to on January 4, 1845, contained the following provisions: First, the Seminoles could settle in a body or separately as they saw fit in any part of the Creek country and make their own town regulations, subject to the general control of the Creek council, in which the Seminoles would be represented. There would be no distinction between the members of the tribes except in their monetary affairs, in which neither could interfere with the other. Second, those Seminoles who had not done so would remove immediately to the Creek country. Third, all contested cases between the tribes concerning the right to property, growing out of sales made before the ratification of the treaty, were subject to the decision of the President. Fourth, since the Seminoles expressed the desire to settle in a body on Little River, some distance west of the residence of most of those already in the Creek Nation, all would have rations issued to them during removal to the new lands and would receive subsistence for six months thereafter. Those who were not in the Creek country before the issue of rations began were to be excluded, except those in Florida, who were given twelve months to remove and join the tribe. Finally, the Seminoles were to receive $1,000 per year for five years, to be paid in agricultural implements to replace the property they had left in Florida.[60] The treaty was ratified on March 6.

While the treaty may have preserved the social integrity of the Seminoles, it left much to be desired concerning their political identity. Like so many treaties, it was simply words on a page. It did not remove the fear of oppression in the hearts of the Seminoles, who had made concessions to the Creeks in order to obtain a land for their exclusive settlement. Neither did it effectively remove the major source of difficulty between the Seminoles and Creeks: the title to and control of the blacks in the Nation. In fact, bringing the Seminoles under the general control of Creek laws in many ways would serve only to aggravate the issue.

Why did the Seminoles give in to monetary inducements after having held out so long? Undoubtedly, as Armstrong had suspected, their general state of poverty, compounded by floods during the preceding summer, had had much to do with it. An additional reason was an apparent weakening of the bond between the Seminoles and the blacks.

Basic to the fear of the Creeks had been the Seminole desire to protect the blacks. They must have known that the treaty would ultimately prove disastrous for the Africans; Creek enforcement of laws under the new political arrangement could in no way work for their advancement. For a time, the common suspicion and fear of the Creeks had maintained the bond between the Indians and blacks—a bond which had been created in a good measure by the exigencies of the American threat in Florida, the Indians' uncertainty preceding the Second Seminole War, and the war itself. However, in the West, there was neither an American threat nor a war. The Indians had begun to distrust some of the interpreters who had been their close advisers and allies in Florida. During the next few months the distrust between Indians and blacks would become more widespread, and the blacks would be left more and more to their own devices to protect themselves.

NOTES

1. Charles J. Kappler, comp., *Indian Affairs: Laws and Treaties* (2nd ed., Washington: Government Printing Office, 1904), 2: 291, 249-250; Angie Debo, *The Road to Disappearance* (Norman: University of Oklahoma Press, 1941), 101-102; Grant Foreman, *Indian Removal* (Norman: University of Oklahoma Press, 1932), 380; Edwin C. McReynolds, *The Seminoles* (Norman: University of Oklahoma Press, 1957), 234.

2. William Armstrong to T. Hartley Crawford, September 10, 1842, 27 Cong., 3 Sess., *House Executive Document 2,* 445; Crawford to Armstrong, April 10, 1844, in National Archives Microfilm Publications, *Microcopy M574* (Special Files of the Office of Indian Affairs, 1807-1904)-13, Special File 96: Seminole Claims to Certain Negroes, 1841-1849 (hereafter cited as *File 96*).

3. Armstrong to Crawford, September 10, 1842, 27 Cong., 3 Sess., *House Executive Document 2,* 443-444.

4. Foreman, 380; Ethan Allen Hitchcock, *A Traveler in Indian Territory: The Journal of Ethan Allen Hitchcock, late Major-General in the United States Army,* edited by Grant Foreman (Cedar Rapids, Iowa: The Torch Press, 1930), 92.

5. Crawford to Joel R. Poinsett, January 4, 1839, 25 Cong., 3 Sess., *Senate Document 88,* 2, 3.

6. Crawford to Armstrong, April 10, 1844, in *File 96.*

7. 26 Cong., 1 Sess., *Senate Document 1,* 472.

8. Armstrong to Crawford, October 1, 1840, 26 Cong., 2 Sess., *House Executive Document 2,* 314; Arbuckle to McIntosh, June 7, 1840, and June 8, 1840, and General Matthew Arbuckle to Mic-ca-nup-pa and other Seminole Chiefs, May 11, 1840, National Archives Record Group 393 (Records of the United States Army Continental Commands, 1821-1920), *Second Military Department,* Letters Sent (hereafter cited as *2nd LS*).

9. Arbuckle to McIntosh, June 8, 1840, and Arbuckle to James Logan, July 19, 1840, *2nd LS;* John Love to Logan, July 3, 1840, National Archives Microfilm Publications, *Microcopy M234* (Records of the Office of Indian Affairs, Letters Received)-923, A899-40. *Microcopy M234* is hereafter cited as *M234,* followed by the roll number.

10. Armstrong to Crawford, October 17, 1840, *M234*-923, A899-40.

11. Mark A. Cooper to John Bell, May 17, 1841, *M234*-923, C1411-41; Crawford to Bell, June 7, 1841, National Archives Microfilm Publications, *Microcopy M348* (Records of the Office of Indian Affairs, Report Books)-2, 420. *Microcopy M348* is hereafter cited as *M348,* followed by the roll number.

12. General Thomas S. Jesup to Bell, June 9, 1841, National Archives Record Group 393, *Fort Gibson,* Volume "Indian Affairs," 5, and *File 96.* Love made inquiry into the matter again in the spring of 1842 and in 1844, when it came before the Creek council. Again, on the testimony of Coa Hadjo, Cloud, Micanopy, Nocose Yohola, and Passockee Yahola, the council declared the blacks to be the property of Mah-pah-yist-chee and Mah-kah-tist-chee, the daughters of Tuskeneehau. T. F. Foster to Secretary of War, January 7, 1842, *M234*-226, F251-42; Crawford to Foster, January 21, 1842, National Archives Microfilm Publications, *Microcopy M21* (Records of the Office of Indian Affairs, Letters Sent)-31, 389 (hereafter cited as *M21*); W. T. Colquitt to John C. Spencer, *M234*-289, C1710-42; Crawford to Spencer, May 13, 1842, *M348*-3, 142; C. D. Pryor to Charles H. Dean, April 10, 1856, *M234*-802, D153-56.

13. J. C. Watson to Poinsett, November 22, 1839, Watson to Crawford, December 6, 1839, Richard W. Habersham, Lott Warren et al. to Poinsett,

July 2, 1840, E. A. Nisbet to Poinsett, July 2, 1840, and Watson to Poinsett, July 25, 1840, *M234*-225, W1099-39, W1010-39, H727-40, N83-40, and W1226-40; Crawford to Poinsett, April 8, July 1, and July 9, 1840, *M348*-2, 59, 141, 143; Watson to Poinsett, January 11, 1841, and John H. Watson to Poinsett, February 24, 1841, *M234*-226, W1351-41 and W1372-41; Crawford to Poinsett, February 27, 1841, *M21*-30, 143.

14. A. Iverson to Crawford, February 27, 1841, *M234*-226, I714-41; Poinsett to Arbuckle, March 2, 1841, *M21*-30, 152; Crawford to Bell, August 10, 1841, *M348*-2, 476.

15. Bell to Armstrong, March 24, 1841, *M21*-30, 184; Report of Committee on Indian Affairs, April 12, 1842, 30 Cong., 1 Sess., *House Report 724*, 2, hereafter cited as *Report 724*.

16. Bell to Crawford, April 29, 1841, and J. C. Watson to Bell, July 7, 1841, *M234*-226, W1433-41 and W1519-41; *Report 724*, 2. Watson became convinced that the conditions on the frontier would not permit him to take the blacks, and he again sought recourse in Congress. In April of 1842, he succeeded in getting a favorable report from the House Committee on Indian Affairs. By that time, he was claiming the value of the blacks in the market at the time they should have been delivered, or about $60,000 plus $6,000 in expenses. The committee, recognizing that Watson's purchase was a speculation, and in view of the small price at which the blacks were purchased, recommended an appropriation of $21,604 to cover the purchase price, interest, and expenses. Watson to Bell, July 7, 1841, *M234*-226, W1519-41; Crawford to Bell, August 10, 1841, *M348*-2, 476; Crawford to Spencer, January 19, 1842, *M348*-3, 83; Watson to Crawford, February 18, 1842, *M234*-289, W1715-42; *Report 724*, 2. No appropriation was forthcoming, however. The claim was again presented in 1849 and 1852. In that latter year, the Congress voted an appropriation. In arguments in the House, opponents of the appropriation said that the slaves were not plunder and therefore did not come under Jesup's agreement with the Creeks. Proponents argued that the blacks were plunder and the slaves of the Seminoles. When the vote was taken, some of the antislavery members of the House voted for it, justifying their act on the grounds that they were not buying slaves but were fulfilling the government's word to the Indians and to Watson who bought the slaves in good faith. Joshua R. Giddings, *The Exiles of Florida* (Columbus, Ohio: Follett, Foster and Company, 1858), 234-250.

17. Arbuckle to Mic-ca-nup-pa and other Seminole Chiefs, May 11, 1840, *2nd LS*.

18. Statement of David Barnet, February 2, 1842, *M234*-226, H1074-42; Head Men and Warriors to Secretary, July 25, 1843, *M234*-227, D830-43; Arbuckle to McIntosh, May 10, 1840, *2nd LS;* Captain John Page to

Crawford, September 6, 1842, *M234*-289, P1158-42. Polly Barnet was
formerly the wife of Chief Bowlegs, who in 1819 manumitted her and
her two children Margarita and Martiness; the papers were recorded in
1822 in the office of the clerk of St. Johns County, Florida. In 1854,
the following descendants of Polly were considered free by the Seminoles:
Grace, Lydia, Mary Ann, Nancy, and Cuny, all daughters of Margarita;
Grace's two children; Lydia's three children; Many Ann's child; William,
George, and Robert, the sons of Martiness; Becky and Dave, both children
of Polly; Becky's child. J. W. Washbourne's Statement, October 14, 1854,
M234-801, D709-54.

19. General Zachary Taylor to Logan, September 9, 1841, National
Archives Record Group 393, *Second and Seventh Military Departments,*
Letters Sent (hereafter cited as *2nd & 7th LS).*

20. Jesup to Spencer, December 28, 1841, and January 18, 1842, 27
Cong., 2 Sess., *House Document 55,* 2, 3.

21. John Ross to Bell, April 12, 1841, and Jesup to Bell, May 3, 1841,
M234-800, R58-41; Crawford to Armstrong, July 17, 1841, *M21*-30, 440.

22. Crawford to Armstrong, July 17, 1841, *M21*-30, 440; Armstrong
to Crawford, September 30, 1841, 27 Cong., 2 Sess., *House Executive
Document 2,* 316.

23. George W. Clarke to Lieutenant Colonel R. B. Mason, February 5,
1842, and March 14, 1842, *Fort Gibson,* Letters Received (hereafter cited
as *Gibson LR*), Box 1.

24. Pierce M. Butler to Mason, March 20, 1842, and Lieutenant W. W.
J. Bliss to Mason, March 27, 1842, *Gibson LR*, Box 1.

25. Butler to Mason, March 31, 1842, *Gibson LR,* Box 1.

26. J. C. Stambaugh to Crawford, March 30, 1842, *M234*-226, S3148-42.

27. Bliss to Mason, April 11, 1842, and Bliss to Colonel S. Kearny,
May 13, 1842, *Gibson LR,* Box 1.

28. *Laws of the Cherokee Nation: Adopted by the Council at Various
Periods* (Tahlequah, Ind. Ter.: Cherokee Advocate Office, 1852), [Pt. 2],
18, 19, 37 (hereafter cited as *Laws*).

29. *Laws* [Pt. 2], 44, 53, 55.

30. Armstrong to Crawford, October 1, 1840, 26 Cong., 2 Sess., *House
Executive Document 2,* 314; Kenneth Wiggins Porter, *The Negro on the
American Frontier* (New York: Arno Press and The New York Times,
1971), 323-324; Page to Crawford, September 6, 1842, *M234*-289, P1158-
42; Statement of P. M. Butler, April 16, 1845, *M234*-800, B2452-45.

31. The event was not an insurrection or revolt; however, the attempted
escape of the slaves resulted in an armed clash between Indians and slaves.
Since the event has been known historically as a revolt, perhaps because

the blacks robbed a store and stole guns, ammunition, and supples, the term has been retained.

32. Norman Arthur Graebner, "The Public Land Policy of the Five Civilized Tribes," *Chronicles of Oklahoma,* 23 (Summer 1945), 110; Graebner, "Pioneer Indian Agriculture in Oklahoma," *Chronicles of Oklahoma,* 23 (Autumn 1945), 241; Carolyn Thomas Foreman, "Early History of Webbers Falls," *Chronicles of Oklahoma,* 29 (Winter 1951-52), 460. Some of the Seminoles in the Illinois bottoms were still there as late as 1847. Marcellus Duval to Colonel Gustavus Loomis, April 29, 1846, *Gibson LR,* Box 2; Loomis to James McKisick, May 18, 1847, *Fort Gibson,* Volume "Indian Affairs," 25.

33. *Laws* [Pt. 2] , 71.

34. Armstrong to Crawford, September 10, 1842, 27 Cong., 3 Sess., *House Executive Document 2,* 445.

35. Thomas L. Judge to Armstrong, February 25, 1843, *M234*-800, A1417-43.

36. Crawford to Judge, March 9, 1843, *M21*-33, 355; Major Ethan Allen Hitchcock to Spencer, June 1, 1842, *M234*-226, H1047-42; Crawford to Page, July 30, 1842, *M21*-32, 358; Page to Crawford, September 6, 1842, *M234*-289, P1158-42.

37. Page to Crawford, September 6, 1842, *M234*-289, P1158-42; J. B. Luce to Armstrong, March 7, 1845, and LeGrand Capers to Crawford, March 4, 1843, *M234*-806, A1789-45 and C1923-43; Foreman, 384. At New Orleans, Toney had applied for his money and was promised it, but the boat had left before the money could be obtained. Upon reaching the Indian country, he again applied for it, but the money was not paid. It was denied him again in 1845. At that time General Worth wrote, "In respect to that scoundrel *Toney,* I only regretted that it was not lawful to have him shot instead of emigrating him." Judge to Taylor, July 28, 1843, *Gibson LR,* Box 2; Crawford to Armstrong, April 3, 1845, and April 29, 1845, and Crawford to Colonel W. J. Worth, April 3, 1845, *M21*-36, 277, 331; Worth to Crawford, April 12, 1845, *M234*-806, W2623-45.

38. Head Men and Warriors of the Upper Towns to Secretary, July 25, 1843, *M234*-227, D830-43; Armstrong to Crawford, May 22, 1843, *M234*-800, A1457-43.

39. Colonel William Davenport to Taylor, June 15, 1843, *Second and Seventh Military Departments,* Letters Received (hereafter cited as *2nd & 7th LR*), Box 5; Bliss to Davenport, June 21, 1843, *Gibson LR,* Box 1; Davenport to McIntosh, July 5, 1843, *Fort Gibson,* Letters Sent (hereafter cited as *Gibson LS*).

40. Dawson to Crawford, August 5, 1843, *M234*-227, D830-43.

41. Judge to Armstrong, September 15, 1843, and Armstrong to Crawford, September 30, 1843, 28 Cong., 1 Sess., *House Executive Document 2,* 415, 424-425.

42. Judge to Crawford, October 22, 1843, *M234*-800, J1350-43.

43. Crawford to Armstrong, April 10, 1844, *File 96.*

44. Crawford to Armstrong, January 24, 1844, and Armstrong to Dawson, January 24, 1844, *M21*-34, 446, 457; Statement of Judge, February 21, 1844, *2nd & 7th LR,* Box 5; Judge to Crawford, April 23, 1844, *M234*-800, I1449-44.

45. Dawson to Captain Nathan Boone, April 10, 1844, *Gibson LR,* Box 2. Siah Hardridge, who was one of the most persistent slave hunters among the Creeks, was probably the same man as Joseph Siah Hardridge, a brother-in-law of the well-known Creek leader George Stidham. Joseph Siah Hardridge was reputedly among those who killed William McIntosh, the former chief of the Creeks. Hardridge died near present Yahola, Oklahoma, in 1868. Loney Hardridge (Interview), March 24, 1937, *Indian-Pioneer History* (Oklahoma City: Indian Archives Division, Oklahoma Historical Society), 2: 316.

46. Dawson to Boone, April 10, 1844, *Gibson LR,* Box 2; Lieutenant James N. Belger to Loomis, April 3, 1844, *Gibson LS.*

47. Dawson to Boone, April 10, 1844, *Gibson LR,* Box 2; Boone to Dawson, April 8, 1844, *2nd & 7th LR,* Box 5.

48. Bliss to Dawson, May 13, 1844, *2nd & 7th LS.*

49. Crawford to Armstrong, April 10, 1844, File 96 and 28 Cong., 2 Sess., *House Executive Document 2,* 323-325.

50. Crawford to Armstrong, April 10, 1844, *File 96,* and 28 Cong., 2 Sess., *House Executive Document 2,* 323-325.

51. Micco Nupper, et al., to Commissioner, April 20, 1844, *M234*-800, M194-44; McReynolds, 251-252; Jesup to William Wilkins, May 22, 1844, *File 96.*

52. Jesup to Wilkins, May 30, 1844, *M234*-800, J1482-44, and *Fort Gibson,* Volume "Indian Affairs," 6.

53. Crawford to Wilkins, May 20, 1844, and Crawford to Armstrong, June 17, 1844, 28 Cong., 2 Sess., *House Executive Document 2,* 325, 326-327; McIntosh, et al., to Dawson, June 8, 1844, *M234*-800, M1973-44.

54. Judge to Armstrong, August 26, 1844, 28 Cong., 2 Sess., *House Executive Document 2,* 471.

55. Alligator, et al., to Crawford, May 16, 1844, Mason to Roger Jones, July 10, 1844, and Jesup's endorsement, August 2, 1844, *M234*-800, A1624-44 and M1973-44.

56. Mason to Jones, July 10, 1844, and Judge to Boone, August 31, 1844, *M234*-800, M1973-44 and J1684-45; Jones to Arbuckle, August 3, 1844, *Gibson LR,* Box 2; Statement of Boone, November 28, 1846, *Fort Gibson,* Volume "Indian Affairs," 25.

57. Judge to Armstrong, August 26, 1844, 28 Cong., 2 Sess., *House Executive Document 2,* 471; McReynolds, 252.

58. Judge to Armstrong, August 26, 1844, and Armstrong to Crawford, October 1, 1844, 28 Cong., 2 Sess., *House Executive Document 2,* 252, 454.

59. Seminole Memorial, December 28, 1844, *M234*-800, Frame 626.

60. Treaty of January 4, 1845, National Archives Microfilm Publications, *Microcopy T494* (Documents Relating to the Negotiation of Ratified and Unratified Treaties with Various Indian Tribes, 1801-1869)-9, Documents Relating to the Negotiation of the Treaty of January 4, 1845, with the Creek and Seminole Indians, Frames 235-243.

A breakdown in relations

Most of the Seminoles removed to their new homes in the spring of 1845
and by fall were well established in the Little River country, where they
settled in twenty-five towns or bands, built cabins, and planted crops.
About eight miles north of Little River they built a council house and
about two miles from that the agency and blacksmith shop. Each town
had its own headmen and town laws; a general council of the tribe had
supervisory control over all of the towns. A majority of the headmen,
with approval of Micanopy, could pass laws to govern all of the Seminoles,
provided that the laws did not conflict with those passed by the Creek
general council. The principal chief's executive council consisted of Wild
Cat, who was Micanopy's "counsellor and organ" and assisted him in
making decisions, Tussekiah, Octiarche, Pascofar, Echo Emathla, and
Passockee Yohola.[1]

The lateness of their removal in 1845 had prevented them from making
a full crop. Scarce provisions and the hard winter of 1845-46 caused many
to suffer, but in 1846 crops were better. Each town had a town field held
in common by the band. Some individuals had fields apart from these.
Most of the labor in reestablishing the Seminoles in their new land was
done by the blacks, who set about, as well as they could under the circumstances, to rebuild the kind of relationship which had existed between them
and the Seminoles before the war. They moved off to themselves in small
groups and began farming corn, beans, pumpkins, melons, and rice, raising
livestock, and paying tribute in produce to their masters. Like the Semi-

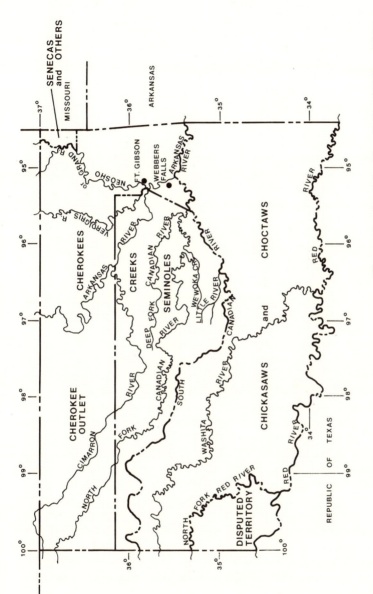

Western Lands of the Five Civilized Tribes, 1845

noles, they built rough log cabins, furnished with stools, mortars and
pestles, hominy baskets, a few pots, sofkee dishes, wooden spoons, and
beef-hide beds.[2]

BLACK INTERPRETERS

Of course, some of the blacks had done other things besides farming.
Several still worked as interpreters, and as such continued—or sought to
reestablish as the case might be—the type of influence they had formerly
had over the Seminoles. Foremost among them was Abraham. In 1840
Captain John Page engaged him to accompany a Seminole delegation to
Florida, but because of his former services to the United States, some of
the Seminoles in Florida harbored hard feelings against him. Therefore,
the chiefs asked to choose other interpreters. In the West, Abraham remained the confidant of and interpreter for Micanopy, his old ally, and
in February 1843 had become the government's interpreter at the Seminole subagency. As an interpreter, Abraham had evidently commanded a
good deal of respect among the Indians, for late that spring, he and Micanopy
came from the Deep Fork "for the purpose of using their influence" in
persuading the Seminoles still living in the Cherokee Nation to remove to
the Creek country. Abraham's name appears as interpreter on the Treaty of
January 4, 1845. A few months later, however, ex-officio Seminole Subagent Gideon C. Matlock dismissed him, apparently for drunkenness:
"Abram is very much addicted to the use of ardent spirits; so much so that
he is entirely incompetent for a Government Interpreter. He was unable to
render me any assistance upon the days of issue, being upon the ground
intoxicated, and engaged in broils and dissensions with the Indians themselves. Besides, Abram has by no means the confidence of the Seminoles."
In Abraham's words, he led "an uncertain and unhappy life" because of
old enmities. While he may have been out of favor with some of the Seminoles, he apparently retained the confidence of Micanopy and others. His
disfavor as an interpreter was short-lived. He had the confidence of
Marcellus Duval, the new Seminole subagent, who in April of 1846 wanted
to send him to try to persuade the Seminole stragglers in the Cherokee
country to remove to their own lands. However, Abraham "could not be
spared during council."[3]

Gopher John was also an important interpreter during the early years in the West. In addition to his activities in Washington, he was called on almost daily by the Seminoles living in the Cherokee Nation from 1843 to 1845. Often the only interpreter at Fort Gibson, John could not ignore their requests. The Seminoles sent him with talks to the Cherokees and to United States officials. John was not hired officially as an interpreter, but Cherokee Agent Pierce M. Butler felt that his services had been so extensive that he ought to be paid.[4] In 1844 and 1845, however, John's reputation among the Seminoles had suffered.

Cudjo also acted as an interpreter. The extent of his activities in the West is uncertain; however, as late as summer of 1845, he was acting as interpreter for the Seminole chiefs, when he and Abraham interpreted a message from them to General Jesup, who was visiting Fort Gibson.[5]

EFFORTS TO ESTABLISH FREE STATUS

While it may have appeared for a short time that the blacks would be able to reestablish their former relationships with their Indian masters and allies, their efforts were never carried to fruition. Some sought to establish their free status through their own efforts. Some with obvious foresight and distrust of the word of officials had come to the West with scraps of paper on which the various officers had recorded statements concerning the circumstances of their surrender. In an attempt to establish their freedom, and perhaps because they had begun to distrust the Seminoles' ability to resist the Creeks, many had given the papers to the agent or the commanders at Fort Gibson to be recorded. Those who had failed to get papers had officials record their own statements.

The records of Fort Gibson and of the Seminole agency reveal the desperate struggle of many blacks to safeguard against a return to slave status. On April 17, 1841, for instance, Abraham had bought his sixteen-year-old son Washington from Micanopy and later emancipated the youth. Primus, the striker in the Seminole blacksmith shop, and his wife Hannah claimed freedom under the proclamation of General Jesup. They had surrendered to Zachary Taylor, who filed a statement with the clerk of Hillsborough County, Florida, certifying their claim to freedom. Tena, the wife of July, had also surrendered to General Taylor and claimed freedom for her and her five children under Jesup's Proclamation. Taylor's statement, recorded in the clerk's office, Hillsborough County, Florida, formed the basis for their claim.[6] All of these blacks had their papers recorded, as well, in the West.

Others who had their freedom papers recorded at Fort Gibson included Gopher John, Joseph, and Toney Barnet. John's papers show that upon the death of his master in Florida, he became the property of the Seminole chiefs, who in February 1843, gave him his freedom. John also had recorded papers signed by Lieutenant J. T. Sprague, stating that when John first surrendered in 1837, ninety head of his cattle were taken by the army. John was not paid for them or for his services as interpreter after his surrender. There was also a statement by General Taylor saying that John had surrendered under Jesup's promise of freedom. In November 1844, Joseph called on Colonel Richard Mason at Fort Gibson and asked Mason to write to Washington regarding his "free papers." He had been stolen from A. J. Forrester by the Seminoles, but had run away from them and had given himself up to Worth. He served as a guide and interpreter for the army for about two years and was sent to the West as a free man. A board of officers had valued Joseph at $450, and Forrester had been paid. He was not claimed by anyone but wanted "free papers" for his own safety and protection. As a final example, Toney Barnet, who had been the object of much contention between the Seminoles and Creeks, was given a letter of protection in January 1845. He was free by virtue of Jesup's Proclamation, his purchase by his wife, and the directive of the commissioner of Indian Affairs. The Seminole subagent was given strict orders not to allow anyone to interfere with Toney; any claims made by the Creeks were against the government and not against Toney.[7]

SLAVE RAIDS

These early attempts to establish rights to freedom resulted, in part, from the continued difficulties concerning slave property between the Seminoles and Creeks. Slave raids by Creeks in 1844 had shown the blacks that their claims to freedom were fragile and that they were vulnerable. Slaving activities had been suspended during the negotiation of the Treaty of January 4, 1845, but during the following spring, some of the Creeks resumed them. Slaving raids, more than anything else, unsettled the blacks and prevented them from reestablishing their former relationships with the Seminoles, for they drove a wedge between the blacks and the Seminoles, as the blacks turned more and more for protection to the military officials at Fort Gibson.

In early March, Dembo Factor, who had been captured in 1844 by Siah Hardridge, complained at Fort Gibson that Hardridge was again trying to capture him and run him off to Texas. Claiming protection under Jesup's Proclamation, he asked Colonel Richard Mason to secure his "free papers" for him. A similar claim was made at the same time by Hardy, a former slave of Nelly Factor; he, too, was presumably being claimed as a slave by Hardridge. Mason issued a paper giving Hardy protection by the army until his case could be heard and forbidding anyone to interfere with him.[8]

The appeals of Hardy and Dembo reflect the blacks' growing distrust of the Seminoles. They found a sympathetic ear in Mason, who believed the charges made by them and Gopher John, who painted a dismal picture of the condition of the blacks. According to them, the Seminoles still held in bondage, and sold to whomever they chose, many blacks who claimed to be free. They had been slaves before emigration, had been removed with the Indians, and had been settled among them in the new lands; to the Indians their status had not changed. Mason was sympathetic because conflicts over the status of these blacks had been a constant concern of military officials on the frontier. Mason felt that something should be done promptly for the blacks whom the government had pledged its faith to protect. They were harassed by various claimants—whites, Seminoles, and Creeks. They lived with uncertainty and suspense, running and skulking about to evade their pursuers. Mason called for an end to the harassment and recommended to Adjutant General Roger Jones severe punishment for those who pursued blacks. One major difficulty in the matter was the fact that no one seemed to know exactly which of the blacks really fell under the protection of General Jesup's Proclamation. Therefore, Mason suggested that the "free papers" of all those entitled to them be sent to Fort Gibson and that the commanding officers of the military posts in the area be given specific instructions concerning the apprehension of any person interfering with those who had "free papers." Mason's sentiments were endorsed by General Matthew Arbuckle.[9]

Military officials had tended to support the blacks and protect them against slavers. Dembo had learned the year before that the army would serve as his protector, and he and others began to call on the officers more often for protection. Mason's action during the spring of 1845 signaled a turning point in relations between blacks and Seminoles. As the blacks turned to the army for help, they became more critical of their former protectors.

In May 1845, Rose (the widow of Plenty) and August came to the post, claiming freedom under Jesup's Proclamation and complaining that Hardridge was trying to take them and several of Rose's children as slaves. Rose asked Mason's intervention. She was apparently not considered free by the Seminoles, for in March 1840, Micanopy, Coa Hadjo, and Black Dirt had signed a statement saying that Rose and her children were the property of Polly, a niece of Coa Hadjo. Nevertheless, Rose found Mason sympathetic to her pleas. He again asked for prompt action to fulfill Jesup's pledges to the Seminole blacks, in order to save them from being "hunted like wolves," and he wanted Hardridge placed in irons. But the measure was too harsh for General Arbuckle, who issued another warning to Hardridge to stop kidnapping blacks and warned the Creeks that the army would take action against Hardridge unless he did so.[10] The warning was apparently sufficient, at least for the time being.

Shortly after the episode with Rose, Mason and Gopher John went to Washington. John, who was losing faith in the Seminoles, hoped to persuade the government to allow him and his people to return to Florida and settle. Although John had acted as interpreter at Fort Gibson since he had taken up residence there, his position among the Seminoles remained delicate and precarious. He continued to engender hostilities, and there had recently been a second attempt upon his life. Thomas L. Judge, the Seminole sub-agent, expected the Indians to try again. John also sought pay for the horse which had been shot from under him in the first attempt on his life as well as for his services as an interpreter. Cherokee Agent P. M. Butler had written Commissioner Crawford that John had been called on almost daily as an interpreter by the Seminoles who had resided in the Cherokee Nation, since he was the only interpreter there at times and could not avoid their requests. But John seemed willing. Although Butler had no authority to hire an interpreter, he felt that John should be paid for his services. But the commissioner would not act on the basis of Butler's memorandum. He asked Butler to file an account, and in reply, Butler was for some reason less praising of John than he had been in the memorandum. Butler now said that until John's return from Washington in the summer of 1844, he had not resided steadily at Fort Gibson. Upon his return, John had become "obnoxious to many of the Seminoles, particularly his former owners who in consequence of some offensive language shot his horse under him and would have taken his life if not prevented." John had then fled to the post for protection. From about October 15, 1844, to April 15, 1845, John was often called on to interpret, particularly from the signing of the treaty until the removal of the Seminoles to Little River.[11]

JESUP'S VISIT TO INDIAN TERRITORY

While Gopher John was in Washington, an event occurred in the West which profoundly affected the status of the "free" blacks, widened the developing breach between the blacks and Seminoles, and created discontent among the Seminoles and Creeks. General Jesup, now the quartermaster general, visited the Indian Territory concerning the construction of stone buildings at Fort Gibson. Hearing that Jesup was there, the Seminoles came to the post, arriving on the opposite side of the Arkansas the day after Jesup had left for Fort Smith on his return to Washington. On July 27, 1845, Micanopy, Wild Cat, Alligator, Tiger, Old-Bear, The Broom, and George Cloud sent a message of greeting after Jesup. Abraham and Cudjo translated. Wild Cat also sent a personal greeting, complaining that the President had promised him, while he was in Washington, to feed the Seminoles for nine months after their removal to the Deep Fork but that the treaty of 1845 had provided for but six months. He also complained that his people were hungry and did not expect to make much corn. His talk was interpreted to the chiefs sentence by sentence by the blacks, and each statement received the full sanction of those present. Abraham also sent a complaint that "his conduct in Florida in favour of the whites, has procured him many enemies, and that he leads an uncertain and unhappy life."[12]

While at Fort Gibson, General Jesup had sent word to the blacks, many of whom the Seminoles still claimed as slaves, that they were free under his promises in Florida. He asked them to come to Fort Gibson to talk with him, but he left before they arrived. Nevertheless, he left a list of those whom he considered free. During the succeeding weeks, the blacks stopped working for the Indians, and nearly all of the men, many of them with their families, went to the military reserve at Fort Gibson, where they sought the protection of the army and worked at what jobs the army could give them. Sixty or seventy of them worked at the erection of new stone buildings at the post. Of course, the situation was less than pleasing to the Indians.[13]

It was aggravated by slaves who obviously had no claim to freedom
but who joined the Seminole blacks on the reserve. A good case in point
was Elsa and her two-year-old son, Benjamin. Elsa had lived among the
Seminoles in Florida and, during removal, had been sold by her Seminole
owner in Arkansas. Later, when Halleck Tustenuggee emigrated, Elsa
persuaded him to buy her and take her into the Seminole country with
him. Yet, when the Seminole blacks went to the reserve at Fort Gibson,
Elsa and Benjamin went with them. Halleck Tustenuggee appealed for
their return, but his case was just one of many. In March 1846, Marcellus
Duval, the new Seminole subagent, reported almost daily complaints about
the Seminole blacks on the reserve. The Indians felt that injustice had been
done them, contrary to their understanding at the time of removal. Like
Colonel Mason, Duval wanted the papers of the legitimate claimants to
freedom sent to him so that he could have a certain base from which to
act.[14] However, Duval's motives were not as altruistic as Mason's; strongly
proslavery in his sentiment, Duval was interested in finding which blacks
were free so that the rest could be returned to the Indians as slaves.

General Jesup intervened for the blacks on April 8, 1846, by informing
General Arbuckle that he had succeeded in getting the case of the blacks
placed before the President, who would decide whether they were to be
separated from the Seminoles and removed to another country or be
allowed to occupy, as they had in Florida, a separate village in the Seminole country. The latter was what Jesup claimed to have promised them.
He asked Arbuckle to prevent any interference with them at Fort Gibson
until the President made a decision.[15] On the basis of this request, Arbuckle
ordered the commander of the post to extend protection to those on the
military reserve.

Jesup also issued a statement clarifying the promise he had made the
blacks concerning their property while he was commander of the army in
Florida. He had promised them that when they separated from their
Seminole masters and surrendered, the government would replace the
property they left with the Indians—axes, hoes, drawknives, handsaws,
pots, kettles, etc. The blacks had complained that they had not been paid
and that their goods had not been replaced.[16]

Jesup's intervention in 1846 was apparently the result of Gopher
John's activities in Washington. He had been there for almost a year,
but about the time of Jesup's letter to Arbuckle, he decided that he
must return to his family, leaving the affairs of the Seminole blacks in
Jesup's hands. As John prepared to leave for the Indian country, he

sought to avoid the bad feelings that had developed against him on his
return from his previous trip. He had the chief clerk in the quartermaster
general's office write a statement that his activities in Washington had
concerned his own affairs and those of the blacks, that he had not meddled
in Seminole affairs, and that on his former visit with Wild Cat, Alligator,
Tiger Tail, and Tustenuggee, he had acted only as interpreter for them.
The statement was given "so that all may know the Seminoles have nothing to complain of in reference to his visits." In spite of the statement,
John found trouble awaiting him when he returned to the Indian Territory.
Shortly after he had left, Wild Cat's brother had taken a horse from John's
wife Susan. John could not go into the Nation after it because he was
afraid the Seminoles would kill him. Neither could he protect his livestock
which ran on the Deep Fork and which the Seminoles began to kill.[17]

REFUGE AT FORT GIBSON

John and the other blacks remained at Fort Gibson under the protection
of orders from General Arbuckle, who had no official orders from the
government in the matter. His action was simply a favor to General Jesup.
When Marcellus Duval learned that, he laid the matter before William
Medill, the new commissioner of Indian affairs. The Indians wanted action,
he said. They still claimed many of the blacks, but if they were not the
property of the Indians, Duval thought that they should be removed from
the Indian country "as they are most certainly under present circumstances,
a nuisance to adjoining tribes, and will be eventually to the people of
Arkansas as a harbor for runaway slaves." Not all of them, however, were
on the military reserve. Some remained in their villages on the Deep Fork
and Little River. Those at Deep Fork were almost unanimous in their
desire to remain there, provided they could have a tract of land of their
own. Although it was not the best land that could have been selected, they
had built houses, cleared fields, and herded over a thousand head of stock.
They were reluctant to move to the post, because they would have to give
up their improvements and leave their horses and cattle, which ran in the
woods. Lieutenant Ralph W. Kirkham at Fort Gibson characterized the
blacks as "honest, temperate, and industrious as could be expected from
the habits which they acquired living with the Indians in Florida."[18] It
is uncertain whether Duval's proslavery comments accurately reflect the
Seminole attitude or indicate the beginnings of an obsession with the

destruction of the enclave of blacks, an obsession which had fully developed
a few months later.

MORE RAIDS BY SLAVE HUNTERS

Despite the protection extended to them, the blacks at Fort Gibson
were not safe from slave hunters. In August 1846, raiders stole a black
from the post reserve, but a party of dragoons pursued them and returned
the man. Such events kept the blacks in a constant state of excitement.
Other conditions tended to disrupt the daily lives of some of them. In one
instance, the Cherokee John Drew decided to sell all of his slaves, among
whom were Billy and Bob, the sons of August, who was a brother of
Dembo Factor. Drew had purchased them five or six years earlier, and
although Lieutenant Kirkham felt that they had as much right to protection as the others at the post, they were to be sold with the rest. Toney
Barnet had also lost two sons, one of whom had been sold shortly after
removal. Toney had not seen or heard of him since. The other, also named
Toney, had been sold to a Cherokee, who had sold him to Mrs. Susan
Coody, another Cherokee whose farm was near the post. Toney Barnet,
who was free, was anxious to have his children free as well.[19]

Wannah had also lost two children. A sister of Gopher John, she claimed
freedom for herself and her five children under Jesup's Proclamation.
However, that claim was not substantiated by the old Seminole Passockee.
According to him, Wannah had been given to the original owner's young
daughter, who was reared by her mother's sister, Colkeechowa. Wannah
emigrated to the West with the girl, who had died in 1844. Until that
time, according to Passockee, there had been no claim to Wannah, but
upon her mistress' death, Jim, the half-blood son of Colkeechowa, laid
claim to her and her children. Wannah had had two children before removal;
she then married Sam Mills, a slave whom Jim also claimed, and by the
time Jim laid claim to her and her family, she had three boys and two
girls, including Daphney, Andrew, Limus, and Sarah. Fearing that Jim
would sell her family, Wannah had gone to Fort Gibson and asked Colonel
Mason to present her claim to freedom to the War Department for a decision. He did so, and on March 11, 1845, issued a proclamation, warning
all persons not to molest Wannah or her family until their case was decided.[20]

But Jim defied Mason's proclamation and sold Limus and Sarah. Sam
Mills and the remaining children fled to Fort Gibson for protection. Wannah

joined them later and stayed for some time with her brother's family at the post. Jim claimed that he had brought Wannah in when he surrendered before the battle of Okeechobee under the proclamation that all Indians who came in voluntarily with their slaves would be secure in that and other property. The post commander was inclined to believe Jim's claim, but old Passockee felt that it could be founded only on Jim's mother's right, which Passockee did not feel was legal.[21]

He was supported by General Jesup, to whom the case had been referred. According to Jesup, Sam Mills was not a slave, having been freed by Jim's mother; Jim did not bring in a single black during the war. Under Jesup's policy, Jim was entitled to only that property which he brought in and nothing more. As for Wannah, she had surrendered to the Shawnee Indians who were fighting for the United States during the war and therefore came under Jesup's promise of freedom. Toney Barnet and other blacks said that Wannah had surrendered alone and voluntarily before the battle of Okeechobee. Jim, they said, had nothing to do at that time with the slaves of Colkeechowa, who was still alive; and when his mother surrendered, Jim stayed with Alligator and fought at the battle. Needless to say, Wannah's case was typically confused. In spite of her claim to freedom, whatever its base, Jim sold the two children Limus and Sarah to Siah Hardridge, who treated them badly. In July 1846, Colonel Gustavus Loomis, the new commander at Fort Gibson, asked Chief Roley McIntosh to return them while Loomis tried to persuade Hardridge to relinquish his claim. Wannah had told Jim that she would never live with him again, and he reluctantly agreed to give up all claim to her and her remaining children for $1,300. It was an exorbitant price, but nothing less would satisfy him. He promised not to sell them until the government took up their case.[22]

While such slaving activities went on, the blacks on the reserve grew afraid to go out into the country to secure provisions for fear they would be stolen by those who claimed them as slaves. A number of them had gained employment during the preceding months while permanent stone buildings were being erected at the post, and the results of their labor can be seen today in the old commissary building maintained on the post grounds by the state of Oklahoma. By the fall of 1846, however, the construction was completed, and as time passed, their stocks of provisions grew low. They asked Colonel Loomis for rations to prevent starvation. Loomis, like his predecessors, was sympathetic and successfully requested permission to issue them "a small quantity as their wants may need."[23]

Slaving activities continued during the winter of 1846 and 1847. Cherokee John Drew and Daniel Coody requested delivery of slaves on the reserve but were told to await the decision of the President. Some of Mrs. Susan Coody's blacks ran away, including Toney Barnet's son Toney, who came to the post for protection; however, the commanding officer told them to go back to their mistress and not to come to the post again. In December 1846, further word came concerning Wannah's children. Hardridge had confused the issue by selling them to another Creek, who, it was learned, intended to put them on a steamboat and send them downstream for sale. Loomis declared that no sale of them would be legal and warned that if they were found, they would be returned to their parents. Loomis once more appealed to Chief McIntosh to have the children delivered. Two months later, Loomis issued a proclamation protecting Latty (or Lemo) and his family from a group of Creeks who had been trying to buy them from the Seminole who claimed them.[24]

SEMINOLE COMPLAINTS

While these slaving activities were going on, Seminole Subagent Marcellus Duval, who was in Washington, had taken the complaints of the Seminoles to the President. Many blacks who had been with them until Jesup came west in 1845 had left their service. They wanted the President to have the blacks returned, for they claimed that Jesup's Proclamation was illegal and that he had made promises to the Indians which were just as binding as those made to the blacks. They believed that Wild Cat was right when he once said of Jesup, "He liked the negroes better than the Indians." Instead of insuring the safe delivery of all of their property in the West as he had promised, Jesup had caused much of their slave property to leave them and go to Fort Gibson.[25]

With his proslavery sentiments, Duval foresaw dangers in confirming Jesup's promises to the blacks and began a campaign to undermine those promises. If the blacks were free, he argued, they had no right in the Creek and Seminole country, and those Indians, joined by the Cherokees, would drive the blacks out. Arkansans would object to a colony of free blacks so close to their boundary. What would the government do with them? What northern state would welcome three hundred free blacks, and would the blacks want to go north? Could the government afford to go into the colonization business of its own accord and ship them to

Africa? Duval concluded, "The consequences of the subject going into Congress anyone can foresee, and I desire to avert the calamitous excitement which it would cause, shaking the Union to its center—a perfect 'firebrand' to be thrown among the discordant and combustible materials on the floor of Congress."[26]

Harriet Bowlegs, the owner of a large number of slaves, was one of the Seminoles who complained of losing slave property by the protection granted the blacks. Harriet claimed to have surrendered to Jesup under provisions of the Fort Dade agreement and was told by him, various officers, and the black interpreters Abraham and Toney that, since she had surrendered and brought in her slaves, her property would be secure. She arrived in the West with about thirty slaves. The blacks had stayed with her until Jesup's visit to the Indian country, when they deserted her and went to the reservation at Fort Gibson. In the fall of 1846, Harriet wrote to Duval that she was impoverished. Her house was falling into ruin, and the only corn she had was what she and two orphan children she had taken in could raise themselves. Every time she went to Fort Gibson to ask the blacks to help her, they refused, saying that they were free and could do nothing for her.[27]

In January 1847, Duval presented Harriet's case to Commissioner William Medill, stating, rather condescendingly, that the blacks were a problem "of more importance than probably you are aware of, having a direct bearing on the feelings and conduct of the Seminoles, not to say anything of the ultimate condition of the negroes." When he learned that Superintendent Armstrong had been requested to report on the matter, Duval said that Armstrong could give no information which was not already before the department. From this point on, apparently for personal reasons, Duval worked hard to keep other officials from investigating the situation and to maintain his authority in the matter. Throughout the following spring, he called on the officers at Fort Gibson for a list of those blacks who were entitled to protection by the government, but by June, he had received no reply.[28]

MARCELLUS DUVAL VS. COLONEL LOOMIS

Duval continued his criticism of the military officers during the fall of 1847. The slaveholding Seminoles had continued to complain, and Duval felt that he had not got sufficient response from Colonel Loomis. Therefore, he made that officer the point of much of his criticism. In Duval's view, Loomis not only persisted in protecting many blacks who were not entitled to it but also granted them immunities and privileges nowhere granted by law to slaves or free blacks in the slave states or territories. Loomis himself assisted in teaching them to read and, Duval thought, to write. He kept a Sunday school as well. Duval said that the effects of such activities could be felt by every man who owned slaves in the Indian country. "Any sensible man," he said, "can see the evil of it."[29] Of course, "any sensible man," in Duval's view, was a proslavery man.

Duval's criticism was unjustified. As far as protecting the blacks was concerned, Loomis was under direct orders from General Arbuckle. Also, he had kept a copy of the list of blacks for Duval for some weeks and, when Duval failed to pick it up, had given it to Creek Agent James Logan who had also requested it for the Creek chiefs. According to Logan, the Creeks were becoming excited about the blacks on the reserve, and in the summer of 1847, there was much talk among them of seizing all of the blacks and making slaves of them, thereby forcing the government to act and decide the question at once. Loomis realized that a settlement of the question was necessary, but the problem became more complex each day. Speculators were trying to get the names of those protected and were making claims whether they had valid ones or not, as in the case of Wannah's two children. Loomis' concern in settling the matter was prompted, in part, by news in June that the children had been taken to Fort Smith and sold for whiskey. Loomis asked General Arbuckle to investigate and requested their return or a deduction of $2,000 from the next annuity payment to the Creeks, since it was Hardridge who had taken them in the first place.[30] Such requests as the latter, no doubt, accounted in part for the Creeks' desire to put a swift end to the controversy. But the end was several months in the future.

As talk of Creek interference increased and slaving activities continued, more blacks called at Fort Gibson for their "free papers" and for protection during the fall of 1847. In September, Jack (son of Rose and Plenty) claimed that his father had purchased the freedom of him and his brothers Cuffy and Wahn and that the papers had been recorded in Florida. Jack asked Loomis to secure them for him. Gopher John asked Loomis to obtain the "free papers" of his mother, who John had heard was detained in Florida as a slave. In late October Loomis extended protection to Nancy and her child, and in November to sixteen blacks who claimed to be free persons in the Creek Nation. They had been property of Sally Stidham until July 3, 1841, when she made a will giving them their freedom and recorded it in the Crawford County Courthouse at Van Buren, Arkansas. In 1847, some of her distant relatives were trying to break the will. While the matter of the will was pending, a Creek named Potostee attempted to capture the blacks as slaves. They left all their property and fled to the post, where Loomis gave them a room. He sought permission to issue rations to them, for it was the opinion of Creek Agent Logan that they were free because he had written the will.[31]

At about the same time, an event occurred that further angered the Creeks. Kibbett, a Seminole black living at Fort Gibson, had gone into the Creek Nation, abused and threatened Joseph Smith because of a personal grudge, stole a mare from Smith, and returned to the military reserve. James Logan asked Colonel Loomis to turn Kibbett over to the Creeks for trial. Although Kibbett admitted taking the mare as ransom for one of his own, which Smith allegedly had, Loomis refused to turn him over without Arbuckle's permission because he was not sure that the Creeks had jurisdiction in the case.[32]

His refusal angered McIntosh and the other Creek chiefs, who claimed the right to try any of the blacks who committed crimes in their country. Logan became alarmed, for by the second week in December, the Creek chiefs were in "an ill humor" about the blacks. He was afraid that trouble would erupt if it appeared that the army was screening the blacks from trial. General Arbuckle apparently saw the danger, too, for Kibbett was delivered to the Creeks during the following week.[33]

RAIDS ON THE MILITARY RESERVE

In the spring and summer of 1848, raids continued on the settlements of blacks in the military reserve. In January, Katy, who had lived for two years on the reserve, complained to Loomis that "some Indian" was trying to sell her. A relative of Murray, the interpreter for General Taylor, and a niece of July, who was killed by the Indians while acting as a guide and spy for the army, Katy had been guaranteed her freedom by Jesup's promises to Murray. When Jesup came to Fort Gibson in 1845, she was living at the post and cooking for one of the officers, yet her name did not appear on the list he had made because he thought she was dead. When Jesup was consulted on her case, he insisted that her name should have been on the list. One night in April, a party entered the reservation and carried off

Katy and her two children. Major B. L. E. Bonneville, in charge of the post, sent out two parties in search of them, but because there were so many persons coming and going from the post, it was difficult to find their trail. He did learn, however, that the blacks had been sold by the Seminoles for "a trifle" to a man named Wilson. Wilson had applied to Bonneville for them some time earlier, but the major had refused him and awaited the decision of higher authorities. When informed of the event, Arbuckle directed Bonneville to try to recover the blacks, to confine their abductors for trial if possible, to take others who had engaged in the illegal transaction, and to protect those blacks entitled to the protection of the government if it meant bringing them into the garrison and placing a guard over them.[34] Katy was subsequently returned to the post.

A few days after Katy's abduction, there was a raid on the military reserve at Fort Smith, Arkansas, where some of the Seminole blacks had hired out as free laborers. Union McIntosh sent his overseer to Fort Smith in search of Joe, a Seminole black he claimed. Finding that Joe was employed in the quarters of Arbuckle's aide-de-camp, Lieutenant F. F. Flint, the overseer sent a constable who took Joe away, despite Flint's protests that Joe was under the protection of the government. Joe, who had waited on several officers at Fort Gibson, was the son of Primus and Hannah, both claiming to be free under Jesup's Proclamation. Bonneville, who had their "free papers" on file, believed that Joe was entitled to protection by the government.[35]

Despite Bonneville's efforts to protect the blacks, further raids were made on the Fort Gibson reservation during the summer of 1848. By that time, Jesup had given up the idea of succeeding in protecting them, for when Bonneville reported a slave raid in July, Jesup wrote in return: "Faith of the government is pledged for the protection of the Seminole negroes and its attention has been frequently called to the subject without avail."[36] Jesup was aware that matters were taking an official turn against the blacks he had long sought to keep faith with and to protect. To this point, controversies over the Seminole slaves had been local, although they had been played out against the backdrop of the larger national controversy over slavery. Duval had done a great deal to bring the conditions at Fort Gibson to the attention of officials at Washington, while maintaining that he did not want them to become an issue of national debate. He succeeded; the bureaucratic machinery was turning in Washington to return the Seminole blacks to bondage. Because they had severed relations with the Seminoles by moving onto the reservation, the blacks could no longer view the Indians as their friends and could not rely on them for help.

NOTES

1. Lieutenant R. W. Kirkham to General Thomas S. Jesup, August 20, 1846, National Archives Record Group 393 (Records of the United States Army Continental Commands, 1821-1920), *Fort Gibson,* Volume "Indian Affairs" (hereafter cited as *Gibson Indian Affairs*), 18; Jesup to William Medill, July 13, 1848, National Archives Microfilm Publications, *Microcopy M234* (Records of the Office of Indian Affairs, Letters Received)-801, J96-48. *Microcopy M234* is hereafter cited as *M234,* followed by the roll number.

Not all of the Seminoles removed. Some remained in the Cherokee Nation in the bottoms of the Grand and Illinois Rivers. In April of 1846, the Cherokees complained that they were killing Cherokee livestock. Marcellus Duval to Colonel Gustavus Loomis, April 29, 1846, *Fort Gibson,* Letters Received (hereafter cited as *Gibson LR*), Box 2. Some were still there a year later. Colonel Gustavus Loomis to James McKisick, May 18, 1847, *Gibson Indian Affairs,* 25; Marcellus Duval to T. Hartley Crawford, September 30, 1845, 29 Cong., 1 Sess., *House Executive Document 2,* 530-531; Duval to Medill, October 15, 1846, 29 Cong., 2 Sess., *House Executive Document 4,* 278.

2. Duval to Medill, October 15, 1846, 29 Cong., 2 Sess., *House Executive Document 4,* 279, 281.

3. Captain John Page to Crawford, September 6, 1842, *M234*-289, P1158-42; Thomas S. Judge to William Armstrong, April 26, 1843, *M234*-800, A1451-43; Crawford to Armstrong, August 23, 1843, National Archives Microfilm Publications, *Microcopy M21*(Records of the Office of Indian Affairs, Letters Sent)-34, 206; Colonel Richard B. Mason to Lieutenant W. W. J. Bliss, April 13, 1843, *Fort Gibson,* Letters Sent (hereafter cited as *Gibson LS*); National Archives Microfilm Publications, *Microcopy T494* (Documents Relating to the Negotiation of Ratified and Unratified Treaties with Various Indian Tribes, 1801-1869)-9, Documents Relating to the Negotiation of the Treaty of January 4, 1845, with the Creek and Seminole Indians, Frames 239ff; Gideon C. Matlock to Armstrong, July 18, 1845, *M234*-800, A1865-45; Kenneth Wiggins Porter, *The Negro on the American Frontier* (New York: Arno Press and The New York Times, 1971), 324-325, 335; Duval to Loomis, April 29, 1846, *Gibson LR*, Box 2. *Microcopy M21* is hereafter cited as *M21,* followed by the roll number.

4. Statement of Pierce M. Butler, April 16, 1845, *M234*-800, B2452-45.

5. Porter, 335. In 1840 and 1841, Cudjo attempted to collect $420 from the government for his services as interpreter in Florida. Armstrong to Crawford, June 18, 1841, *M234*-289, A1030-41; Crawford to Armstrong, July 21, 1841, *M21*-30, 456.

6. Porter, 323; Statement of Mason, June 19, 1842, *Gibson LR,* Box 1; Armstrong to Crawford, June 12, 1845, *M234*-800, A1838-45; Copy of Statement, September 15, 1840, *Gibson Indian Affairs,* 3.

7. See various papers relating to Gopher John (or John Warrior), *Gibson Indian Affairs,* 1-2; Mason to Brigadier General Roger Jones, November 3, 1844, *Gibson LS;* L. Thomas to Mason, December 18, 1844, *Gibson LR,* Box 2, and *Gibson Indian Affairs,* 8. In April 1845, Joseph applied for pay due him for his services as a guide to the army in Florida. This time, investigation showed that as soon as Joseph had arrived at head-quarters, Forrester had appeared and claimed him and payment for his services while with the army. Because of the critical state of affairs, the army would not give Joseph up but made a bargain with Forrester whereby Joseph would be purchased and sent west. Joseph had due him about two hundred dollars at the time. It was agreed that the amount would be applied toward the purchase price. In effect, Joseph had been working out his freedom thus, the army ruled that he had no money coming for his services. Mason to Jones, April 2, 1845, *Gibson LS;* Le Grand Capers to Captain J. T. Sprague, April 30, 1845, *Gibson Indian Affairs,* 10; Jones to Mason, May 8, 1845, *Gibson LR,* Box 2; Armstrong to Seminole Agent, January 25, 1845, National Archives Record Group 393, *Second and Seventh Military Depart-ments,* Letters Received (hereafter cited as *2nd & 7th LR*), Box 6.

8. Mason to Jones, March 5, 1845, *Gibson LS.*

9. *Ibid.*

10. Mason to Lieutenant James H. Prentiss, May 21, 1845, *Gibson LS;* Statement of Micanopy and others, March 16, 1840, *Gibson LR,* Box 1, and *Gibson Indian Affairs,* 10. Rose's children included Wahn, Jack, Sally, Rachael, Caesar, and Jesse. See Appendix, List C, Numbers 42-49. Prentiss to Mason, May 28, 1845, *Second and Seventh Military Departments,* Letters Sent (hereafter cited as *2nd & 7th LS*).

11. Roley McIntosh to Mason, March 14, 1845, *Gibson LR,* Box 2; Judge to Crawford, April 27, 1845, Casey to Commissioner, May 28, 1845, Statement of P. M. Butler, April 16, 1845, and Butler to Crawford, July 25, 1845, *M234*-800, J1684-45, C2309-45, B2452-45, and B2528-45; Crawford to Armstrong, May 29, 1845, Crawford to Judge, May 29, 1845, *M21*-38, 416; Crawford to Casey, May 29, 1845, and Crawford to Butler, June 3, 1845, *M21*-36, 417, 424.

12. Charles O. Collins to Jesup, and Talk of Micanopy and others, July 27, 1845, reprinted in Porter, 334-337.

13. Duval to Medill, March 24, 1846, *M234*-801, D1059-46; Duval to James K. Polk, December 21, 1846, National Archives Microfilm Publications, *Microcopy M574* (Special Files of the Office of Indian Affairs, 1807-1904)-13, Special File 96: Seminole Claims to Certain Negroes, 1841-1849 (hereafter cited as *File 96*). The list of blacks made by Jesup is reproduced as List K in the Appendix.

14. Duval to Medill, March 24, 1846, *M234*-801, D1059-46. Duval, a native of Alabama, replaced Thomas Judge as subagent to the Seminoles in the late winter of 1845-1846. William Medill was confirmed as commissioner of Indian affairs on January 3, 1846.

15. Jesup to General Matthew Arbuckle, April 3, 1846, *File 96; Official Opinions of the Attorneys General of the United States* (Washington, 1852), 4: 723-724, hereafter cited as *Official Opinions*.

16. Statement of Jesup, April 9, 1846, *Gibson Indian Affairs*, 17.

17. Gad Humphreys to Mason, December 5, 1845, Statement of William A. Gordon, April 13, 1846, Loomis to Duval, May 3, 1846, and Kirkham to Jesup, August 20, 1846, *Gibson Indian Affairs*, 15, 17-18; Jesup to Arbuckle, April 8, 1846, *File 96*. John instituted claims for his losses, but there is no evidence that any claim was ever paid. The claim for the horse seems to have been thwarted by Duval, who refused to hold up the annuity or take the amount out of it. John raised the claim in 1846, 1847, and 1848. At the latter time he presented for a second time the claim for the use of his wagon during the removal. Duval to Medill, June 2, 1847, and Jesup to Medill, July 13, 1848, *M234*-801, D38-47 and J96-48; Duval to Loomis, June 7, 1847, *Gibson LR,* Box 3; Loomis to Casey, June 11, 1847, *Gibson LS*.

18. Duval to Commissioner of Indian Affairs, July 10, 1846, *M234*-801, D1091-46; Kirkham to Jesup, August 20, 1846, *Gibson Indian Affairs*, 18.

19. Kirkham to Jesup, August 20, 1846, *Gibson Indian Affairs*, 18.

20. Kirkham to Jesup, August 20, 1846, and August 26, 1846, and Statement of Mason, March 11, 1845, *Gibson Indian Affairs*, 21, 18-19, 9; Captain A. Cady to Jones, March 18, 1846, *Gibson LS*.

21. Cady to Jones, March 18, 1846, *Gibson LS;* Kirkham to Jesup, August 26, 1846, *Gibson Indian Affairs*, 21.

22. Jones to Arbuckle, April 22, 1846, *2nd & 7th LR,* Box 6; Loomis to McIntosh, July 20, 1846, and Kirkham to Jesup, August 20, 1846, *Gibson Indian Affairs*, 18-19.

23. Loomis to Lieutenant F. F. Flint, October 29, 1846, *2nd & 7th LR,* Box 6.

24. Kirkham to John Drew, November 1, 1846, Kirkham to Susan Coody, November 6, 1846, Loomis to James McKisick, November 28, 1846, Loomis

to McIntosh, December 17, 1846, and Statement of Loomis, February 14, 1847, *Gibson Indian Affairs,* 22-23, 24.

25. Duval to Polk, December 21, 1846, *M234*-801, P5-47, and *File 96; Official Opinions,* 4: 723.

26. Duval to Polk, December 21, 1846, *M234*-801, P5-47, and *File 96.*

27. Records of the Seminole Subagency, Book A, p. 5, listed the following slaves as the property of Harriet Bowlegs and her daughter Betsy on September 30, 1837: Old Primus, who remained in Florida as interpreter by order of General Taylor; Old Davy; Ned; John (Ned's brother); Jack; Adam; Daily (dead); Scipio (dead, brother of Daily); Noble (brother of Scipio and Daily); Boston; Dennis; Sharper; Murria or Muria (wife of Miccopotokee's Ned) and her children; Polly; Amy; Davy; Rufile; Jim; two infants, Dahlia and Eliza; Flora (mother of Dennis above); Flora (wife of King Cudjo and mother of Ned and John above), and her children; Sam (little boy, sold to Cudjo); Matilda (infant sold to Cudjo); Juba (daughter of Flora and sister to Dennis) and her children; Abby or Cumby; Old Rose (dead, mother of Jack); Hagar (mother of Boston, above) and her children; Delia; Fanny; Lucy; Adam; Bella; Jacob. Transcript of record, enclosed in Duval to Medill, January 26, 1847, Harriet Bowlegs to Duval, September 26, 1846, and List of Negroes claimed by Harriet Bowlegs, *File 96.*

28. Duval to Medill, January 26, 1847, *File 96;* Duval to Arbuckle, June 27, 1847, *2nd & 7th LR,* Box 8.

29. Duval to Medill, October 15, 1847, *M234*-801, D65-47.

30. Loomis to Flint, July 20, 1847, *Gibson Indian Affairs,* 26.

31. Loomis to Humphreys, September 13, 1847, and Loomis to Jones, September 13, 1847, and Loomis to Jones, September 14, 1847, *Gibson Indian Affairs,* 28, 31; Logan to Loomis, November 23, 1847, *Gibson LR,* Box 3.

32. Statement of Tustenuggee Micco, December 9, 1847, and Logan to Loomis, December 6, 1847, *Gibson LR,* Box 3.

33. Logan to Loomis, December 9, 11, and 15, 1847, *Gibson LR,* Box 3.

34. Loomis to Jesup, January 21, 1848, and Jesup to Loomis, February 17, 1848, *Gibson Indian Affairs,* 34, 35; Major B. L. E. Bonneville to Flint, April 21, 1848, *2nd & 7th LR,* Box 7; Flint to Bonneville, April 23, 1848, *Gibson LR,* Box 3.

35. Flint to Bonneville, May 1, 1848, *Gibson LR,* Box 3; Bonneville to Flint, May 3, 1848, *2nd & 7th LR,* Box 7.

36. Jesup to Bonneville, July 21, 1848, *Gibson Indian Affairs,* 36.

6

Return to bondage

Even if General Jesup and military officers on the frontier had not intervened on behalf of the blacks, it is not likely that they could have reestablished their former relationship with the Seminoles. The circumstances which
created their alliance did not exist in the West, and the threat of being captured and sold into slavery kept them unsettled. Had the slaving raids not
occurred, it is not likely that the Seminoles could have reestablished their system of slavery because of the proximity of the Creeks and the civil control they
exerted over the Seminoles. At any rate, all attempts to renew old ties ended
with the flight of the blacks to Fort Gibson, which finally severed the close
relationship between them and the Seminoles. The longer they were separated from the Indians, the more they assumed that they were free and the
more they disliked their former status as slaves, however relaxed their relationship with their masters may have been. Because of the separation, the
Seminoles began to lose their sense of attachment to the blacks and to look
at them as property much as the Creeks looked at their own blacks. Some
Seminoles sold their blacks without a qualm, often for a trifle.

WIDENING THE BREACH

Duplicity of proslavery officials of the Bureau of Indian Affairs helped
to widen the developing breach between the blacks and Seminoles. Foremost among those officials was Marcellus Duval, whose motives became
clearer in the winter of 1847-48. He was apparently intent on getting title

to some of the Seminole blacks. But first, he had to remove them from
the government's protection. Thus, in December 1847, he had renewed
his efforts to have them removed from Fort Gibson and returned to the
Seminoles. The Seminole chiefs had received the claims of various Seminoles
to consider what should be done but had not reached any conclusion.
Finally, they asked Duval to represent them in Washington, and when he
could not because of his duties, they sent his brother, W. J. Duval, instead,
an arrangement which later proved expensive to both the Seminoles and
the blacks they claimed.[1] It gave Marcellus Duval a personal interest in the
blacks, whom he sought more zealously than ever to return to a state of
servitude.

Marcellus Duval blamed the government's failure to act on antislavery
men in the North. Nearly a year earlier he had urged President Polk to take
action, but he had not. "Why the matter was allowed to slumber in a pigeon-
hole I can't say," wrote Duval, "but believe it was because being a subject
which most of the northern men are afraid of, it was thought to be easiest
to let it pass with as slight a notice as possible inasmuch as there could be
legally no other decision than that the negroes were slaves and subject to
the Indians." Slaveholding friends of Duval, such as former Congressman
Waddy Thompson of South Carolina, had advised Duval that he could
seize the blacks as fugitives, but Duval had declined because he feared that
if the military opposed him, the Indians would be "very apt to commit some
unlawful act" because they would feel that they had the backing of their
agent. Duval did not want to attempt anything he could not carry out,
for then he would lose his authority among the Indians. In his view, the
situation had national significance: "By emancipating these slaves, (had
we the right to do so) an inducement would be held out to all slaves in
our southern community in time of war to take part with our enemies—
until some General should see proper to *buy them off by promises of
freedom.*" He once more asked President Polk to order the blacks returned
to the Seminoles.[2]

The military officials, too, had begun to search for a solution to the
problem, but their sympathies, as usual, were with the blacks, rather than
the Indians. In early December 1847, Gopher John and Toney Barnet
expressed their belief to Colonel Gustavus Loomis that the blacks would
never be left unmolested to enjoy their freedom among the Indians or in
the Indian country. As spokesmen for their people, John and Toney said
that they were willing to emigrate to any place where they would be un-

molested. They wanted Loomis to seek the aid of General Jesup. Loomis
was too involved with the blacks to be objective. He knew from claims
presented to him that some Indians and whites were very eager to get their
hands on the Seminole blacks; others used claims to create discontent
among the Indians. Loomis had nothing but praise for the blacks. During
the preceding summer, they had raised large amounts of corn and rice on
the reserve. For the past two or three months, some of them had assembled
every Sunday for a Sabbath school, at which Loomis "tried to give what
instruction as would tend to make them better men and women." Some of
them were trying to learn to read the Bible. Loomis wanted the government to pay for their removal or persuade some benevolent society to
transport them to Africa.[3]

General Matthew Arbuckle endorsed the suggestion. He believed that
since the blacks were being issued rations at public expense and were the
source of constant complaints from the Seminoles and from the neighboring tribes, it would be far more economical and the well-being of the country
would be promoted if the government would send them to New Orleans
and put them on a boat for Africa. Whatever was done, he felt that justice
required some provision for those who had surrendered voluntarily during
the war.[4]

JESUP'S SUPPORT FOR THE BLACKS

Meanwhile, W. J. Duval was pressing the issue in Washington. Secretary
of War William L. Marcy asked Jesup for a full report concerning this
action during the Seminole War. On April 3, 1848, Jesup reviewed his
career in Florida, the promises he had made to both the Indians and the
blacks, and the classes of blacks who had been removed to the West under
the terms of the agreements. He insisted, as he had always done, on his
right as commander of the armed forces in Florida to receive those who
surrendered under his terms. In the case of the blacks, their surrender had
erased their Indian masters' claims to them. Jesup maintained that he would
have sent the blacks to the West, even if the Indians had remained in
Florida, and claimed for them the same protection which they would have
received had their masters not surrendered and emigrated. He wanted them
settled in a separate village under the protection of the United States
with an agent to see to their needs. "The question with me," he said, "is

not of national obligation merely, but of personal honor; and if the power exists in this country I am resolved these people shall have protection— if neither the War Department nor the President has the power to protect them it is my purpose to bring their case immediately before Congress."[5]

Shortly thereafter, the Creek delegation at Washington said the blacks at Fort Gibson and Little River had become a "positive nuisance" to the Creeks. They did not argue Jesup's right to free the blacks by proclamation; they simply wanted the question of title settled so the blacks could either be removed from the Creek country or placed under the control of their laws. According to the Creeks, the blacks were apparently without controls and violated the laws of the United States and of the Creek Nation with impunity; they were "idle and worthless" and brought whiskey into the Nation, stole, and induced slaves in surrounding areas to run away. Blacks who committed crimes were given asylum at Fort Gibson, the Creeks said. Many of the blacks were claimed by whites, who the Creeks felt should be given an opportunity to process their claims before a Creek tribunal, since Creek law extended to the Seminoles. If the blacks were declared free under Jesup's Proclamation, the Creeks wanted to know if they would then come under the jurisdiction of the Creek laws as other free blacks did.[6] By the time the Creeks made their complaint, the matter had been referred to John Y. Mason, Acting Attorney General of the United States, for an opinion.

When Marcellus Duval found that the matter had been referred to Mason, he took it upon himself to present the views of the Seminoles to the government, ostensibly "to protect them against the interference in their affairs of all persons not brought directly in contact by official obligations," meaning, of course, Jesup and the army officials on the frontier. However, because of his brother's involvement, Duval had a personal stake in the matter. He argued that until the blacks were offered protection by the army, every government action after their surrender or capture in Florida had recognized them as slaves and not as free blacks. In the negotiations which led to the Treaty of 1845, for instance, one of the reasons the Seminoles did not want to come under the laws of the Creeks was the matter of their slave property. A clause had been inserted to give the President power to determine who had title to the slave. Such a clause would have been unnecessary, Duval argued, if the blacks had been free. They had been, in fact, returned to the status they occupied before the war. Upholding Jesup's promises was tantamount to confiscation of private property. "I believe," Duval wrote, "the confiscation of the *private property* of those in our own country in the *slightest degree* under our control, is not only demonstrable to be unjust & illegal, but so absurd and monstrous a position as not even to require an argument." Should the blacks be declared free, he believed the Indians would drive them out of the territory. The government could not colonize them; therefore, the only apparent alternative would be to continue them on the reserve at public expense. They would be much better off, Duval argued, under the system of "benevolent slavery" practiced by the Seminoles. Duval ended his proslavery argument with a final blast at Jesup who he claimed called upon the government "to protect his personal honor, by desiring them to confirm an illegal & unjust act."[7]

Duval was wrong in asserting that every government action subsequent to the surrender or capture of the blacks had recognized them as slaves. Commissioner C. A. Harris had approved the convention of Fort Dade, and by its failure to disapprove Jesup's other agreements with the blacks, the government had in effect given its approval to them. It had also been General Taylor's policy as commander of the Second Division at Fort Smith to insist on a strict fulfillment of the provisions made to the blacks in Florida. Finally, departmental directions to Armistead and Worth in 1841 and 1842 had sent many slaves, the property of whites in Florida, to the West as free persons.

ATTORNEY GENERAL MASON'S OPINION

Attorney General Mason delivered his opinion on June 28, 1848.[8] He divided the slaves of the Seminoles into five classes: those protected under the agreement at Fort Dade, March 6, 1837; those brought in by their owners; those captured by the Creek warriors; those who were the property of white men but had not been returned to their owners before emigration; those captured by the army, including the ones who voluntarily came into the American camp; those whom Alligator brought in under an agreement supposedly made with Jesup.

In Mason's opinion, only those in the last class came within the scope of General Jesup's Proclamation. They were completely at the mercy of the Executive branch of government. As persons, slaves had no legal power to contract and could not, therefore, enter into an agreement or treaty.

As property, they were like any other movable property captured from an enemy. It was quite within the power of the Executive to return the prisoners or booty to their former owners and reestablish their antebellum status. In fact, in Mason's opinion, that had been done with one notable exception among the Seminole blacks.

The de-facto restitution had occurred because the government had not acted at once regarding Jesup's Proclamation. Under orders from the general, the blacks had emigrated with their Indian masters, and the government approved the act and defrayed the expenses. The government had recognized the blacks' slave status in 1845 when the treaty was made by the United States and the Seminoles and Creeks, with no stipulation to carry out Jesup's agreements with the blacks. In fact, the government took no action whatsoever until 1846 when protection was granted by the officers at Fort Gibson; by that time, Mason decided, the government had exhausted the Executive power in the matter and left the President no recourse but to deal with the problem under his powers granted by the act regulating trade and intercourse with the Indian tribes. The President could not recapture or reclaim the blacks without a new treaty with the Seminoles.

Beyond these legal questions, Mason believed that there was no such thing, in the states where slavery existed, as the qualified freedom which Jesup had supposedly promised the blacks. Even in the broadest sense of its powers, the government had no authority to give or to execute such a promise as Jesup's. In view of these facts and the objections of the Creeks to settlement of free blacks among the Seminoles, Mason declared the blacks the property of the Seminoles. "I do not perceive," he wrote, "on what principle you can interfere to deprive the Seminoles of their property, to give their slaves any 'qualified freedom.' " The terms of Jesup's promises were too uncertain, and it would be impossible to identify the blacks. Freeing the blacks would be impractical in view of "its legal repugnance to the lawful rights of the Indians; and of the acts of the government on the subject, which, under three distinct administrations, by orders and acquiescence through a space of ten years, have established what was to be done by the government in regard to the Indians and negroes." It was Mason's opinion, then, that the military authorities should restore the blacks to the condition which existed before Jesup's letter to Arbuckle on April 8, 1846, asking that the army intervene for the protection of the blacks.

Mason had pointed out that the only written documents containing the promises made to the blacks were Jesup's statements written after the fact. He asked Jesup to detail the agreements, but the general was ill and could not comply for several days. By that time, Mason had already made his decision concerning the fate of the blacks, and Jesup lost his long-fought battle in their behalf. President Polk approved the opinion on July 8, 1848.[9]

With this decision, the government had broken its promises to many of the blacks. It must be granted that Jesup's policy was new and unpopular in the slaveholding South, but the government had upheld the promises by supporting Jesup's actions. That the government could have acted in favor of the blacks is certain. It had done so in many prominent instances such as the cases of Toney Barnet, Gopher John, and Abraham. Apparently, however, as the possibility of armed resistance to a change of status decreased and the bond between the Seminoles and blacks became weaker, proslavery officials thought it safe to have the blacks declared slaves, just as Jesup had thought it safe to declare them free over a decade earlier.

PART OF THE NATIONAL DEBATE

While Mason's decision suggests the influence of Duval, it can be explained as simply a by-product of the national debate over slavery. John Young Mason of Virginia was the only member of John Tyler's Cabinet retained by President Polk. He had served as Attorney General from March 1845 until September 1846, when he became Secretary of the Navy. He was replaced by Matthew Clifford of Maine, who resigned on March 18, 1848, to become commissioner to Mexico. Clifford was replaced by Isaac Toucey of Connecticut, but in the interim, Mason, still Secretary of the Navy, heard the case. The opinion was rendered on June 28, the day before Toucey entered upon his duties. Thus, Mason, a Southerner, was apparently called upon to render a proslavery opinion between the terms of two Northern men. An opinion in favor of the blacks, as Duval suggested, would have been politically explosive.

That some of the Seminole blacks became the subject of the national debate over slavery cannot be doubted, for the representatives of J. C. Watson had revived his old claim to the blacks captured by the Creeks. On the day of Mason's opinion, the House Committee on Claims recommended an appropriation of the purchase price, plus 6 percent interest from 1838 until the date of payment. A minority report was filed by Representatives John Cromwell, J. A. Rockwell, William Nelson, and David Wilmot, who objected to payment of the claim on the ground that the purchase was a mere speculation, and Watson, knowing the risk, should have to assume the loss. They also questioned the legality of Watson's agreement with the Creek warriors and took up the old argument that the blacks were prisoners of war. "It was not in the power of the government agents," they said, "either with or without the sanction of the executive department, to transform prisoners of war into slaves, whether these prisoners belong to the aboriginal, American or African race, and then, for a stipulated price, to consign them to perpetual bondage." The current national debate over slavery was further reflected in the report, for the committee members argued the old questions of whether slaves were property or men and whether slavery was a state institution with which the federal government had no right to interfere, either to abolish or to sustain.[10] The minority report made one pertinent point regarding the blacks involved in the claim: A change in their condition would be extremely harsh.

When Watson's agents heard of Mason's opinion, they applied for delivery of those Watson claimed among the blacks covered by the decision. Marcellus Duval objected. In his usual manner, he denied Jesup's right to permit the Creeks to confiscate Seminole property without the consent of Congress. The government had, in effect, refuted his right by removing the blacks with the Seminoles and returning them to their original owners. They were never in Watson's possession; any claim he had was with the government and not the Seminoles. It would be impossible to deliver the blacks because they could not be identified, and if they were taken, the Indians whose blacks were captured by the Creeks would suffer while those whose blacks were captured by the army would not. The titles to many blacks had been transferred since removal. Even if all these obstacles could be overcome, Duval argued, to turn the blacks over to Watson would disturb the Seminoles.[11] Watson's application was denied.

RETURNING THE BLACKS TO THE SEMINOLES

In early August 1848, Secretary Marcy instructed General Arbuckle to deliver the blacks, in Duval's presence, to the chiefs, who were to deliver them to their proper owners. The only exception was Abraham and his family, who were apparently free by virtue of the special promise made to them. Those who were not apparently the property of the Seminoles were to be reported to the department along with any claims made to them. The blacks had occasionally worked as laborers at the post and had been supplied with rations. Further support for them from the stores of the post was suspended. The Creeks were informed of the decision, Commissioner William Medill expressing the hope that the decision would bring an end to the long-standing contention between the Seminoles and the Creeks concerning the blacks.[12]

Thus, the Executive machinery was set in motion to return the blacks on the reserve to bondage. There remained the task of carrying out the orders, which were disappointing to General Jesup and catastrophic to the blacks who had for nearly a decade lived with the illusory hope of freedom. The decision was repugnant to the sensibilities of many of the governmental officials on the frontier, and compliance with it was to prove a distasteful task.

If the military and civilian officials on the frontier could have kept the Attorney General's decision secret, no doubt they would have preferred to do so. The blacks on the reservation, as well as those who remained among the Seminoles, were armed, and over the years had developed a strong sense of independence, especially those on the reserve. Their imminent return to slavery and exposure to sale would make them restless. The Indians, bent on having the blacks returned with a clear title as slaves, would be anxious to have the matter settled and would likely make premature sales. Slave traders who purchased, or hoped to purchase, them would flock to the vicinity of the post and to the Seminole country, and premature sales would likely result in raids on the black settlements. It was the hope of officials to avoid any of these situations, for any change in the status of the blacks before they were returned to the Seminoles would probably result in the complication, if not delay, of their return.

As long as the status of those on the reservation had remained unsettled, the blacks had steeled themselves against the worst possibility—that they would be returned to the condition of slavery. Some purchased themselves or were purchased by others. For example, in the fall of 1847, Gopher John bought John from Wild Cat, and Robin purchased himself from William Grierson.[13]

Gopher John had remained at the post and acted as an interpreter after his return from Washington in 1846. He was not under formal contract, but every time the Indians came to the post, they sought him out, and he consented to interpret to get them to leave him alone. In the summer of 1847, Colonel Loomis had applied unsuccessfully for a compensation for John.[14] However, John gained an important advantage from the position he occupied at the post: As interpreter, he was most aware of the direction which events were taking in the spring of 1848.

In early June, he sent a list of complaints to General Jesup: For a few goods and a little whiskey the Indians made false titles to the blacks; Katy and her two children had been stolen recently; and the Indians stole the blacks' horses. John had concluded from talk about the post that they would probably be given back to their old masters. To defend himself against such an event, he wanted to establish his "claim to freedom on another title" than Jesup's Proclamation. About five years earlier the Seminole council had freed him and written emancipation papers which were properly witnessed. The papers had been recorded by Subagent Thomas L. Judge, from whom John wanted Jesup to obtain them. Jesup, of course, felt sympathy for the blacks, but for the first time he was critical of them. He felt that those at the post had weakened their own cause by allowing blacks who were not included in Jesup's arrangement to join them and that some of their actions had made the Creek chiefs complain to the President about the blacks' "intereference" with Creek women and about other outrages. Jesup wrote, "I will do all I can for those of them under my arrangement but I am apprehensive that I will fail in protecting them." Commissioner Medill could not locate John's "free papers." However, Duval, who was then in Washington, thought that they were in his office and promised to deliver them to John when he returned to the Indian country. John was evidently not satisfied, especially with Duval handling the matter. Therefore, he asked Wild Cat to make a statement that he had been given his freedom by Wild Cat and the other head chiefs and to reaffirm the bill of sale for John, whom Gopher John had purchased from Wild Cat in 1847.[15]

SPECULATORS' PLOTS

By this time, Mason's decision concerning the blacks was known in the West. Slave speculators immediately began to plot the capture of some of the blacks. General Arbuckle sent confidential instructions to Captain W.

S. Ketchum, then commanding Fort Gibson, to prevent the sale or removal of any of the blacks claiming freedom under Jesup's Proclamation. Slave traders who attempted to take them were to be warned that no transactions would be valid until the blacks were returned to the Seminoles. Duval was due to return to the Indian country in mid-September, at which time Arbuckle hoped finally to end the matter.[16]

Ketchum could effectively guard those blacks on the reservation, but he had no control over those who, though claiming freedom, had remained in their camps in the Seminole country. As Arbuckle had feared, slavers began their raids before Duval returned to his post. During the first week in September a party of fifteen Cherokees led by Bill Drew and some Creeks, including Union McIntosh and Joe Smith, made a raid in the Seminole country and carried off Clary and her children Pussy, Rose, Caesar, Sarah, and Tenny, all the property of Micanopy. They claimed to have made the raid under orders of Chief Roley McIntosh. Ketchum asked McIntosh to hold the blacks until Duval returned to the territory with orders for the settlement of the title, warning him that any sale made before the settlement would not be recognized. Micanopy appealed for a settlement of the matter in council.[17]

McIntosh claimed that a Creek citizen was simply trying to secure his slaves and employed a company of men to go to the Seminole Nation to get them. Nevertheless, he assured Ketchum that the blacks would be kept in the country until title to them could be settled. McIntosh's promises did not satisfy Ketchum. He sent troops to McIntosh's home for Pussy, Rose, and Caesar who were at Union McIntosh's and for Sarah at William Whitfield's nearby. Ketchum had learned that the Indians had beaten Clary when they made the raid, had stolen a gun from Thomas, Clary's husband, and had stolen a horse, saddle, and bridle belonging to a free black named Margaret. Ketchum demanded the return of those items. By mid-September, Ketchum had all of the family except Sarah inside the pickets at Fort Gibson. Sarah remained at Whitfield's, supposedly ill and "under the operation of medicine" for fever, but Whitfield promised to bring her in at first opportunity. The property of Thomas was still at Union McIntosh's and that of Margaret was still at Whitfield's. Ketchum firmly insisted on its return but at the same time assured the Creeks that the recent show of military strength was simply to insure that the blacks would not be run out of the territory and was, therefore, not a cause for the Creeks to become alarmed.[18]

The personal property in question was significant because it exemplified one of the important bases of contention between the Creeks and Seminoles. Laws of the Creek Nation were in effect in the Seminole country, and those laws prohibited blacks from owning horses and weapons. Yet the Seminoles had continued to allow their blacks to hold such property. Still unwilling to yield on this point, they insisted on the return of the property. Ketchum reassured them that the army would not allow raids to continue in their country and promised Micanopy to keep Clary and her children inside the garrison and give them rations until "the Negro business" was settled. To lessen excitement among the Seminoles, he tried to reassure the chiefs by saying that he believed the Creeks did not intend to sell them out of the territory. Ketchum also continued to give refuge to those who came to the post. Only a few days earlier, for instance, Jesse, Silla, and their four children had come from the Seminole country, asking for and receiving protection from slave speculators.[19]

Despite Ketchum's efforts, the property which had been taken during the raid kept tensions high between the Seminoles and Creeks. Late in September, Micanopy sent a message to Roley McIntosh, saying that if he would have the property returned, the Seminoles would "all be pleased."[20]

Occurring at a time when harmony between the tribes was desperately needed, this episode disturbed General Arbuckle. In an attempt to prevent other incidents, he directed Ketchum to keep on the reserve all of the blacks reported free on the list General Jesup had left at the post. They were not to be permitted to leave without instructions from "proper authority," presumably Arbuckle himself. Others not on the list, not on the reservation, and not claimed by the Seminoles, whether they were free blacks or runaways who had emigrated with the Seminoles and continued to reside with them, were to be brought in and kept on the reserve until the entire matter was settled.[21]

UNREST AMONG THE BLACKS

As time passed, the blacks on the reservation became restless, and the military authorities became uncertain that they could be contained. Brevet Lieutenant Colonel D. S. Miles, commanding the post in mid-November, found himself obligated to issue rations to nearly all of them, despite Arbuckle's orders in August that the commander was not to

issue rations except to prevent their starving. He expected them to sub-
sist by farming and by employment obtained near the post. Although the
blacks had diligently tended their crops, a drought during the summer
caused their harvest to be small. By late fall, their provisions had run out,
and they were destitute.[22]

They were anxious to have their cases settled. Excitement was at a
feverish pitch as they heard rumors that the government had decided to
turn them over to the Seminoles en masse without deciding their freedom.
The Seminoles, who looked at the blacks more and more as property, had
begun to sell them to anyone who would speculate on their purchase,
and, according to Miles, there were many such speculators among both the
Creeks and Cherokees. Miles could see the outcome. Coercion would be
necessary to make the blacks obey the decision of the government, and
there would be confusion and great disorder among the conflicting claimants
of Creeks and Cherokees who had purchased them from the pretended
Seminole owners, sometimes for prices as low as a bottle of whiskey. Thus,
Miles felt that the garrison at Fort Gibson was too small to be respected
and suggested an increase in its size.[23]

Duval came to the post on November 30 and talked with Miles, some
of the speculators who had gathered there, and a few of the blacks. He
sent messages to the rest of the blacks, trying to quiet their fears about
being turned over to sharpers. At the Seminole agency, Duval called a
council of the chiefs, who decided to go to Fort Gibson to receive the
blacks from the government on December 22. The blacks would be taken
back to the Seminole country before they were turned over to their respective owners by the chiefs.[24] On the night the chiefs arrived at Fort Gibson,
Micanopy died. His death represented another setback for the blacks, for
whom Micanopy had always demonstrated affection.

General Arbuckle intended to start for the post when he found that the
Indians were ready to meet him and do business. Meanwhile, the commandant was to make the chiefs comfortable and issue rations to them
and the blacks if necessary until Arbuckle arrived. However, about the
appointed time, an injury prevented Arbuckle from going to Fort Gibson,
and he appointed Brigadier General William G. Belknap to meet with the
chiefs in his stead. Arbuckle expected protests from certain white claimants,
especially W. E. Love and a man named Blake, against the delivery of the
blacks. Belknap was to receive their protests for submission for government
action, but he was not to allow their protests or those expected from the
Creeks to interfere with transfer of the blacks.[25]

Belknap was ordered to update the list of blacks on the reserve, with indications if they claimed to be free. Such claims were to be examined carefully, for Arbuckle was convinced that many were not legally claimed by any person and were justly entitled to be free, at least from Indian masters. He especially wanted Belknap to render any service he could to Gopher John, who was anxious to purchase his wife and children, in making an arrangement with their owner. When the chiefs were ready to leave the post with the blacks, Belknap was to provide them subsistence until they reached their towns.[26]

BLACKS TURNED OVER TO THE SEMINOLES

As Arbuckle suspected, the Creeks sought to delay the transfer. McIntosh, Benjamin Marshall, and others asked Belknap to arrange a council with the Seminoles before the blacks were turned over to them. No meeting was held, however, and on January 2, 1849, the blacks were turned over to the Seminoles. The chiefs were apparently satisfied with the instructions from the War Department, and the blacks seemed willing to obey them. W. E. Love presented a demand for those blacks he claimed as the heir of Hugh Love, but Belknap refused his demand.[27]

Nearly 260 blacks were officially turned over to the Seminoles as slaves. Of that number, over half were on the military reservation at Fort Gibson, and the remainder were mainly at the Deep Fork and Little River with a few at the North Fork and Arkansas rivers. The government list also carried the names of fourteen free blacks, sixteen blacks who had been sold out of the Indian country, and thirty-four who had died. The free blacks were Gopher John, Romeo, Sarah, Sandy, Peter, Lucy, Rufile, Jack, Cuffy, Judy, and Sam Mills.[28]

Surprisingly, the transfer had gone smoothly, in spite of rumors that the blacks would be distributed among the different claimants as soon as they were delivered to the chiefs. At first, they had vowed to die where they were rather than assent to being given up. Arbuckle had anticipated an escape attempt or some other difficulty in making the transfer. However, after consultation with Belknap, the blacks understood that they would be permitted to live in towns as they had formerly done and that they would not be sold or otherwise disposed of without their consent. The chiefs were told that the blacks would be turned over with that expectation;

the chiefs did not object, thereby virtually making a promise to that effect. The chiefs tried further to allay the fears of the blacks by telling them that they would remain with the Seminoles and be treated kindly. It is doubtful that the Seminoles were entirely sincere, but with their assurances, the blacks agreed to live with the Indians as they had previously done. In General Arbuckle's opinion, these understandings were the basis of the smooth transfer and the reason why the blacks, though armed, did not resist.[29]

Some of those who previously had been on the military reserve had voluntarily gone back to the Seminoles before the transfer. There remained the problem of transporting the nearly 150 who had not. Their movement was held up by unusually cold weather, the chiefs allowing the blacks to remain at the post until the snow and ice melted off. The Seminoles asked for wagons to carry the women and children as far as the North Fork, going by way of the old black settlement on the Deep Fork. Original orders had guaranteed transportation only as far as the Deep Fork. Without wagons to complete the trip the blacks would be detained there for some time, away from the Seminoles. Both the Indians and the blacks objected to that, saying they feared that some of the blacks might be run off by Creek claimants who had no title to them. The Seminoles wanted the government to help them move the blacks on to Wewoka Creek, about twelve miles from the Seminole subagency, to which point most of those then living at Deep Fork intended to move during the winter. The cold weather persisted, and the chiefs sent the black men out first to prepare cabins at the place designated for them and planned to remove the women and children later.[30]

ADVICE TO THE BLACKS

When preparations were being made to transfer the blacks to the Seminoles, the military authorities had told the blacks that they were to conduct themselves properly and to do nothing to create any disturbance. In all cases where they felt themselves to be wronged, they were to appeal to the agent. If any armed parties of slave hunters tried to seize them while they were en route to the Seminole country, however, they were to defend themselves. During the weeks following the transfer, this advice was transformed by rumor to a mandate to kill, if possible, Creeks or anyone else who might come among them to try to execute their slave

claims. On April 2, 1849, Wild Cat appeared at Arbuckle's office at Fort
Smith, intoxicated and complaining that the army had given the blacks
improper and unfriendly council.[31]

Arbuckle asked for clarification. Belknap, in fact, had told the blacks
that if attacked *by whites* on their way to the Seminole country, they
could defend themselves. However, on April 3, he informed them in the
presence of Marcellus Duval, the new chief Jim Jumper, and others that
if the Indians did them any wrong on their arrival in the nation, they must
not try to right it themselves but appeal to the chiefs and finally to the
agent, who would obtain justice for them. Belknap directed his words to
both the slaves and the free men, just a few days before they departed.[32]

The free blacks in the group sought extra protection of their rights.
Toney Barnet had secured a pass, placing him under "the especial protection of the government," granting him the right to settle in any part of
the Seminole country, and protecting him from being molested by anyone. Major Pinkney Lugenbeel also directed Creek Agent James Logan to
see that Toney was protected from molestation by any of the Creeks and
to recover two guns taken from Toney by the Creeks. Gopher John, likewise somewhat uncertain about his future and not wanting to be cut off
from Fort Gibson, was given a pass by Major Lugenbeel on April 8 "to
pass and repass from the Seminole country, his place of residence to this
post or to any other portion of the Indian country where his necessary
business might take him." Upon his arrival in the Seminole country, John
had Chitto Harjo make a new bill of sale for John's nephew Andrew, whom
he had bought in January. Finally, August had Wild Cat, Passockee Yohola,
Halleck Tustenuggee and other chiefs, in the presence of Abraham and
Marcellus Duval, sign his manumission papers.[33]

Upon reaching the Seminole country, the blacks began to defy the
authority of the Indians. In spite of urgings from Chief Jim Jumper, they
were slow in removing from the Deep Fork to the place where the Seminoles wanted them to settle. When they finally moved, most did not settle
at the location chosen by the Indians, twelve miles from the agency; instead,
they settled on Wewoka Creek, thirty miles from the agency. That action
was particularly objectionable to the chiefs, but the Seminoles decided
to allow the blacks to settle after their own fashion until the chiefs decided
in council who were the owners of the various families. They informed
the blacks that when the decisions were made, they would be turned over
to their owners.[34]

Thus, the blacks settled in small towns in the Seminole country, mainly at Deep Fork and Wewoka. Most, however, were at the latter under the leadership of Gopher John. They retained their arms and lived with no control from their Indian masters, resolved to protect themselves from slaving activities. They had developed a strong sense of independence. There were the years of thinking that they were free under Jesup's Proclamation, the three years of protection by the military authorities at Fort Gibson, the verbal agreement of the chiefs with General Belknap not to sell the blacks without their consent, and the directive to protect themselves against slaving activities. Thus, they evidently considered themselves free and merely wards of the Indians.[35] Settled apart in towns of their own and armed and living independently, they lacked only one thing—a leader. He soon emerged in the person of Gopher John, who had settled at Wewoka Creek.

NOTES

1. Marcellus Duval to James K. Polk, December 1, 1847, National Archives Microfilm Publications, *Microcopy M574* (Special Files of the Office of Indian Affairs, 1807-1904)-13, Special File 96: Seminole Claims to Certain Negroes, 1841-1849 (hereafter cited as *File 96*).

2. *Ibid.; Official Opinions of the Attorneys General of the United States* (Washington, 1852), 4: 723 (hereafter cited as *Official Opinions*).

3. Colonel Gustavus Loomis to General Thomas S. Jesup, December 7, 1847, National Archives Record Group 393 (Records of the United States Army Continental Commands, 1821-1920), *Second and Seventh Military Departments,* Letters Received (hereafter cited as *2nd & 7th LR*), Box 7, *File 96,* and National Archives Record Group 393, *Fort Gibson,* Volume "Indian Affairs" (hereafter cited as *Gibson Indian Affairs*), 32.

4. General Matthew Arbuckle to Roger Jones, January 29, 1848, in *File 96.*

5. Jesup to William L. Marcy, April 3, 1848, *File 96.*

6. Benjamin Marshall, Tuckabatche Micco, G. W. Stidham, and George Scott to William Medill, April 26, 1848, *File 96.*

7. Duval to John Y. Mason, May 20, 1848, *File 96.*

8. *Official Opinions,* 4: 720-729.

9. Jesup to Marcy, July 1, 1848, and Endorsement, Opinion of John Y. Mason, June 28, 1849, *File 96.*

10. H. W. Hilliard to Marcy, June 23, 1848, National Archives Microfilm Publications, *Microcopy M234* (Records of the Office of Indian Affairs, Letters Received)-228, H819-48; Committee Report and Minority Report, June 23, 1848, 30 Cong., 1 Sess., *House Report 724,* 1-9. *Microcopy M234* is hereafter cited as *M234,* followed by the roll number.

11. Duval to Secretary of War, July 13, 1848, *File 96.*

12. Marcy to Arbuckle, August 5, 1848, and Medill to Duval, August 5, 1848, *Fort Gibson,* Letters Received (hereafter cited as *Gibson LR*), Box 3; Medill to Marshall and others, August 10, 1848, National Archives Microfilm Publications, *Microcopy M21* (Records of the Office of Indian Affairs, Letters Sent)-41, 157. *Microcopy M21* is hereafter cited as *M21* followed by the roll number.

13. Statement of Wild Cat, September 25, 1847, *Gibson Indian Affairs,* 37. This was the same John who had been claimed by A. J. Forrester a few years earlier. Statement of William Grierson, December 27, 1847, *Gibson Indian Affairs,* 34.

14. Loomis to Lieutenant F. F. Flint, July 10, 1847, *Gibson Indian Affairs,* 27; Medill to Loomis, September 6, 1847, *Gibson LR,* Box 3, and *M21*-40, 53.

15. Gopher John to Jesup, June 10, 1848, *M234*-801, J102-48; Jesup to Captain B. L. E. Bonneville, July 28, 1848, *Gibson Indian Affairs,* 36. Captain Bonneville endorsed John's letter, saying that the blacks had many horses stolen and that they were quiet people who farmed rice and corn for their own use and for the troops. Medill to Gopher John, August 2, 1848, *M21*-41, 137, and *Gibson Indian Affairs,* 37; Statement of Co-ah-coo-chee, August 21, 1848, *Gibson Indian Affairs,* 38.

16. Flint to Captain W. S. Ketchum, September 4, 1848, *Gibson LR,* Box 3.

17. Ketchum to Roley McIntosh, September 8, 1848, *Gibson Indian Affairs,* 38.

18. McIntosh to Ketchum, and William Whitfield to Ketchum, September 14, 1848, *Gibson LR,* Box 3; Ketchum to McIntosh, September 11 and September 13, 1848, *Gibson Indian Affairs,* 39. Margaret may have been the daughter of Polly Barnet, the wife of Toney, and therefore free by virtue of her manumission by old Chief Bowlegs in 1819. Statement of J. W. Washbourne, October 14, 1854, *M234*-801, D709-54.

19. Ketchum to McIntosh, September 28, 1848, and Ketchum to Micanopy, September 24, 1848, *Gibson Indian Affairs,* 41, 40.

20. Ketchum to McIntosh, September 28, 1848, *Gibson Indian Affairs,* 41. The property in question had not been returned as late as January of 1849. James Logan to General William Belknap, January 30, 1849, *Gibson LR,* Box 3.

21. Flint to Ketchum, September 25, 1848, *Gibson LR,* Box 3.

22. Flint to Ketchum, August 21, 1848, *Gibson LR,* Box 3; Lieutenant Colonel D. S. Miles to Flint, November 17, 1848, *2nd & 7th LR,* Box 7.

23. Miles to Flint, November 17, 1848, *2nd & 7th LR,* Box 7.

24. Duval to Arbuckle, December 1, 1848, and Duval to Arbuckle, December 11, 1848, *2nd & 7th LR,* Box 7.

25. Flint to Captain C. L. Stevenson, December 11, 1848, and Flint to Belknap, December 19, 1848, *Gibson LR,* Box 3.

26. Flint to Belknap, December 19, 1848, *Gibson LR,* Box 3.

27. McIntosh, et al., to Belknap, December 27, 1848, Belknap to Arbuckle, January 3, 1849, W. E. Love to Belknap, January 3, 1849, *Gibson LR,* Box 3.

28. List of Negroes Turned Over to the Seminole Chiefs at Fort Gibson, C. N., Jan'y 2nd 1849, *File 96;* the list is reproduced as List K in the Appendix.

29. Arbuckle to Jones, January 8, 1849, *File 96;* Arbuckle to Jones, July 31, 1849, and Flint to John Drennen, August 13, 1849, 33 Cong., 2 Sess., *House Executive Document 15* (hereafter cited as *Document 15*), 22, 26.

30. Duval to Arbuckle, January 3, 1849, *2nd & 7th LR,* Box 7; Francis N. Page to Assistant Adjutant General, November 18, 1854, *Document 15,* 10; Duval to Medill, January 18, 1849, in *M234*-801, R437-49.

31. Flint to Belknap, April 2, 1849, *Gibson LR,* Box 3.

32. Belknap to Flint, April 4, 1849, *2nd & 7th LR,* Box 7.

33. Statement of Pinkney Lugenbeel, March 1849, and Lugenbeel to Logan, March 26, 1849; Pass, April 8, 1849; Receipts of Harjo, January 11, and May 15, 1849; and Manumission papers of August, May 15, 1849, *Gibson Indian Affairs,* 44-46.

34. Duval to Belknap, June 7, 1849, *Gibson LR,* Box 3; Duval to Arbuckle, July 16, 1849, *File 96;* Arbuckle to Jones, July 31, 1849, *Document 15,* 22.

35. Page to Assistant Adjutant General, November 18, 1854, *Document 15,* 10.

7

Bolt for freedom

The militant stance of the blacks after their return to a state of slavery caused difficulties not only between them and the Seminoles but between the Seminoles and the Creeks as well. The Seminoles were led by a young chief who apparently cared less for the blacks than Micanopy had. The old prewar relationship between Africans and Seminoles was only a memory for both. They had now assumed the positions of master and slave and of armed antagonists. The situation was capitalized upon by Marcellus Duval, who officially considered the blacks as slaves in revolt. However, he had personal motives for wanting them subdued, and his duplicity contributed significantly to the theft and sale of many of them outside the Seminole country and to the desperate attempt by others to escape from the Indian country and seek refuge and freedom outside the United States.

At first, difficulties arose from accusations of horse stealing against the blacks. The Creeks complained that about the time of and during the trek of the blacks to the Seminole country, the blacks stole some horses from Creek citizens. One horse, recovered from an Indian, had been bought from a black, and a horse stolen from the Choctaw Nation was seen among the blacks. However, it was the complaint of a Cherokee that resulted in the first confrontation between the Seminoles and the blacks. He came to the Seminole country to get his stolen pony, bringing evidence and describing the animal.

He named "the notorious thief Joe, commonly called Walking Joe," as the culprit. The chiefs sent two men to Gopher John's town, and when all of the horses were driven up, the one stolen was among them. When

the two Seminoles tried to arrest Joe, he drew a knife, but they succeeded
in disarming and roping him to take him to the council for trial. Before
they could leave, all of the black men arrived, armed with knives and
pistols, threatened the Indians, and set Joe free. They sent Cuffy with
the Indians to give the chiefs a message: To avoid the risk of injury, the
Seminoles were not to come to the blacks' town to arrest one of their men
without first consulting the head men, among whom Gopher John was
the most prominent. The warning angered Marcellus Duval. He sent for
Gopher John, who came to the agency a few days later and blamed the
affair on the "young and unmanageable negroes." Although John had
played a prominent part in the affair, the Indians allowed him to return
to his town without punishment, even though Duval thought "he should
have been whipped at least." After the affair, Walking Joe remained at
large.[1]

DUVAL'S PROSLAVERY VIEW OF AFFAIRS

In Duval's proslavery view, there was potential danger in the situation:
"It must be decided whether the negroes govern or the Seminoles. Should
the Seminoles allow the negroes to go on the Creeks will protest first and
finally interfere which they have a right to do to keep order in the country."
If an Indian should be hurt in a confrontation with the blacks, Duval said
that he could not answer "for the number of negroes who would suffer."
More than all of this, however, he obviously feared the presence of an
enclave of free or independent blacks in a slaveholding territory. He insisted
that they had committed acts for "which the lives of the ringleaders would
be forfeited if committed in a slave state." He wanted them brought into
subjection to their masters and "taught their proper place," but he promised
that they would not be "unnecessarily interrupted" and that he would
protect them "from interference from all persons but their owners & the
authorities of the nation."[2] In view of Duval's personal interest in the
matter, the sincerity of the latter statement is doubtful.

Duval blamed the situation on the military authorities, who he felt
had given the blacks encouragement in their resistance to authority. To
him, military policy had been wrong from the start. Officers had protected
blacks on the Fort Gibson reserve from unauthorized persons and legitimate
owners alike. Duval cited the example of the family of Thomas who had

been taken by their owner D. N. McIntosh from the black town on Deep
Fork in the fall of 1848. The blacks had been taken from McIntosh and
placed in the garrison. The military officers had also allowed the blacks
to keep their weapons in violation of the Creek law, and criminals had been
given up only when the commanders were ordered to do so by General
Arbuckle. The officers allowed the blacks at the garrison to run their livestock in the Indian country, but the blacks rendered no service to their
owners. Finally, Duval thought bad the advice Belknap had given the blacks
at the time they were returned to the Seminoles. While Duval claimed that
it was not good to squander slaves and to sell parents from children and
husbands from wives, he felt that Belknap should never have told the
Indians not to sell the blacks or scatter them unless the blacks wanted to
go—at least, not in the presence of the blacks. For they had construed the
advice to mean that they were still protected by the military, and they
now used military force as a threat against the Indians.[3] Under the present
circumstances, Duval felt that if the military showed the least disposition
to support the blacks, there would be trouble between them and the
Indians.

Of course, Duval's complaint against the army had been long-standing,
because the officers would not let him have his way with the blacks. Like
Duval, General Arbuckle had concluded that the blacks were a problem,
but for different reasons. He felt that many of them had been separated
from the Indians for so long that they would never be "very serviceable"
to them or to anyone else as slaves. They were too independent and insubordinate. He wrote, "In their present position, I regard them as a nuisance
in the Seminole country. They were counselled to conduct themselves
properly when they were turned over, and assured that if they did so,
they should not be cruelly or illegally treated. But it seems they have acted
otherwise."[4]

DISARMING THE SEMINOLE BLACKS

In July 1849, the Seminoles met in council and decided who were the
original owners of the blacks before protection was offered them and who
the present owners were according to the Seminole laws. However, the
blacks refused to be separated or to allow their towns to be broken up
and told the Indians that the army would protect them in their refusal.

The owners began to complain that the government was the cause of the situation. The chiefs, mindful of the fighting ability the blacks had demonstrated during the Florida war, were reluctant to confront the blacks and force their compliance with the decrees of council. Thus, the owners turned to Duval to secure their property and avoid bloodshed, which would no doubt have resulted in the loss of some of their slaves if the Indians had taken the matter into their own hands.[5]

The Creeks, too, began to assert their right to disarm the blacks if the Seminoles did not, insisting that their laws forbade blacks to live in separate towns or to bear arms. The Creeks were apparently influenced by speculators who wanted the blacks returned to the Indian owners, from whom the speculators had bought them. The Creeks' taking the matter into their own hands would force a confrontation with the Seminoles, who vehemently disliked any interference of the Creeks in their affairs, even though they themselves would have liked to see the blacks disarmed. The blacks would certainly resist the Creeks by force. Ostensibly to prevent a confrontation, Duval called upon General Arbuckle to send troops to disarm the blacks. His request was endorsed by John Drennen, the superintendent of Indian affairs for the Western Territory.[6]

Arbuckle had hoped that the army was through with the blacks when they were returned to the Seminoles. He found it strange that the Indians could not control the blacks by forcing them to settle in the desired place and to give up their arms if they were armed contrary to the laws of the Nation. He did not think that troops were necessary but offered to send an officer with Duval to look into the state of affairs and try to get the blacks to surrender their arms peaceably until the matter could be settled.[7]

Arbuckle defended the role of the military officers in the entire matter. Belknap's advice to the Seminoles and blacks had been given at his direction because the general understood that it was the government's intent to allow the blacks to settle quietly in towns as they had formerly done in Florida. In Arbuckle's opinion, if Belknap had not obtained the promise from the Indians to treat the blacks kindly, they could not have been removed from Fort Gibson except in irons. Since their removal, Arbuckle had received no complaints until Duval's came.[8]

Arbuckle knew that Duval and the Seminoles wanted the army to disarm the blacks to save themselves risk and trouble, for he knew that they feared armed resistance if they tried to separate and dispose of the blacks. But Arbuckle now suspected other motives on Duval's part. He had learned that about one third of the blacks had been promised to William J. Duval, the brother of Marcellus, for his services as attorney in getting the blacks returned to the Seminoles. About as many more supposedly had been sold or otherwise disposed of to Cherokees and Creeks, with some United States citizens having an interest in the transactions. The blacks knew of these arrangements and, of course, were determined to resist their fulfillment.[9]

Piqued at Arbuckle's refusal to send troops, Duval angrily refused the general's offer of an investigating officer, saying that the only proper investigation would be his own, and returned to his agency. Arbuckle instructed Belknap to watch the situation closely. While he hoped to settle the conflict quickly, he had doubts because the blacks had been separated from the Indians too long and believed that they would be freed by the government.[10]

Arbuckle's suspicions of Duval were heightened a few days later when Belknap reported that it was the general impression in the Seminole country by trader P. H. White and a lawyer from Van Buren named Johnson one third of the negroes provided him by the Indians for his agency in having them restored to the Seminoles by the government." Belknap also learned that Duval had been accompanied from Fort Smith to the Seminole country by trader P. N. White and a lawyer from Van Buren named Johnson and that these men had proposed to the Creek subchief Benjamin Marshall to disarm the blacks. Marshall had refused the proposal. Belknap expected no trouble from the Creeks, "in fact no trouble at all unless from the agents.'

REQUEST FOR TROOPS

On August 10, 1849, Duval renewed his request for troops to disarm the blacks. Arbuckle again refused, expecting no disturbance unless it was produced by "interested persons." He referred specifically to the interference of White and Johnson. Lieutenant F. F. Flint, Arbuckle's aide-de-camp, wrote to John Drennen, "Most of the trouble in the Indian country on this frontier has been occasioned by our own citizens, either directly or indirectly and it is much to be lamented." He assured Drennen that Arbuckle considere the "insubordinate and independent position of the negroes as a serious evil" but doubted the propriety of sending troops.[12]

To the Adjutant General, Arbuckle wrote essentially the same thing. He believed that the Seminoles were sufficiently numerous to control their

blacks without military assistance and that it was clearly their duty to
keep the blacks in subjection. He wrote, "They seem to fear that there would
be a loss of life, should they take the matter into their own hands. But what
reason is there to believe that the result would be different should it be
undertaken by others? The negroes well know what to expect after being
deprived of their arms, and they are not disposed to yield peaceably to any.
The *Indians* certainly do not set a very high value on the negroes, as I am
informed that many of them have been disposed of for the merest trifle;
so that it cannot be the blacks whose lives *they* are so anxious should not
be put in jeopardy. In short, I am satisfied that the whole business is kept
in agitation by others, who manifest much restlessness, impatience, and
deep solicitude, respecting the welfare of the Seminoles and their negroes."[13]

Drennen, an Arkansan and a slaveholder, defended Duval's request for
troops. The blacks were slaves in a state of rebellion, and, to him, it was
"the imperative duty of the government to protect the Indian and quell
domestic strife." Drennen questioned P. H. White, who denied having
asked Benjamin Marshall to intervene in the matter. "I am *well aware,*"
Drennen wrote "that great disturbance and much difficulty has arisen in
the Indian country by designing white men, for mercenary purposes; but
I did not think for *one moment* that anything of the kind was intended in
this case, as I made the requisition for troops in good faith, and upon the
statement in writing of a *highly respectable agent of the government.*"[14]
His reference, of course, was to Duval.

Duval's motives became more suspect and his credibility further eroded
in early September, when Wild Cat, Passockee Yohola, and George Cloud
and about fifteen warriors showed up unexpectedly and uninvited at
Arbuckle's office in Fort Smith. They denied Duval's accusation that
Gopher John had encouraged the people of his town to resist the Indians.
In fact, the Seminoles said that they had no complaints against the blacks,
that the blacks were conveniently settled in three towns, that they wished
the blacks to keep their arms so they might hunt to feed their poor families,
and that the blacks might not be disturbed in any way.

The chiefs claimed to have been sent to Arbuckle by the head chief
Jim Jumper. However, they charged that Jumper, a young man who owned
no slaves, had promised one third of the blacks to William J. Duval without the consent or knowledge of the owners of the slaves. Now, they claimed,
Marcellus Duval was saying that ninety would not be enough, since
he and his brother had expended much more money than expected in
prosecuting the Seminole claims. Speaking for the owners, the chiefs main-

tained that the agent was paid by the government and should not expect further pay from the Indians, and they made it clear that if Duval obtained the slaves, the Seminoles would file a claim for their value against the government. They alleged that the agent had threatened to hold up their annuity if the Seminoles did not give up the blacks. Finally, they charged that Duval had asked Chief Roley McIntosh to send some of the Creeks to meet the Seminoles in council, assuring him that if the Creeks approved of disarming the blacks, the Seminoles would help them do it. The Creek Jim Boy was to be at the head of the council which was to have met on September 3 near the black settlements; however, the Seminoles, totally opposed to any interference by the Creeks, refused to attend. Angry at Duval, the chiefs had then sent the delegation to General Arbuckle.[15]

The general advised the Seminoles to remain quiet until he could consult his superiors concerning the use of troops and sent the chiefs with their complaints to Superintendent Drennen's office at the Choctaw Agency. They took with them a letter in which Arbuckle's aide wrote, "The General believes the course adopted by the sub-agent is such as will probably lead to difficulty between the Seminoles and the Creeks, and is therefore of the opinion that your instructions to their agents should be such as to prevent such trouble hereafter, and he cannot doubt your interposition in relation to this matter." Duval had made his overtures to the Creeks in the absence of their agent. Therefore, Arbuckle informed the agent of the situation and asked him to keep the Creeks from interfering until the government could act. Finally, to the Adjutant General, Arbuckle suggested an investigation to find "the persons most directly and deeply interested in carrying into execution the plan proposed by the Seminole sub-agent, and urgently recommended by the acting superintendent."[16]

CLASHES AND CLAIMS

Meanwhile, some of the bolder Seminole blacks had drifted back to the vicinity of Fort Gibson, much to the dissatisfaction of the Creeks who considered them "a worthless, lazy set of vagabonds," who would "give much trouble sooner or later."[17] Other free blacks of the Creek Nation lived in the vicinity. In early October, General Belknap went on an inspection tour, and the slave hunters took the opportunity of his absence from the post to make raids on the blacks. A man named Myers from Fort Smith stole a woman and her three children, who were considered free, the woman having settled on the land as an Indian because her mother was a full-blood Yuchi. Soldiers from Fort Gibson recovered them and captured Myers. Investigation showed that Myers had been taken advantage of in his purchase, and he was therefore released. Then on October 11, Siah Hardridge presented a claim for some blacks he had purchased from Nelly Factor in 1843. He claimed that they were in the Cherokee Nation near the post. Although no claim which predated the return of the blacks to the Seminoles was supposed to be valid, Hardridge attempted to take Dembo Factor, who drew a pistol and a knife; Hardridge's brother wounded Dembo with a shotgun. Hardridge was forbidden to molest the blacks further, but that night he made another attempt to take them, and the blacks drove him off.[18]

Dembo was taken to the post hospital where the surgeon pronounced his wound to be mortal. Later that day, however, Hardridge took him across the river into the Creek Nation, and by the end of the month, Dembo was reported to be recovering. A few days after the raid, a man named Tyrell from the Cherokee Nation, apparently employed by Hardridge, came late at night to the quarters of one of the officers and tried to carry off a woman, swearing "that he would have her if he was compelled to cut off her head." The slavers watched the ferries across the Arkansas to prevent the Seminole blacks from escaping to their own country. General Belknap believed that Hardridge was simply the agent for some trader and had no claim whatever to Dembo. He suggested to General Arbuckle that the Creek authorities be asked for the return of the man.[19]

However, Arbuckle was reluctant to act. Nothing could prevent the Seminoles from selling their slaves even though they had promised not to do so without the blacks' consent. If Dembo had been taken illegally, the owner should demand his return from the Creeks. If any attempt were made to seize blacks about the garrison, Belknap was not to allow them to be taken unless the claimant could satisfactorily prove his title and unless nothing else could be done.[20]

These raids only added to the contention which had surrounded the blacks since their return to the Seminoles. They were assuredly related to the factionalism among the Seminoles, which had long been developing but which now became open. Shortly after the raids, Wild Cat delivered a talk at the North Fork and asked Duval to forward it to the President of the United States. He asked the government to remove his people from the Creek Nation to a place near the Rio Grande. They were tired of living among the Creeks, he said, and the country would suit them better. He believed that he could induce Billy Bowlegs and all of the remaining

Seminoles in Florida to go willingly to the Rio Grande, whereas they would always object to being removed to lands near the Creeks.[21]

Wild Cat's dissatisfaction with affairs in the West had been long-standing. Although he had signed the Treaty of 1845, he smarted under the Creek dominance established by the pact. For some time he had been a chief adviser to Micanopy, and had been expected to succeed the latter as principal chief of the Seminoles. He had laid plans to form a confederacy of the Seminoles and the southwestern tribes with himself at the head.

WILD CAT'S MIGRATION TO MEXICO

Wild Cat evidently got his idea in 1845 and 1846 when he traveled in the Southwest. He first went to Texas in December 1845, with Cherokee Agent Pierce M. Butler and M. G. Lewis on a peace mission to the Comanches. As significant as the success of the mission was the impression the country had made on Wild Cat. Upon their return to the Seminole country, Wild Cat organized another expedition, ostensibly to trade with the western tribes, and left again for the Southwest with Halleck Tustenuggee, Oktiarche, and other Seminoles. After six weeks they returned, and at the council in the summer of 1846, Wild Cat spoke to the Seminoles about the Comanches and other tribes they had met, of the good prospects for trade, and of the friendly attitude of the southwestern tribes. During his travels, he had met the Kickapoos, Lipans, Tonkawas, and Comanches. In 1847, he sent a message to the Secretary of War complaining that the Indian Territory was not a better land than Florida. It was cold and rough. After the annuity stopped, the Seminoles would not know what to do, for the people had become dependent on it. "As for myself," he said, "I can get along well enough, but I am writing for them." In 1848, he sent representatives to the Kickapoos, Lipans, Tonkawas, and Comanches, as well as to the Kichai and Wacos, urging them to come to the Indian country and join the Seminoles.[22]

However, matters did not go as he had expected on the home front. Micanopy died on the night of his arrival at Fort Gibson to receive the blacks from General Belknap. The election of principal chief did not fall to Wild Cat as he had expected but to Jim Jumper, the young son of Jumper, who had died on the way to the West in 1838. Thus, Wild Cat could not ask the wild tribes to join one who was not a chief. He decided, instead, to lead his people south of the Rio Grande and there establish a colony for refugees, including Indians and blacks from Texas, the Indian Territory, and Arkansas.[23] Perhaps he was putting his plans in final shape in the late summer of 1849, when he intervened on the part of the Seminole blacks and protested to General Arbuckle against their being disarmed at Duval's request. He certainly had his plan completed that fall when he asked to be removed to the Rio Grande and to be permitted to induce Billy Bowlegs and the remaining Seminoles in Florida to remove with him.

Shortly after he made the request, the Florida Seminoles afforded him the opportunity to make his break from the Seminole country. The Seminoles in Florida numbered about 350. Under their principal chief Sam Jones and their war chief Billy Bowlegs, they inhabited the Everglades. In the fall of 1849, it was decided that the western Seminoles might be able to induce them to remove, so a delegation was formed, headed by Halleck Tustenuggee. With ten delegates, including three black interpreters—Jim Bowlegs, Toney, and Tom—and Marcellus Duval, Halleck Tustenuggee left North Fork Town on October 16.[24]

Capitalizing on Duval's absence, Wild Cat set about carrying out his plan. He persuaded some of his people and a few Creeks, with a combined strength of twenty to twenty-five warriors, to leave the Indian country and make treaties with the western tribes and with Mexico. Using a hunting pass given him by Duval, he claimed he had permission to go to look for new lands. When in late October the party left the Seminole country, they were accompanied by Gopher John and about twenty other black men and their families. Also in the group were a few slaves belonging to Creeks and Cherokees. Numbering about two hundred, they encamped in the spring of 1850 at Cow Bayou on the Brazos in Texas so that the blacks could make a corn crop, and in the summer of 1850 they went on to Mexico, where they asked admission as settlers.[25] This bolt for freedom by the blacks under Gopher John was by far the most radical event which had occurred in relation to the Seminole blacks. While it may have established the freedom of those who reached Mexico, it proved disastrous to many of those who remained in the Seminole country.

DUVAL'S RETURN

Marcellus Duval and the Seminole delegation did not return to the western Nation until April of 1850. Duval was clearly angered at what he

found. He had left the territory amidst a hail of criticism from both
General Arbuckle and the Seminoles, especially Wild Cat. Now, in light
of Wild Cat's escape from the Nation with a large number of blacks,
Duval saw an opportunity to recoup some of his credibility by saying,
"I told you so." He laid the blame squarely on Arbuckle, whom he had
warned of the consequences of failing to disarm the blacks. He accused
Arbuckle of telling him in July 1849 that he would advise Gopher John
to go to Mexico with all the blacks who were free, that there John would
be a great man, "as a negro was as big as anybody." Duval charged Arbuckle
with aiding and abetting Wild Cat in his scheme.[26]

In the spring of 1850, the Seminoles met in council and asked Duval
to recover the runaways if possible. He knew that going to Mexico to
arrest the blacks would result in bloodshed. He asked the commissioner
of Indian affairs to issue orders for their arrest, for if they were allowed
to settle outside the United States, they would be a harbor for renegade
Indians and runaway slaves and would "destroy the safety of the Texas
frontier." Already rumors were being circulated that several blacks from
the Creek and Seminole Nations planned to leave that fall to join Wild Cat.[27]

In reality, Duval was probably as anxious to recover the escaped blacks
as were the Seminoles because of his brother's interest in them. His claim
to a large number of them dated from a power of attorney, given by
Micanopy and the chiefs and head men to W. J. Duval on November 20,
1847. While he was given authority to prosecute their claims for recovery
of the blacks, no mention was made of recompense. On December 7, 1847,
W. J. Duval was also given the power of attorney for Siah Hardridge, the
Creek who had often raided the blacks' camps to recover the blacks he
claimed.[28] These documents strongly support the accusations of both
Arbuckle and Wild Cat that Marcellus Duval had an ulterior motive in
wanting the blacks disarmed. But slaving activities in the early summer
of 1850 pointed more certainly to the duplicity of Duval, who with other
claimants capitalized on the absence of Wild Cat, the blacks' strongest
Indian defender, and Gopher John, their strongest leader. Without these
two figures, the blacks who remained in the Seminole country were at
the mercy of the Indians.

In early June, a party of slave hunters from the Creek Nation entered
the Seminole country and took three slaves. Among the slavers were Siah
Hardridge and his son, who shot and took away a slave belonging to
Gopher John. D. N. McIntosh captured Jim Bowlegs and Stephen but

had a bill of sale for only the latter. They were rescued, however, by General Belknap. Belknap sent an officer to the Creek Nation to see Chief Roley McIntosh and protest the action. McIntosh, much angered, sympathized with Hardridge, for Gopher John, he said, had "decoyed off a number of negroes" belonging to Hardridge. The Seminole chiefs had supposedly given Hardridge permission to take all of the property left in the Nation by Gopher John. Even if Hardridge had no claim to the wounded black, the Creeks would have supported him because the black resisted and tried to take a gun from Hardridge's son, who shot him. As for Jim Bowlegs, he was a slave and possessed arms and a horse, both of which were prohibited by Creek law. D. N. McIntosh had a bill of sale for Stephen, and thus had the right to take his property anywhere he found it. After defending the Creeks' actions, McIntosh attacked Belknap, who he said had earlier told him that he would have nothing more to do with the Seminole blacks but had gone back on his word and offered them protection. McIntosh accused the blacks of repeatedly breaking the laws of the Creek Nation and the military of asking the Creeks to suspend the laws when it came to the Seminole blacks. If in the army's view the Creeks had no right to make and enforce laws regarding the blacks, McIntosh wanted to know so that the Creek delegation to Washington could work at getting the matter finally settled.[29]

CREEKS AND SEMINOLES AT LOGGERHEADS

On June 24, great excitement was created in the Seminole Nation when another armed party arrived in the vicinity of the black settlement at Wewoka. Among them were Creeks, headed by Union McIntosh and including Hardridge, Tom Carr, Joe Smith, John Sells, and others. There were Cherokees including William Drew, Dick Drew, and Martin Vann. And there were four white men: P. H. White of Van Buren, J. M. Smith of Fort Smith, a trader named Mathews from near the Creek agency, and Gabriel Duval of Montgomery, Alabama. Duval was the brother of Marcellus Duval and had taken over the claim of their brother William, who had recently died. At first, the Seminoles were excited because they did not know the party's purpose; upon learning that they intended to attack the black town, many of the Seminoles were determined to help the blacks defend themselves against the outsiders.[30]

Captain F. T. Dent of the Fifth Infantry was in the vicinity and intervened to prevent a confrontation. He sent word to Marcellus Duval,
asking him to come to the scene, warned Union McIntosh that the action
his party intended would likely start a war between the Creeks and Seminoles, and vowed to interfere to prevent it. Dent persuaded McIntosh to
try to reach some understanding with the Seminole chiefs before he acted.
On the following day, Marcellus Duval told McIntosh and his party to
cross to the north side of the North Fork and wait in the Creek country.
He then called a council of the Seminole chiefs, which McIntosh and four
other Creeks attended. The chiefs agreed to admit the party and to help
them in taking a number of blacks, the exact number Dent could not
learn. As soon as the Seminoles came to the decision, Dent retired from
the scene.[31]

He later learned that about 180 blacks had been taken, but many of
them were kept as prisoners for a short time to prevent their giving information to and supporting others who had fled. All of the prisoners were still
at the Seminole agency on July 15. Apparently, they were all seized by
the Seminoles to be turned over to the Creeks who had camped about
six miles from the black town.[32]

Thirty-four blacks given up to satisfy the claim of William J. Duval
were claimed by Mah-kah-tist-chee, or Molly, who appeared on July 15
at the army departmental headquarters in Fort Smith and filed a complaint.
Molly claimed to own seventy-nine grown slaves "besides many infant
children," who were either inherited or were descendants of slaves inherited
from her grandfather. Molly was the daughter of Tuskeneehau, a Mikasuki
chief, and granddaughter of Kinhijah (also known as Capichee Micco), a
former principal chief of the Mikasukis. At her death, the property would
go to her sister, Mah-pah-yist-chee. She claimed that when her father died,
Miccopotokee was made guardian of the slaves, at which time a half-blood
Creek named Archie Gray began selling the slaves, without apparent title, to
Hugh Love of Georgia. Miccopotokee had not yet removed to the West, so
the claim was settled in his favor in the East. Then in 1844 or 1845, the
western Creek council had decided that the slaves belonged to the two
sisters. There was no other claim to the slaves until recently, when Capichee,
a Seminole lately arrived from Florida, at the urging of Halleck Tustenuggee,
set up a claim to them.[33]

When Molly's husband died, a paper setting forth her right to the property
was taken by Micanopy. At his death it had passed to Duval, then to Halleck

Tustenuggee, and finally to Capichee. Now, by their action, the Seminole chiefs had agreed with Duval that thirty-four of her slaves would be given up to satisfy William J. Duval's claim against the Nation. Thirty-one women and children had been forcibly seized and three men escaped; they were now being sought, and the chiefs had agreed to turn them over when they were taken. Molly claimed that she had had no information concerning the agreement between Duval and the chiefs until Micanopy had died and Jim Jumper informed her of it; however, he had made no mention that her slaves were involved. She did not expect justice from Jumper and the Seminole subagent and asked the army to secure her property for her.[34]

PROPERTY GUARDIANSHIP AMONG THE SEMINOLES

Molly's complaint points out a most complex matter regarding the titles of slaves among the Seminoles. She claimed that Micanopy owned but one slave himself but was guardian of many others, the property of friends. It was general practice for the Seminoles to leave such property in the care of the chiefs if the heirs were either minor, infirm, or incompetent. Sometimes, guardianships lasted many years. Such was the case of many of those under Micanopy's care. After his death, because of the difficulties with the blacks, the chiefs showed little reluctance to give them up to satisfy claimants. Such was also the case of those blacks owned by absentee Seminoles, such as Billy Bowlegs, whose slaves were sent west while he remained in Florida. Perhaps the chiefs thought that he would never emigrate, for there seemed to be no objection, at least among the Creeks, to attempts to take Jim Bowlegs, one of his slaves, and the chiefs seemed willing to allow others to be taken. In July 1850, Duval tried to obtain more of Billy Bowlegs' slaves to satisfy the claim of his brother.

Bowlegs himself had opened the door to fraud in relation to his slaves. In April 1850, he had written to Jim Jumper and the chiefs that it was uncertain whether he would ever go west. Therefore, in order to prevent disputes about the title to his slaves among his relatives in the West, he asked the chiefs, upon his death, to give the property to the nieces of his "poor brother Holatoochee." The chiefs were to designate the most sensible of the three women to take charge of the fifty slaves, whom he had inherited and who were well known to all of the chiefs as his. Bowlegs gave special instructions to the chiefs to protect Hester who had been illegally sold to a Cherokee by his deceased brother It-koh and to allow his slave Jim Bowlegs to have general charge of the slaves under their mistress.[35]

In July 1850, Duval demanded that Belknap give up Jim Bowlegs and Katy and Fanny, whose names were on Billy Bowlegs' list. Duval wanted Jim on an old charge filed by the superintendent of Indian affairs, alleging that Jim had stolen a horse in the Choctaw Nation. Duval claimed to have hired out Katy and Fanny to Major Pinkney Lugenbeel in 1849, with permission and for the benefit of their Seminole owner. When Belknap did not turn over any blacks, Duval accused him of protecting them.[36]

Belknap's story was somewhat different. Jim Bowlegs was not on the reserve at the time and had not been for several days. There were only three black men on the reserve—August, Lewis, and Primus—all of whom possessed "free papers." A few days earlier, Sally Factor had informed Belknap that August was being sought by several slave hunters. She had sold most of her blacks, but she still claimed him. She also claimed Katy and Fanny and asked Belknap to turn them over to her son Billy. The two women were there, employed by an officer. Belknap had refused to give them up because he did not know who owned them. There were several claimants, but Belknap believed that the real owner was Billy Bowlegs.[37]

Duval had hired the women out for Bowlegs' niece, Kith-lai-tsee, or Eliza. However, he was now attempting to recover them for Sally Factor. When Eliza learned that, she protested to the government on behalf of her and her cousins, to whom Bowlegs had willed all his slaves in the event of his death. According to Eliza, Katy had been sold first by a relative of Nelly Factor to General George M. Brooke at Tampa Bay. He had sold her to Gad Humphreys, who kept her until she grew up and had two children. When the war broke out, Humphreys fled from his plantation, leaving his slaves, who were carried off by the Seminoles. Katy and Fanny surrendered with Jumper, and when Humphreys asked General Jesup to return all of his recaptured slaves, Katy and Fanny were not sent. It seems that, as agent, Humphreys had received $2,400 for cattle sold for Billy Bowlegs' mother but had not paid her, having held the money in trust. The two slaves were retained as payment of the debt. According to Eliza, Humphreys agreed to this, and the slaves emigrated as the property of Billy Bowlegs. No other claim was made for them until the Factors made their claim.[38]

White slave hunters also claimed Katy and Fanny. When Duval called for them at the post, they were claimed as well by a trader named Dickson, who had bought them from a well-known slave trader named Nordheimer, who had bought them from a Creek named James McHenry. Both McHenry and Dickson had presented claims for them at various times. Belknap had refused them just as he later refused Duval and vowed to do so until the title became clear. Belknap subsequently turned them over to Dickson, who was the only one of the claimants who could produce a bill of sale.[39]

MEXICO AS REFUGE

The increase in slaving activities which followed the departure of Wild Cat and Gopher John ultimately resulted in nearly three hundred blacks leaving the Indian country for Mexico, including 180 who left under Jim Bowlegs in the summer of 1850. This group was pursued by a party of Creeks and white slave traders, who overtook them near Fort Arbuckle. The blacks resisted, and some were killed. A few escaped, but most of them were captured and brought back to the Seminole country.[40]

Those who remained in the Seminole country were given further hopes of escape when Wild Cat returned in September of 1850. During the preceding July, he, Gopher John, and a chief of the Kickapoo had visited Colonel Juan Manuel Maldonado, the subinspector of the colonies, at San Fernando de Rosas, Coahuila, and asked for land, farming tools, livestock, and munitions. Welcoming them as a possible buffer against the wild tribes who were at that time overrunning the state, Maldonado gave tentative approval to the request, contingent upon approval by the central government. Wild Cat left immediately for the Indian Territory to gather more of his people. On the way he visited the Comanche, Caddo, and Waco, but had little success in getting them to join him. However, he was more successful with the Kickapoo, a large number of whom agreed to join him.[41]

The Kickapoos whom Wild Cat recruited had lived for years beyond the Creek country on the Canadian and had carried on a rather steady trade with the Creeks, buying principally powder and lead from the trading houses on the Little River. In mid-September 1850, they came in for more supplies and brought news to the Seminoles that Wild Cat was on his way and had asked them to meet him and prepare to join him. The Creeks became uneasy because of these events, and rumors circulated in eastern newspapers that Wild Cat had recruited eight hundred Indians to commit hostilities against the whites. Echo Hadjo and Billy Hadjo, the head and second chiefs of Canadian District, reported news of Wild Cat's return to General Belknap and directed the merchants on Little River to sell no more powder to the Kickapoos or other Indians. On September 20, it was reported that Wild Cat was in the Indian country, and all of the chiefs and head men of Canadian District asked Chief McIntosh to "censure the people of this country in his remaining in our midst, as harboring men guilty of outrages on other citizens."[42]

The Creeks were afraid of Wild Cat's influence on the Seminoles and blacks. On September 23, McIntosh informed General Belknap that Wild Cat had held a talk and told the Seminoles that the Mexicans had agreed to give him land and subsistence if he would come and settle in Mexico. "Now he come back with enticing news," wrote McIntosh, "and want to carry his people in that nation; and the negroes, he told them if they emigrate to that country, they will all be freed by the government. This is good news to the negroes. I am told some are preparing to go." Wild Cat claimed that he had four hundred men with him when he was traveling, but he came in with only one woman and a young man.[43]

About the time of Wild Cat's return, rumors of depredations upon whites in Texas spread through the western part of the Creek Nation. One had it that Wild Cat and a small party of his own people and a band of Comanches had crossed into Texas and killed about a hundred people. Wild Cat himself added to the rumors by changing his stories. At one time he claimed to have recruited 1,600 Kickapoos and at another only six hundred. The result was a great deal of excitement among the Creeks, who began to feel the need to check his influence over his people. They called a council on September 23 and again on September 30 at Tuckabatchee to adopt some measure to stop him.[44]

A few days later, Chief McIntosh sent three hundred Creek warriors into the Seminole country to prevent any blacks from leaving with Wild Cat and to detain him until they could find what his mission was. McIntosh assured the Seminole chiefs that the object of the invasion was not to deprive the Seminoles of their blacks but to prevent their escape. At Wewoka the Creeks learned that Wild Cat was still in the Seminole country and that a number of blacks were preparing to leave, but the party returned to the Creek country without accomplishing anything, except that Wild Cat left the Seminole country to keep from being taken. He succeeded in persuading about thirty or forty Indians to go with him.[45]

THE DOWNFALL OF DUVAL

For the most part, Wild Cat's scheme had been disastrous for the blacks who had remained behind, mainly because of the complicity of Marcellus Duval in slaving activities. However, it was the downfall of Duval himself as a government official. When it became apparent that Wild Cat would return to Mexico, Duval wrote to Governor P. H. Bell of Texas, warning him to be on the watch for Wild Cat and the Kickapoos. He also wrote to General George M. Brooke, commanding the Department of Texas at San Antonio, asking him to arrest any Seminole blacks the army found. He sent the message by an agent, whom he hired to go to Texas and assist in arresting all of the fugitive slaves from the Seminole country.[46]

As complaints had continued about Duval's involvement in the matter of slave ownership, he had done some complaining of his own to Luke Lea, the commissioner of Indian affairs. He charged Arbuckle and other officers of being determined to make the Indians dissatisfied with him as an agent. "They are meddling in our business," he had said. Duval laid the blame for Wild Cat's escape and the loss of so many blacks on the interference of the military officers, especially Belknap. In December 1850, he renewed his charge that Belknap had protected Jim Bowlegs and other blacks on the military reserve during the preceding summer, that he was protecting blacks who shot their masters, and that he was aiding and abetting the abolitionists. The act which sparked Duval's anger this time was Belknap's having issued a pass to two blacks to visit Fort Smith to see General Arbuckle. To Duval this was proof of interference in Indian matters. Belknap answered that he had received numerous complaints during the several preceding months from both Seminoles and blacks about Duval's treatment of them. He had ignored the complaints, he said, until the two applied for a pass, and it was given simply to prevent them from being taken by whites, of whom they had expressed some fear.[47]

Belknap charged Duval with slaving activities. He had aided and abetted the raiding party during the summer of 1850, and Belknap suspected that the attempt to arrest Jim Bowlegs was simply a ruse to get possession of him. The charge against Jim was an old one, and it seemed strange to Belknap that Bowlegs had lived near Duval for some years and had even been sent back to Florida as an interpreter for General Twiggs, where he remained for several months, without Duval's attempting to capture him. "It can perhaps be best accounted for," Belknap wrote, "by supposing that as Jim was a very active and intelligent negro, he might have been desirous (*as he and his brother at that time ran out upwards of fifty negroes belonging to the Seminoles, as you are already aware*) of securing Jim also, for his own use." In fact, the Seminoles had complained that Duval and his brother had taken several of their blacks who had never lived at the post under the protection of the government and run them out of the country. Finally, Belknap called "false and malicious" the charge that blacks shot their masters and that the military officials were abetting abolitionism, adding that he "considered an abolitionist as holding as low a place in the scale of moral honesty" as Duval considered him.[48]

Duval's agent in Texas had no success in recovering any of the blacks. In January 1852, Duval learned where many of them were and wanted to go to Texas himself, but his duties prevented it. Thus, the following summer, he gave authority to a man named Captain Adams of Texas to recover the runaways. Duval received no report from Adams, so he finally decided to go to Texas to see how the search was going. This trip was agreed to by John Drennen, the superintendent for the Western Territory. To make recovery easier, Duval claimed, the Indians gave him bills of sale for the blacks, and he gave each one of them a statement as to why the bills were executed.[49] Armed with the documents, he made ready to leave.

Duval's activities had implications for the Seminoles still in Florida. In the summer of 1852, a delegation of western Seminoles, with Abraham as interpreter, were in Florida trying to induce Billy Bowlegs and old Sam Jones to emigrate. The delegation succeeded in getting Bowlegs to go with them to Washington and New York, leaving Florida in August. During the fall, the Indians debated the matter of removal. Harriet Bowlegs, Billy's niece, had sent him a letter from the Indian Territory, saying that Duval had taken off seven more of Bowlegs' blacks. Luther Blake, the special agent to the Indians, kept the letter from Bowlegs to prevent it from angering him and jeopardizing the possibility of removal.[50]

The blacks to whom Harriet referred formed the basis of charges filed against Duval. On May 9, 1852, about the time Duval was preparing to go to Texas, Captain John C. Henshaw, commander at Fort Arbuckle in the Chickasaw Nation, reported that a black named Dennis had come to the post that day asking protection. Dennis claimed that he was formerly owned by Harriet Bowlegs who had set him and several others free. Dennis had a paper signed by General Taylor showing that he and his wife were free by virtue of General Jesup's Proclamation in Florida. He claimed that his Indian protector was absent with a delegation to Billy Bowlegs in Florida and that during his absence Duval and Jim Jumper had been running off the Bowlegs blacks to Arkansas. They had already carried off a number, including Dennis' wife, and were trying to capture him. Their object, Dennis claimed, was to get the blacks out of the country before Bowlegs emigrated. On the basis of the evidence, Secretary of War Charles M. Conrad concluded that Duval was an active participant in the slave trade and recommended that the blacks be protected from those who would take them by force or fraud.[51]

Unaware that these charges had been made against him, Duval set out for San Antonio to confer with Adams, who claimed to have had much difficulty in accomplishing anything because of "obstacles thrown in his way by certain military gentlemen." Unsuccessful in his mission, Duval started back to the Indian Territory. At Austin, he received news of Henshaw's charges against him. Duval wrote to Commissioner Luke Lea that here was more evidence of the "continued intermeddling & illegal course of some of the officers of the army." But Duval never got the chance to answer the charge officially. He was removed from office before he returned from Texas for having been absent too much from his post.[52]

Duval was bitter and vitriolic in his criticism of those involved in his removal. All he had done, he said, was to try to help the Seminoles regain property which they had been illegally and arbitrarily dispossessed of by General Jesup. In the process he had gained the enmity of certain army officers. He now charged Henshaw and the Secretary of War of meddling in affairs not their own. As for the episode concerning Dennis, Duval charged that Henshaw believed the story because Henshaw had once asked Duval to purchase a slave girl for him from among the Seminole blacks and Duval had refused. As for the charges of speculation, he claimed that the bills of sale he had executed in the summer of 1852 were simply for convenience in recovering the blacks in Texas. Finally, Duval felt that his removal was politically motivated. He had helped start and keep up the Fort Smith *Herald* "as a Democratic paper," and he was therefore "violently assailed" in the Van Buren, Arkansas, *Intelligencer,* which he called "the Bastard sheet."[53]

No matter how much Duval protested, the fact remained that after 1847, he had an interest in the disposition of the slaves by virtue of his brother's power of attorney to act for the Seminoles in reclaiming the blacks and the subsequent claim to certain of those blacks as payment for services. Duval was himself a slaveholder, and Henshaw later charged that on his farm near Van Buren, Duval had a large number of slaves from the Seminole Nation, some of whom had claimed freedom under Jesup's

Proclamation and others by the will of Harriet Bowlegs.[54] These combined facts prevented Duval from acting objectively as a representative of the government, and his action contributed in a great measure to the movement of the Seminole blacks from a state of comparative freedom in 1848 to a state of subjection in 1849. It had forced many to flee from the people whose language and way of life they had adopted, and it had resulted in the death of many at the hands of slave hunters or hostile Indians on the southwestern plains.

NOTES

1. Marcellus Duval to General William Belknap, June 7, 1849, National Archives Record Group 393 (Records of the United States Army Continental Commands, 1821-1920), *Fort Gibson,* Letters Received (hereafter cited as *Gibson LR*), Box 3.

2. *Ibid.*

3. *Ibid.*; Duval to William Medill, June 9, 1849, in National Archives Microfilm Publications, *Microcopy M234* (Records of the Office of Indian Affairs, Letters Received)-801, R519-49. *Microcopy M234* is hereafter cited as *M234,* followed by the roll number.

4. General Matthew Arbuckle to Adjutant General, July 31, 1849, 33 Cong., 1 Sess., *House Executive Document 15,* 23 (hereafter cited as *Document 15*).

5. Duval to Arbuckle, July 16, 1849, *Gibson LR,* Box 3.

6. *Ibid.*; John Drennen to Arbuckle, July 20, 1849, National Archives Record Group 393, *Second and Seventh Military Departments,* Letters Received (hereafter cited as *2nd & 7th LR*), Box 7; Lieutenant Francis N. Page to Adjutant General, November 18, 1854, *Document 15,* 11.

7. Lieutenant F. F. Flint to Drennen, July 26, 1849, *Document 15,* 20-21.

8. Arbuckle to Adjutant General, July 31, 1849, *Document 15,* 21-22.

9. *Ibid.*; Page to Assistant Adjutant General, November 18, 1854, *Document 15,* 11.

10. Arbuckle to Adjutant General, July 31, 1849, *Document 15,* 21-22; Flint to Belknap, August 2, 1849, *Gibson LR,* Box 3, and *Document 15,* 23-24.

11. Belknap to Flint, August 8, 1849, *2nd & 7th LR,* Box 7.

12. Flint to Drennen, August 13, 1849, *Document 15,* 25-27.

13. Arbuckle to Adjutant General, August 14, 1849, *Document 15,* 24-25.

14. Drennen to Arbuckle, August 18, 1849, *Document 15,* 27, and *2nd & 7th LR,* Box 7.

15. Flint to Drennen, September 10, 1849, *2nd & 7th LR,* Box 7, and *Document 15,* 28-29; Carolyn Thomas Foreman, "The Jumper Family of the Seminole Nation," *Chronicles of Oklahoma,* 34 (Autumn 1956), 284.

16. Flint to Drennen, September 10, 1849, *2nd & 7th LR,* Box 7; Flint to Colonel Raiford, September 10, 1849, *Document 15,* 29-30; Arbuckle to Jones, September 14, 1849, National Archives Microfilm Publications, *Microcopy M574*(Special Files of the Office of Indian Affairs, 1807-1904)— 13, Special File 96; Seminole Claims to Certain Negroes, 1841-1849 (hereafter cited as *File 96*), and *Document 15,* 31.

17. Captain J. Lynde to Flint, October 12, 1849, *2nd & 7th LR,* Box 7.

18. *Ibid.*

19. Belknap to Flint, October 31, 1849, *2nd & 7th LR,* Box 7.

20. Flint to Belknap, November 9, 1849, *Gibson LR,* Box 3.

21. Duval to Orlando Brown, November 5, 1849, *M234*-289, D247-49.

22. Duval to Medill, October 15, 1846, 29 Cong., 2 Sess., *House Executive Document 4,* 279; Edwin C. McReynolds, *The Seminoles* (Norman: University of Oklahoma Press, 1957), 256-257; Grant Foreman, *The Five Civilized Tribes* (Norman: University of Oklahoma Press, 1934), 244-245; Wild Cat to Secretary of War, March 17, 1847, *M234*-801, C82-47; Kenneth Wiggins Porter, *The Negro on the American Frontier* (New York: Arno Press and The New York Times, 1971), 426.

23. Duval to Medill, June 9, 1849, in *M234*-801, R519-49; McReynolds, 260; Porter, 427; Page to Assistant Adjutant General, November 18, 1854, *Document 15,* 10-11; Muriel Wright, "Seal of the Seminole Nation," *Chronicles of Oklahoma,* 34 (Autumn 1956), 266; Carolyn Thomas Foreman, 283.

24. McReynolds, 265-266; Carolyn Thomas Foreman, 285.

25. Duval to Brown, May 30, 1850, in *M234*-801, D392-50; Page to Assistant Adjutant General, November 18, 1854, *Document 15,* 11; McReynolds, 261-262; Porter, 424, 427. For an authoritative treatment of the activities of Wild Cat, Gopher John, and their people in Mexico, see Porter, 424-459.

26. Duval to Brown, May 30 and 31, 1850, *M234*-801, D392-50.

27. *Ibid.*

28. Power of Attorney to W. J. Duval, November 20, 1847, and December 7, 1847, in *File 96.*

29. Roley McIntosh to Belknap, June 12, 1850, *2nd & 7th LR,* Box 8, and *Document 15,* 16-17.

30. Captain F. T. Dent to Flint, July 15, 1850, *2nd & 7th LR,* Box 8, and *Document 15,* 17-18.

31. *Ibid.*

32. *Ibid.*

33. Statement of Molly, July 15, 1850, *2nd & 7th LR,* Box 8; J. W. Washbourne to Thomas Drew, January 5, 1855, in *M234*-802, D153-56. See List J in the Appendix.

34. Statement of Molly, July 15, 1850, *2nd & 7th LR,* Box 8.

35. William Bowlegs to Jim Jumper and the Chiefs, April 12, 1850, *2nd & 7th LR,* Box 8. Bowlegs' slaves were as follows: Teena and her children, Rose, Bob, and Juan; Juan; Pompey; Jim; Cornelia and her children Nannie, John, Pompey, Teena, and Isaac; brothers and sisters Hester, Fanny, Lizzy, and Frederick; sisters Rina, Peggy, Betta; Viney, Dindy, and Collin, the children of Hester; Sam and Diny, the children of Fanny; brothers and sisters Polly, Davis, Jim, Rufile, Dolly, Lisa and Do-it; Philip and Thomson, children of Polly; Katy and her child Fanny by Sampson; brothers and sisters Andrew, Pussy, Peggy, Jessy, Ned, and Abram; Collins, Sylla, Toney, Hendry, Noya (a girl), the children of Peggy; brother and sister Sharper and Mary Ann; Levi, Jim, Harkless, and three girls, the children of Mary Ann.

36. Duval to Arbuckle, July 29, 1850, *2nd & 7th LR,* Box 8.

37. Sally Factor to Belknap, July 18, 1850, *Gibson LR,* Box 3; Belknap to Page, August 6, 1850, *2nd & 7th LR,* Box 8.

38. Statement of Eliza, August 15, 1850, *2nd & 7th LR,* Box 8.

39. *Ibid.*; Belknap to Page, August 22, 1850, and December 9, 1850, *2nd & 7th LR,* Box 8.

40. Porter, 428; Page to Assistant Adjutant General, November 18, 1854, *Document 15,* 12, 17-18.

41. Porter, 427-428.

42. Echo Hadjo and Billy Hadjo to Belknap, September 18, 1850, *Gibson LR,* Box 3; Echo Hadjo et al, to McIntosh, September 20, 1850, *Gibson LR,* Box 3, and *Document 15,* 31-32.

43. McIntosh to Belknap, September 23, 1850, *Gibson LR,* Box 3, and *Document 15,* 32; Duval to Luke Lea, September 25, 1850, *M234*-801, D451-50.

44. C. J. Atkins to Commandant at Fort Gibson, September 30, 1850, and McIntosh to Belknap, September 23, 1850, *Gibson LR,* Box 3; Duval to Lea, September 30, 1850, *M234*-801, D455-50.

45. Belknap to Page, October 15, 1850, *2nd & 7th LR,* Box 8, and *Document 15,* 32-33; Duval to Lea, December 9, 1850, *M234*-801, D481-50; Duval to Lea, October 25, 1851, 32 Cong., 1 Sess., *House Executive Document 2,* 405.

46. Duval to Lea, December 9, 1850, *M234*-801, D481-50.

47. Duval to Lea, August 22, 1850, *M234*-801, D429-50; Belknap to Page, December 9, 1850, *2nd & 7th LR,* Box 8.

48. Belknap to Page, December 9, 1850, *2nd & 7th LR,* Box 8.

49. Duval to Commissioner, April 8, 1853, *M234*-801, D298-53.

50. Porter, 327-328; Luther Blake to Lea, November 18, 1852, and Agreement with Bowlegs, et al., September 20, 1852, *M234*-801, B149-52 and A6-52.

51. Charles M. Conrad to A. H. H. Stuart, June 18, 1852, *M234*-801, W107-52.

52. Duval to Lea, November 15, 1852, and Duval to Commissioner, April 8, 1853, *M234*-801, D223-52 and D298-53.

53. Duval to Commissioner, April 8, 1853, *M234*-801, D298-53. *The Intelligencer* was started at Van Buren, Arkansas, in 1842, by Van Horn and Stern and later edited by J. W. Washbourne and Cornelius D. Pryor. It was a Democratic paper. The *Herald* was begun in 1847 by John F. Wheeler. In 1851, half ownership went to the Democratic Association of Fort Smith. See Fred W. Allsopp, *History of the Arkansas Press for a Hundred Years and More* (Little Rock: Parke-Harper Publishing Company, 1922), 123, 413.

54. Captain John C. Henshaw to Commissioner, June 7, 1853, *M234*-801, H251-53.

The last slave controversies

By 1853, the struggle of the blacks to establish their rights to freedom or to secure their rights to remain unmolested among the Seminoles was over. Only the bitter denouement remained. There had been perhaps no more insidious force in bringing about the turn of events than the actions of Marcellus Duval. Between the time they were returned to the Seminoles in 1849 and Duval's removal from office, their ranks had been decimated. Nearly all those to whom the title was vague or contested had either run away or had been captured and sold. Their villages had been broken up, and those who remained were scattered. They no longer found sympathy among the Seminoles and were without government protection or the safety of numbers. Left without leaders, those who remained in the Seminole country were vulnerable. For the most part, titles to these latter were clear, but in many cases the titles belonged to Seminole children or women who had guardians assigned to them. It was such cases to which the slave speculators, with the help of some proslavery officials, turned their attention during the 1850s.

THE PRYOR CASE

The decade was dominated by one large but significant case, commonly called the Pryor Case. It involved the slaves of Mah-pah-yist-chee and Mah-kah-tist-chee (Molly), who had complained to the army in 1850 that Jim Jumper had promised thirty-four of them to satisfy William J. Duval's claim for services as attorney for the Seminoles. They were the same slaves who had been the object of the Love claims during the 1830s and 1840s. On April 7, 1853, Molly sold her right to the slaves to Daniel Boone Aspberry, a half-blood Creek. She was very old, and her slaves were only nominally in a state of servitude. They did not work regularly, nor did they give her anything when they did work. They refused to support her in a separate residence and to cultivate fields separately for her, for that was not the old Seminole way. But if she would live with any of them, they would support her, so she went from slave family to slave family. As time passed, she became less satisfied with the arrangement and looked for a way to control the blacks and force them to support her. Aspberry persuaded her to place the title in his name so he could have legal control over them. They made a bill of sale with the understanding that Aspberry would capture as many as he could, sell them, and pay Molly $100 for each one he caught. Molly's sister Mah-pah-yist-chee died during the following summer, and her slaves passed to Molly, who sold that interest to Aspberry in September.[1]

Before Aspberry could capture a single black and pay her any money, Molly died. Since Aspberry had the bill of sale, he decided to pursue the claim. The only problem was that the blacks knew the circumstances of the title. They did not claim to be free, but neither did they recognize Aspberry as their master because he had paid Molly nothing and therefore sent him word that they would resist to the death any attempt to capture them. Some of the Seminoles apparently backed them in their defiance because Aspberry was a Creek. He offered certain citizens of the United States an equal share in the blacks if they would bring their influence to bear on authorities in the Creek and Seminole Nations and took the claim before the Creek council, who decided that the sale was valid and that he had a right to the slaves. The chiefs ordered the Creek Indian police to deliver them.[2]

In November 1853, Aspberry, thirty other Creek policemen, and a few whites went to Molly's home, captured over a score of blacks, and killed a youth who tried to help his mother escape. The Seminole chiefs had a claim to the blacks, since the women had died without issue, but the Creeks insisted that their laws were the only ones in force and that the Seminoles had no say in the matter. The Creeks had recognized Aspberry's title and approved of the raid. A few days later, Aspberry sold the blacks to white men in Arkansas.[3]

Although Seminole Agent B. H. Smithson feared trouble when the whites came to the nation to get the blacks, it did not occur, and those captured were taken to Arkansas. Alarm spread to other slaves in the area. Aspberry and his group remained in the Seminole country for a while to try to take the rest of the blacks he claimed, but because of the excitement that prevailed, they had to leave for their own safety. Aspberry's associates refused to aid him further; he then made offers to others for assistance, but to no avail.[4]

Aspberry had agreed to sell twenty-five of the blacks to two white men named Bright and Perkins, who had helped to capture them. They took twelve and left ten with Aspberry, including Scipio, William, Bob, Betty, Lucy, and her four children. Others whom Aspberry claimed remained uncaptured in the Seminole country: Scipio, Betsey, Hetty, Patty, Rhoda, July, Flora, Guide, Pompe, Sanches, Ishmael, Lucy and child, Betsy (second by that name), Ben, and William. In view of the probable difficulty in capturing these blacks, Aspberry apparently decided that Bright and Perkins had given up the idea of taking any more. He offered to sell his claim to the remaining blacks to Cornelius D. Pryor, a United States citizen and trader at North Fork, Creek Nation. Pryor investigated and, thinking that Bright and Perkins had withdrawn from the business, accepted the proposition.[5]

Archibald H. Rutherford, a clerk in the office of the western superintendent of Indian affairs, hearing that Aspberry had settled the claim, wrote for his share of the profits. He was apparently one of the officials who had brought pressure to bear in the Indian country to help Aspberry get his claim. There is some indication that Agent Smithson knew of the relationship between the two, for Rutherford wanted Aspberry to give his pay for "services" to Smithson. In lieu of money, Rutherford wanted a slave worth $350, and Aspberry made out a bill of sale for a black named Willie Bob.[6]

PRYOR-ASPBERRY AGREEMENT

In February 1854, the matter became more complicated when Perkins insisted on keeping his interest in the slaves. Pryor had spent a great deal of effort in trying to obtain the slaves, so he sought payment for his losses and release from the agreement with Aspberry. To avoid loss, Aspberry proposed to turn over to Perkins all of the slaves he had except one and to let Pryor have the sixteen still at large in the Seminole country. With everyone apparently satisfied, Aspberry hired agents to collect the money due him from Pryor, when Pryor succeeded in getting possession of the blacks. He empowered them to call on the Creek Indian police to keep the blacks in the country until they were paid for.[7]

With this claim apparently settled, Aspberry continued other slaving activities. He was responsible for at least one raid in the spring of 1854. About the middle of April, a group of Creeks attacked at night the home of George Noble, a free black in the Seminole country, killing Noble's oldest son and capturing the rest of the family. They also destroyed his store of corn, killed a brood sow, and stole a horse and three ponies. Noble, who had been freed by Harriet Bowlegs, was absent in Florida. In the preceding December, Lieutenant John Gibbons and Smithson had urged Noble to go with the Seminole delegation to Florida to try to induce the remaining Seminoles to emigrate. Noble had refused at first because he had feared for the safety of his family, whom Aspberry had allegedly purchased. Gibbons and Smithson promised Noble that they would protect his family from molestation and wrote Creek authorities regarding Aspberry, who claimed to hold a title. Under those circumstances, Noble agreed to go. After he had gone, Aspberry sold the claim to another Creek; Noble's family was stolen, taken to Louisiana, and sold. When Noble returned and found his family gone, he appealed to Superintendent Thomas S. Drew for aid in recovering them, but the appeal was fruitless.[8]

There were more raids on the Seminole blacks during the summer of 1854. That fall, reports circulated that a large number of Creek and Seminole blacks were preparing to run off in the following spring, one group proposing to go to Mexico and another to Canada. Military officials pledged to cut off any attempt to escape. About this time, some of the blacks who had been claimed by Aspberry appealed to Pryor to purchase all of them from Aspberry. They proposed to find purchasers for themselves in the Creek and Seminole Nations; some of them had relatives who were free and would assist in paying Pryor a fair price for their freedom. Aspberry agreed to the purchase, apparently thinking that if the sales could be made, all parties involved would be paid and, therefore, satisfied. On November 24, 1854, Aspberry made out a bill of sale and took Pryor's promissory note for $7,800.[9]

Pryor went to the Seminole country to try to dispose of the blacks to persons there. The new Seminole agent, J. W. Washbourne, who was Pryor's former business partner, was absent, and Pryor ran into difficulties. He informed some of the blacks of his purchase and told each one to select a purchaser whom he was willing to live with; those who could pay a fair price for freedom would be liberated. They were satisfied, but told him that some of the Seminoles objected to the arrangement and disputed Aspberry's title. One was Halleck Tustenuggee, who agreed to meet Pryor at the Creek council in December and have the matter submitted for decision.[10]

During his discussions with Halleck Tustenuggee, Pryor learned that Halleck and Necksucky claimed to be guardians of the blacks but made no claim of ownership, and Pryor was willing to let the Creek council consider the case. But when the Creek council met on December 26, Halleck failed to attend. Pryor applied to Washbourne to have the blacks delivered to the nearest point within the reach of the civil process so that he might establish his title in a court of law, but Washbourne simply referred the matter to Superintendent Drew.[11]

APPEAL TO SUPERINTENDENT DREW

Supported by a letter from Washbourne, Pryor appealed personally for aid from Drew on January 6, 1855. He claimed title to Scipio and Sancho, William, Prince, Cyrus, Lucy and her four children, Betsy and her four children, Thamar and her seven children, Rhody and her infant, all of whom were under the control of Necksucky and Halleck Tustenuggee, as well as five others who were in the Creek country.[12] Drew, however, had little favorable to say about Pryor's claim. He had received many complaints during the previous year about the trouble caused among the Seminoles by raiding parties from the Creek Nation. From what he could learn, Aspberry had never paid anything when he "purchased" the blacks, and Drew therefore doubted the legality of the claim. Drew also dismissed Washbourne's endorsement of Pryor's claim, and wrote to Commissioner George W. Manypenny: "I am compelled, however, to make many allowances for his kindly disposition towards Pryor for his utter ignorance of the local affairs of these people as he has not been among them but for a few weeks at a time since his appointment." Drew asked for a full investigation since the claim had caused so much disturbance between the Creeks and Seminoles.[13]

Drew would take no action until he heard from the commissioner of
Indian affairs and advised Pryor to talk to the Seminoles again. Pryor
attended the annuity payment at the Seminole agency and prevailed upon
Halleck Tustenuggee to bring the matter before the chiefs and the agent.
The Seminoles did not dispute the title but were offended at the manner
in which part of the blacks had been taken from the country. They resented
the interference of the Creeks. Pryor failed to get Halleck to bring the
matter before the Creek council then in session at Tuckabatchee, where
the Creek Agent W. H. Garrett, Washbourne, and the chiefs could investigate. However, he succeeded in obtaining a written statement that the
violence perpetrated during the capture of the blacks had been the act of
officers of the Creek Nation. Armed with that statement, he visited Drew
again in March 1855.[14]

INVOLVEMENT OF THE SEMINOLE CHIEFS

Pryor was convinced that Halleck and the other Seminoles planned to
sell the blacks, and he feared that when spring came, the blacks would leave
for the Rio Grande and try to join Wild Cat's band. To appease him, Drew
directed Halleck and the other chiefs to see that the blacks were not taken
out of the country by traders or allowed to leave for the plains until Pryor's
claim could be settled.[15]

Pryor was supported in his claim by Creek Agent W. H. Garrett, who
held that Aspberry's claim had been validated by the Creek chiefs, that
they had issued an order to the Indian police to capture the blacks for
Aspberry, and that the rumors of violence and disorder in the capture
were not substantiated by his investigation. Garrett saw no reason why
the blacks should be kept in the Seminole country and felt that the government was obligated to take "prompt and decisive steps in breaking up the
settlement of negroes in that country which for years past has been notorious
as a safe refuge and harbor for every fugitive slave for hundreds of miles
around." If Pryor claimed title to the blacks, he should be offered an
opportunity to prove it.[16]

It was the custom of the Seminole chiefs to levy a tribute upon large
estates in the country; upon the extinction of heirs, as in the present case,
the town chiefs claimed the property and, in cases of minors, became guardians of the property. Halleck Tustenuggee now claimed one hundred dollars
tribute for each black before he would permit their removal from the Nation.

Pryor could not pay the tribute, and the Creeks expressed a willingness to send their police to take the blacks. Drew directed Garrett not to permit any such act until instructions came from Washington.[17]

John Jumper, who affirmed Molly's title, had tried to prevent her from selling the blacks to Aspberry. He asked Pryor to attend the Seminole council on March 29, when the chiefs debated, finally agreeing to Pryor's claim. What they found objectionable was Molly's failure to follow the old custom of obtaining the consent of the chiefs to sell her slaves. At the time of her grandfather's death, he had asked the town chiefs to keep the property together so that the slaves could "make corn for his children." Since she had sold them in spite of Jumper's advice, the chiefs felt that they had done their duty.[18]

Washbourne was away from the agency. The chiefs told Pryor to come with his papers after the agent returned, point out the blacks, and take them. They would hold the Nation bound for their safekeeping. They gave him Robert, or Bob, whom Pryor had agreed to liberate for $300. Robert paid Pryor, who gave him his "free papers," and the council approved the act. The chiefs appointed Halleck Tustenuggee and Passockee Yohola to aid Pryor by delivering the other blacks to him at Billy Harjo's place, but when Pryor went to meet them, they failed to show up.[19]

SEMINOLES RECOGNIZE PRYOR'S CLAIM

By their action regarding Bob, the Seminole chiefs had recognized Pryor's claim to all of the blacks. But they began to hesitate. When Halleck and Passockee Yahola failed to meet him, Pryor returned to Jumper with a list of the blacks and asked the chief for a copy of the proceedings of the council. Jumper refused, saying that he did not like to sign papers in the name of the chiefs. Passockee Yohola was under subpoena to appear in federal court at Van Buren and would be there in a few days. Jumper suggested to Pryor that Passockee Yohola make a statement before the superintendent. Pryor returned to Arkansas and found the chief, but the superintendent was gone. Pryor decided to have the chief make a statement before the United States district attorney, but Washbourne interfered. The agent was angry at Superintendent Drew for having written the commissioner that Washbourne was ignorant of Seminole affairs and was often away from his post. He was also angry at Garrett, whom he felt Drew had instructed to act in the matter without Washbourne's approval. Washbourne vowed to tell the Seminoles not to attend any council called and presided over by Garrett, and he sent Passockee Yohola home, instructing him to make no statements.[20]

Pryor convinced Washbourne that he had had nothing to do with Drew's criticism of Washbourne, and Washbourne finally agreed to call a council and investigate. His letter giving Pryor the date of the council arrived late, and Pryor missed the meeting, at which it was agreed that the matter was entirely under Creek laws. Pryor alleged that by bribing Halleck and Passockee Yohola, parties who wished to purchase the blacks themselves had convinced Washbourne that the blacks belonged to the minor children of Charley Brown who had died a few years earlier, that Brown was Capichee Micco, the original owner, and that Mah-kah-tist-chee was only acting as guardian for his children in the West while he remained in Florida. Pryor charged that Halleck and Passockee Yohola were paid to get the matter taken before the Creek council and that Creeks Chilly McIntosh and Watt Grayson would get the blacks.[21]

It was true that Washbourne had referred the whole matter to the Creek council on the basis of a paper signed by Marcellus Duval saying that the blacks belonged to Capichee Micco. But when Pryor showed up a few days later, he showed Washbourne a copy of the statement that Molly had made before the military authorities in 1850, alleging that Marcellus Duval and Jim Jumper were trying to deprive her of her slaves, and Washbourne became convinced that he had been deceived.[22]

THE CREEK COUNCILS

Pryor attended the Creek council, though protesting that the case should not be settled by the Indians but by the agents. In conversation, the Seminoles denied saying that Charley Brown was Capichee Micco, for the latter had died many years earlier in Florida and had appointed Miccopotokee as guardian of the blacks. When the council met, the Seminoles showed that Capichee Micco had indeed died, that Tuskeneehau was his son, and that Miccopotokee was the guardian of the property until his death, when he turned the property over to Micanopy as guardian of the property of Mah-kah-tist-chee and Mah-pah-yist-chee. Charley Brown was only distantly related to Capichee Micco and had no right to the property. At that point the Seminoles stopped the investigation and denied having given Washbourne permission to have it presented to the Creek council, refusing to be bound by a decision by the Creeks. The proper place, they said, was before the Seminole agent and Seminole council.[23]

Meanwhile, Jumper had sold one of the blacks. Washbourne instructed the Seminoles not to sell any more and called another council, at which the Seminoles insisted that there were other heirs of Capichee Micco who would contend for part of the estate. Halleck said that they were the grand-children of Capichee Micco and therefore jointly entitled with the children of Tuskeneehau. Halleck Tustenuggee told the council that Capichee Micco had eight children. Then he named fourteen. One heir was present, Sharp-kee, the daughter of Chitto Larni, son of Capichee Micco, but she had got her property before removal. Creeks Chilly McIntosh and Watt Grayson were on hand and contested the right of Molly to sell the blacks. The chiefs thereupon declined to decide the question and asked to have the matter sent back to the Creek council. Washbourne decided to do so, and the Seminoles said that they would abide by the decision.[24]

Pryor attended the Creek council at Hillabee Square, but the Seminoles did not. No further action was taken until the meeting of the Creek council in December of that year, when the Seminoles again requested an investiga-tion. Pryor had accused Chilly McIntosh of bribing Halleck Tustenuggee, and there was apparently some substance to his accusation. By the time the council met, McIntosh had purchased all of the claims adverse to that of Mah-kah-tist-chee and Mah-pah-yist-chee, except one. Halleck Tustenuggee and Passockee Yohola testified that there were other legitimate claimants, while others testified that none were living except Sharp-kee or that no such persons were in the Seminole country. They also testified that when Capichee Micco had died, the property had been divided equally, the council rendering judgment; the property in question had belonged to Mah-pah-yist-chee. Nevertheless, the council found in favor of the alleged heirs, a decision which dissatisfied the Seminoles.[25] That meant, in effect, that the council recognized Chilly McIntosh's claim, and the case rested for the time being.

WILLIAM FACTOR'S RAID

Since Aspberry's raids in the Seminole country, there had been only one notable slaving raid on the Seminole blacks. In the late summer of

1855, William Factor, one of the best-known interpreters in Florida and one of the blacks named in the Solano and Papy slave claim in the 1840s, became a slave hunter himself. Factor and his wife Nancy lived in Sebastian County, Arkansas. In 1852, he made a claim through Senator W. K. Sebastian of Arkansas for losses he and his mother Rose Factor had sustained during the Seminole war. They owned personal property amounting to $2,000, part of which was destroyed by the Seminoles and part by the American troops to prevent the Seminoles from getting it. There was never any doubt about the loyalty of the Factors. In 1854, Factor was paid three hundred dollars, and seven hundred dollars was sent to Superintendent Drew, who had been beseiged by Factor's creditors. This amount was subsequently paid to Factor, but another $1,000 was retained by the department and ordered paid to the administrator of Rose Factor's estate, Joseph Vandever. Factor never saw any of that money.[26]

While Factor was deserving in this instance, he was generally considered an unsavory character, and the success he had had in prosecuting the claim no doubt influenced him to set about pressing others in his own way. Many of the latter, however, had no base. One involved old Abraham, who Factor claimed had been involved some thirty years earlier in the sale of five blacks belonging to Black Factor. Although he had sold his claim to the five blacks several times, William Factor nevertheless persuaded some young Creeks to help him get satisfaction from Abraham. In the summer of 1855, he made a night raid on Abraham's family, whom Abraham owned, capturing Abraham's wife and three children. Having failed to get them all, Factor brought suit against Abraham before the Creek council. Agent Washbourne denied that the claim had any basis, and the Creeks decided that Abraham was not responsible to Factor for the slaves lost in Florida.[27]

Washbourne had nothing good to say about Factor, calling him "a hybrid Seminole and negro." He wrote: "He is a scoundrel unwhipt of Justice, or rather he *has* been whipped several times by both Creeks and Seminoles, once in my presence, for horse-stealing." He had also allegedly murdered a Cherokee and several years earlier had allegedly burned a Creek woman to death. He was an outlaw who did not "dare show his head in daylight in the Seminole nation." Neither did Washbourne have much good to say about Abraham. For several months before the seizure, Abraham and his family had been living near Fort Arbuckle in the Chickasaw Nation, where they were working. In December 1855, Abraham fled to the post, leaving his family at home, saying that Factor was after him again. Washbourne

believed upon investigation that Abraham had nothing to fear and simply
wanted attention: "Old Abram has been spoiled by notice paid him by U.S.
officers heretofore, and he thinks himself a personage entitled to great attention, but as negro influence has proved greatly prejudicial to the welfare
of both Seminoles and Creeks, I have set my face against it, and am glad
to know that Agent Garrett and the Creek chiefs did the same long before
I went into office."[28]

THE PRYOR CASE AND SUPERINTENDENT CHARLES DEAN

In the spring of 1856, Pryor renewed efforts to acquire the blacks he
claimed. If he had found little sympathy in Superintendent Drew, he found
less in Charles W. Dean, who had replaced Drew in the spring of 1855.
Ironically, it was apparently a case similar to Pryor's which had resulted
in Drew's dismissal. Through administrative error and bureaucratic delay
in 1854, Drew had allowed a group of slave hunters from Van Buren to
enter the Creek Nation and take several members of a family of free blacks
named Beams. Early in 1855, Senator R. W. Johnson of Arkansas requested
Drew's removal. He left office on April 17.[29]

During the year after Dean's appointment, Pryor approached him several
times with his claim, but Dean refused to act because he was not sure of
Pryor's title. If it was good, Dean was not sure it was the department's place
to obtain the blacks for him. On April 10, 1856, Pryor again asked for
assistance in prosecuting his claim for thirty-seven blacks. Pryor had at no
time before claimed that many. Undoubtedly, the claim was based on a new
agreement which he negotiated with Aspberry a few days earlier, in which
Aspberry relinquished all right and title to the blacks named in his former
bill of sale to Pryor on November 24, 1854.[30]

This time, Dean forwarded the papers relating to the claim to Commissioner George W. Manypenny for instructions. Of particular concern to
Dean was the fact that the bill of sale from Molly, although alleged to have
been recorded in both the Seminole and Creek agencies, had never been
produced. Also, it had not been shown that Aspberry had paid anything
for the claim. As for Pryor's financial circumstances, Dean wrote, "I would
about as soon believe him were he to assert that he had paid cash in hand—
seven million dollars for the negroes as that he had paid seven thousand
dollars for them." It was impossible for him to have raised that much;
in fact, he had not paid Aspberry anything but had given him a note.[31]

Embittered by his failure to get the blacks, Pryor turned on his former friend, Washbourne, and blamed him for his failure. Pryor tried to find delinquencies in the agent's official capacity. He told Washbourne that he had evidence to support charges of misconduct in office, but Dean would not have his agent intimidated. Dean considered Pryor a man "destitute of honorable principles" and "prompted by a sentiment of vindictive malice." He no longer traded but remained in the Creek Nation for the sole purpose of speculation in slaves, causing much dissatisfaction among the Seminoles. Dean asked W. H. Garrett to have Pryor expelled, but the Creek agent could not since no complaint had been made against Pryor by the Creeks. In May, Pryor filed a formal complaint, charging Washbourne with repeated absences, juggling accounts by overcharging, spending contingent funds for traveling, causing dissatisfaction among the Creeks and Seminoles, and mishandling annuity funds.[32]

GROWING INTEREST OF WHITE SLAVERS

Pryor's claim and the difficulty it had caused among the Indians as well as among officials of the United States in the Western Territory exemplified the growing interest of whites in the Seminole blacks since they had been turned over to the Seminoles in 1849. Slaving was a lucrative business, and the interest of slave hunters in the slaves of the Indians had grown as the risks involved had decreased after Wild Cat's departure. Their boldness was perhaps bolstered by an opinion of Attorney General Caleb Cushing, approved by President Franklin Pierce on March 6, 1854. Growing out of a case related to the Beams family in the Choctaw Nation, the opinion said that the Fugitive Slave Law of 1850 applied to the Indian Territory. Citizens of the United States could enter the territory to recover any person who owed them services under the laws of the states.[33]

In the early summer of 1856, a number of citizens of Van Buren, Arkansas, made plans to form a company to buy up claims to the Seminole slaves as well as to blacks generally in the Indian Territory. This proposed organization caused Dean to write to Commissioner Manypenny concerning the problem.[34]

Dean maintained that the government should take some action to control slave hunting in the Indian Territory in order to preserve peace and harmony there. One Arkansan, for instance, had recently "bought for a song" a claim to a family of Seminole free blacks who had lived in the country for years, were considered free, and could prove it. The head of the family had been employed by the government in both Florida and the West. It was only through influential friends that the family succeeded in keeping the purchaser from trying to enforce the claim. Dean believed that it was the system of slavery in the Seminole country that had made such incidents possible. According to Dean, the blacks were slaves in name only. They lived with their masters or not as they pleased, they worked if and when they pleased, they made their own bargains, they came and went as they pleased, they sat at the table with their masters, and spoke to them as though they were equals. "Proper subjection," according to Dean, was rare. Because of this lifestyle, little benefit was realized from the slaves; they were really of little value beyond "an imaginary distinction that attaches to the name of master." Dean was quite right in asserting that the system of slavery of the Seminoles had attracted slave hunters. However, the system as he described it was no longer widespread and was probably based on his knowledge of the Pryor Case, which had arisen because old Molly had not been able to control her slaves and had sold them to Aspberry.

Dean did not lay the blame for slaving activities entirely on the whites. When the Indians were isolated from the whites, there was no trouble among them about titles, but the whites were abetted by the shrewder Indians in getting possession of titles. Many times oppression resulted, especially of women and children, who lost their property. The degraded position of Indian women and the relationship of the guardian as it existed in the Indian country were simply means "whereby the guardian, if so disposed, possesses himself of the property of the ward." This practice was increasing. Dean charged that many members of the Creek delegation to Washington were slave speculators. Among them was Chilly McIntosh, who had bought up the adverse claims in the Pryor case. Evidence showed that he could not have a shadow of a claim, yet he was "quietly and engergetically prosecuting the claim." Dean asked Manypenny if the Indians' trade in slaves with the whites might not be checked or if Congress could render void all contracts for slaves with the Indians.[35]

A SEPARATE SEMINOLE NATION

In the summer of 1856, the Seminoles finally achieved an objective they had sought since their removal. On August 7, they signed a treaty which dissolved the weak union that had existed between them and the Creeks since the Treaty of 1845 and established a separate Seminole Nation. They received over two million acres, the boundaries of which ran from the mouth of Pond Creek on the Canadian, north to the North Fork, up that stream to the southern boundary of the Cherokee Outlet, west to the 100th meridian, south to the Canadian, and along the Canadian to the mouth of Pond Creek. Satisfied that they could finally control their own affairs, the Seminoles built a new council house, a new agency, and substantial homes. They made good crops and made strides in educating their youth.[36]

The separate Seminole Nation came too late for most of the blacks who had removed with the Indians. Had the government granted it at the first, perhaps the blacks could have been saved. Instead, they became part of the price the Seminoles had to pay for a land of their own. The Creeks, and the whites who had encouraged them, no longer cared if the Seminoles were among them, for they had achieved their objective, too; they had separated most of the blacks from the Seminoles and had carried or driven them out of the territory.

But not all slave controversies were entirely settled. Early in 1857, Pryor renewed his claim and the charges against Washbourne through Senator R. W. Johnson of Arkansas. Elias Rector, the new superintendent for the Western District, was at first inclined to support Pryor's claim, but when he fully investigated the matter, Pryor failed to show the kind of hard evidence that Rector wanted to see. As for Washbourne, Rector could find no reason to censure him. Pryor raised the matter one last time in April of 1859, again without success.[37] With that ended over six years of wrangling and dissension over a single case.

In the summer of 1858, the last contingent of Seminoles, including Billy Bowlegs, emigrated from Florida. As preparations for that removal began, claims were set up for blacks alleged to be among them. Following the policy of his predecessors in 1841 and 1842, Commissioner Charles Mix directed Elias Rector, who was to conduct the Indians to the West, not to do anything regarding the claims for slaves that would delay "the all important and permanent object of effecting removal of the Seminoles from Florida." If blacks came in with the Indians and Rector was satisfied they belonged to white claimants, he was authorized to turn them over to their owners with the consent of the Indians. However, if to do so would cause any difficulty, he was simply to disregard the claims and ship the blacks off with the Indians and pay the owners. When the contingent of

165 Indians left Florida, only two blacks went with them, one of them an old man in Bowlegs' party. There was no difficulty concerning the blacks, and no claims were made for them. Neither were there any rumors of other blacks being harbored among the Indians who remained.[38]

Bowlegs' emigration came almost a decade after the visit of the delegation attended by Marcellus Duval in 1849-50. During the years that had elapsed, most of Bowlegs' slaves in the West had run off to Mexico or had been stolen and sold by slavers who set up claims to them. The years of conflict over the status of the Seminole blacks had taken their toll. Of the nearly five hundred who had emigrated and their descendants, it is impossible to say how many remained. One contemporary traveler estimated that in 1860 there were 1,000.[39] However, that figure is entirely too high in view of the attrition of their numbers in the preceding two decades.

Those blacks who remained with the Seminoles apparently engaged in farming in much the same way that they had for years. They raised horses, cattle, hogs, and poultry and owned oxen, wagons, farming tools, and guns.[40] Whatever security Seminole control of their own destiny may have brought to the remaining blacks was short-lived. Outside the Indian country, the national debate over the slavery question was about to turn into war, and the status of Seminole blacks, as well as that of their counterparts in the states and other Indian nations, was to be decided on the battlefield.

NOTES

1. Charles W. Dean to George W. Manypenny, April 29, 1856, National Archives Microfilm Publications, *Microcopy M234*(Records of the Office of Indian Affairs, Letters Received)–802, D153-56; C. D. Pryor to Thomas S. Drew, January 6, 1855, in *Microcopy M234*-833, D782-55. *Microcopy M234* is hereafter cited as *M234,* followed by the roll number.

2. Dean to Manypenny, April 29, 1856, *M234*-802, D153-56; A. H. Rutherford to Manypenny, December 6, 1853, *M234*-801, D476-53.

3. Dean to Manypenny, April 29, 1856, *M234*-802, D153-56.

4. B. H. Smithson to Manypenny, November 24 and 27, 1853, in *M234*-801, D476-53; Dean to Manypenny, April 29, 1856, *M234*-802, D153-56.

5. Daniel B. Aspberry to Bright, February 16, 1854, in *M234*-802, M383-57.

6. Rutherford to Aspberry, January 27, 1854, in *M234*-802, M383-57; Edwin C. McReynolds, *The Seminoles* (Norman: University of Oklahoma Press, 1957), 274.

7. Aspberry to Bright, February 16, 1854, and Aspberry to Atkins and Hay, n. d., in *M234*-802, M383-57; McReynolds, 274.

8. Drew to Manypenny, October 25, 1854, *M234*-801, D709-54; Carolyn Thomas Foreman, "The Jumper Family in the Seminole Nation," *Chronicles of Oklahoma,* 34 (Autumn 1956), 285.

9. Major G. W. Andrews to Post Adjutant, November 23, 1854, National Archives Record Group 393 (Records of the United States Army Continental Commands, 1821-1920), *Fort Gibson,* Letters Received (hereafter cited as *Gibson LR*), Box 3; Pryor to Dean, April 10, 1856, in *M234*-802, D153-56; *Foreman Transcripts* (Oklahoma Historical Society, Indian Archives Division), 7: 71.

10. Pryor to Dean, April 10, 1856, in *M234*-802, D153-56.

11. Pryor to Drew, January 6, 1855, in *M234*-833, D782-55.

12. *Ibid.;* J. W. Washbourne to Drew, January 5, 1855, in *M234*-802, D153-56.

13. Drew to Manypenny, January 29, 1855, *M234*-833, D782-55.

14. Pryor to Dean, April 10, 1856, in *M234*-802, D153-56.

15. *Ibid.;* Drew to Manypenny, March 14, 1855, *M234*-833, D816-55.

16. W. H. Garrett to Drew, February 12, 1855, in *M234*-833, D816-55.

17. Drew to Manypenny, March 14, 1855, in *M234*-833, D816-55.

18. Pryor to Dean, April 10, 1856, in *M234*-802, D153-56.

19. *Ibid.*

20. *Ibid.*

21. *Ibid.*

22. *Ibid.*

23. *Ibid.*

24. *Ibid.*

25. Pryor to Dean, April 10, 1856, in *M234*-802, D153-56.

26. W. K. Sebastian to Commissioner, May 1, 1852, *M234*-801, S90-52; Drew to Manypenny, October 24, 1854, Charles E. Mix to R. McClelland, July 9, 1855, and McClelland to Mix, July 5, 1855, *M234*-801, D708-54, I1068-55, and I1053-55. In 1858, Factor hired Thomas S. Drew, the former superintendent then a lawyer at Fort Smith, to make inquiries about the remaining $1,000, threatening suit in the Court of Claims if the money was not paid. According to Drew, Rose Factor was never a citizen of Arkansas and had no real or personal estate there. She died in the United States garrison on the military reserve at Fort Smith. Therefore, Vandever had no estate to administer, and Factor did not authorize him to draw the money. M. Thompson to Jacob Thompson, December 6, 1858, *M234*-802, T346-58.

27. Washbourne to Dean, January 24, 1856, in *M234*-802, D92-56.

28. *Ibid.*

29. Drew to Chief and Head Men of the Creek Nation, July 27, 1854, George Butler to S. A. Worcester, November 22, 1854, Franklin Pierce to McClelland, January 6, 1855, and Statement of Drew, April 16, 1855, in National Archives Microfilm Publications, *Microcopy M574*(Special Files of the Office of Indian Affairs, 1807-1904)-13, Special File 277. *Microcopy M574* is hereafter cited as *M574,* followed by the roll number. For details of the Beams case, see Daniel F. Littlefield, Jr., and Mary Ann Littlefield, "The Beams Family: Free Blacks in Indian Territory," *Journal of Negro History,* 61 (January 1976), 16-35.

30. Pryor to Dean, April 10, 1856, in *M234*-802, D153-56; *Foreman Transcripts,* 7: 71. In 1856, Pryor claimed Sancho, Scipio, Ishmael, William, Billy, Cyrus, Sampson, Jim, Teanear, or Tenny and her eight children, Lucy and her four children, Nancy and her four children, Betsy and her four children, Hetty, Rhody, Thamar and her two children.

31. Dean to Manypenny, April 29, 1856, *M234*-802, D153-56.

32. Dean to Manypenny, May 30, 1856, and Washbourne to Manypenny, May 8, 1856, *M234*-802, D171-56 and W64-56.

33. Opinion of C. Cushing, February 18, 1854, and Jefferson Davis to Worcester, October 7, 1854, in *M574*-75, Frame 1482 and Choctaw I727-54; S. Cooper to Commanding Officer, Fort Gibson, May 4, 1854, *Gibson LR,* Box 4.

34. Dean to Manypenny, June 24, 1856, *M234*-802, D180-56.

35. *Ibid.*

36. McReynolds, 277-281.

37. Pryor to R. H. Johnson, February 14, 1857, Jacob Thompson to Acting Commissioner, June 12, 1857, Rector to Commissioner, June 24, 1857, Rector to Denver, July 7, 1857, and Rector to Denver, September 17, 1857, *M234*-802, I503-57, I596-57, R270-57, R274-57, and R341-57; Charles E. Mix to Jacob Thompson, June 6, 1857, National Archives Microfilm Publications, *Microcopy M348*(Records of the Office of Indian Affairs, Report Books)-10, 224; J. W. Denver to Elias Rector, June 17, 1857, National Archives Microfilm Publications, *Microcopy M21*(Records of the Office of Indian Affairs, Letters Sent)-57, 57 (hereafter cited as *M21,* followed by the roll number); Mix to M. Thompson, April 7, 1859, *M21*-60, 415.

38. Resolution, December 29, 1854, Howe to S. R. Mallory, April 20, 1858, L. B. Dunn to Mix, July 7, 1858, and D. L. Yulee to Commissioner, July 16, 1858, *M234*-802, Y29-58, M452-58, D56-58, and Y33-58; Mix to Rector, April 30, 1858, and Mix to Yulee, July 10, 1858, *M21*-58, 503, 191; Mix to Rector, May 5, 1858, *M21*-59, 8-9. Carolyn Thomas

Foreman erroneously reports that Bowlegs took forty slaves to the West in "Billy Bowlegs," *Chronicles of Oklahoma,* 32 (Winter 1955), 527.

39. Michael F. Doran, "Population Statistics of Nineteenth Century Indian Territory," *Chronicles of Oklahoma,* 53 (Winter 1975-76), 501. The Seminoles refused to allow a census of the blacks in their Nation in 1860. However, eight Seminole households enumerated with the Creeks that year listed fifty-four. After the Civil War, sixty-two Seminole blacks, most of them heads of households, applied for payment for losses during the war. Most of the Seminole blacks escaped to the Union lines during the war. An 1867 census of them contained only 333 names. National Archives Microfilm Publications, *Microcopy M653*(Federal Population Census Schedules)-54, Arkansas [Slave Schedules] ; *M574*-11, File 87: Loyal Seminole Claims.

40. *M574*-11, File 87.

Civil war and emancipation

It is perhaps ironic that slavery—the cause of constant conflict between the Seminoles and the United States and the Creeks for decades—was to engage them in another major conflict, which they had done nothing to bring about. To the Seminole blacks, the Civil War proved the most important war in their history. For those who survived it, it achieved what the Second Seminole War had promised but failed to do: It finally ended their slavery and made them free men.

CONFEDERATE OVERTURES

By late January 1861, politicians in Arkansas were looking toward secession and wanted to make sure that they had Indian allies on their western flank. Governor Henry M. Rector asked John Ross, principal chief of the Cherokees, to support Arkansas in its action. His words applied to the Seminoles and the other slaveholding tribes as well as to the Cherokees: "Your people, in their institutions, productions, latitude, and natural sympathies are allied to the common brotherhood of the slaveholding States. Our people and yours are natural allies in war, and friends in peace. Your country is salubrious and fertile, and possesses the highest capacity for future progress and development by the application of 'slave labor.' " Rector went on to say, "It is well established that the Indian country west of Arkansas is looked to by the incoming administration of Mr. Lincoln as fruitful fields ripe for the harvest of abolitionism, free-soilers, and northern mountebanks. We hope to find in you friends willing to co-operate with the

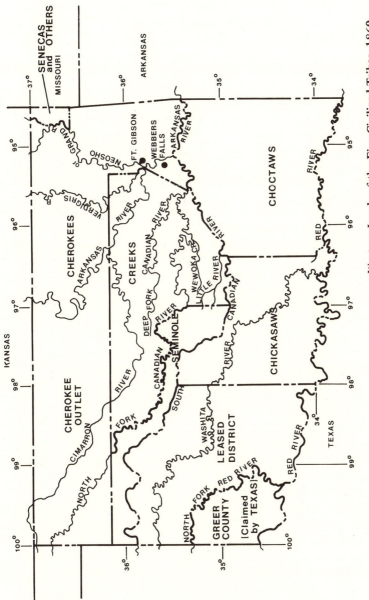

Western Lands of the Five Civilized Tribes, 1860

south in defence of her institutions, her honor, and her firesides, and with whom the slaveholding States are willing to share a common future, and to afford protection commensurate with your exposed condition and your subsisting monetary interests with the general government."[1]

The Five Civilized Tribes were receptive to Confederate overtures. The reason seemed simple in retrospect to John T. Cox, special Indian agent in the Indian Territory in 1864. During the Buchanan administration, people of southern sympathy held or had access to every governmental office within the Southern Superintendency of Indian Affairs. They influenced all sources of information. To sway their sympathy, postmasters told the Indians that the old government had fallen and otherwise undermined the Indians' confidence in the United States. Military necessity led to the abandonment of posts, government stores, and ordnance depots in the West, and the government was unfortunately late in recognizing the need to assist the Indians in resisting the overtures of the Confederates. The Indians felt abandoned. Albert Pike of Arkansas was sent to the Indian Territory as a commissioner for the Confederate government, and before the end of 1861 he had concluded a treaty with each of the Five Civilized Tribes. In March 1861, international councils were held at the Creek agency and at the North Fork, and in April the Choctaws and Chickasaws went over to the Confederate side. The rest of the tribes vacillated. The Creeks finally signed a treaty on July 10.

The Seminole full bloods—a majority of the tribe—for the most part remained pro-Union. In March, they voted in council not to meet with the Confederates. Albert Pike then negotiated secretly with John Jumper, the principal chief, who with twelve other town chiefs signed a treaty on August 1, while other town chiefs, such as John Chupco and Billy Bowlegs, refused to sign.[3]

Many of the Creeks also remained loyal and rallied around the aged Opothleyohola. Douglas H. Cooper, the former United States Choctaw agent, tried to persuade the loyal Creeks and Seminoles to defect to the Confederates, but he failed. Therefore, in November 1861, he led an armed force of Choctaws, Chickasaws, and Texans and marched on Opothleyohola's camp. However, by the time they arrived at North Fork town, they found Opothleyohola gone.[4]

FLIGHT TO KANSAS

Upon receiving news of Cooper's approach, the old chief had decided to leave the Creek Nation, pass through the Cherokee country, and take refuge in Kansas. In his party were Seminoles under Halleck Tustenuggee, John Chupco, and Billy Bowlegs and several hundred Creek and Seminole blacks. The escape of these people has been treated often, and their struggle has been described in terms all but epic. They were overtaken three times and fought battles with Confederate troops: at Round Mountain on November 19, at Chustolasah on December 9, and at Chustenahiah on December 26, 1861. In these battles, the Seminoles bore the brunt of much of the fighting. The last battle was costly. The Confederates captured about 160 women and children, and the loyal Indians lost nearly all their goods and livestock. The weather was bitter, and snow was on the ground. In their retreat before the Confederate army, the loyal party suffered greatly. Many froze to death, and the trail was marked by bodies.[5]

When the loyal party arrived in Kansas, they were poor and had nothing. They were tired but anxious to fight the rebels, although the President had not called on the loyal Seminoles to take up arms. During the winter of 1861 and the following spring and summer, thousands of Indians and blacks were driven from their homes because of their loyalty to the government. They were ineffectual in their resistance to the disloyal Indians and the white troops from Texas and elsewhere who sought to hold the Indian Territory for the Confederacy. Ultimately, about two thirds of the tribe and nearly all their blacks joined the loyal refugees in Kansas. Other blacks took refuge in the Cherokee country and later sought protection at Fort Gibson.[6]

Some of the blacks, however, were less fortunate. Upon the breaking out of hostilities, the Confederate Seminoles passed a law reenslaving all the free blacks in the Nation and taking their property from them. Cooper's army, as well, took a number of blacks captive.[7] Later, the southern Seminoles took their slaves to the Red River in the Chickasaw Nation to prevent their escaping to the north.

In November 1861, the authorities at Richmond appointed an agent to the Seminoles. When the Reverend J. S. Morrow arrived at the agency in September 1862, he found the buildings, archives, and records in the charge of "a free mulatto man. He had done all he could to preserve them, but everything was in confusion, the old agent having been absent about a year."[8]

By 1862, the Confederates were having trouble keeping all of the promises made in treaties with the Five Civilized Tribes. At Jefferson Davis' insistence, S. S. Scott, the Confederate commissioner of Indian affairs, visited the Indian Territory and assured the tribes that even

though the exigencies of war had prevented the Confederate States from
fully complying with the treaties, there was no doubt that they would.
In a follow-up letter, Scott wrote to the leaders of the Five Civilized
Tribes: "Slavery with you is as obnoxious to the fanaticism of the north
as it is in the Confederate States, and could that government subjugate
them and deprive them of their slaves, it would not be long in taking yours
from you also. But this is not all. After having dispossessed you of your
slaves, it would fasten upon your rich and fertile lands and distribute them
among its surplus and poverty-stricken population, who have been looking
toward them with longing hearts for years."[9]

In Kansas, the refugee Seminoles and blacks were given subsistence
through money appropriated from funds held in trust for the Indians of
the Southern Superintendency who had joined the rebels. They were mainly
women, children, and old men, the able-bodied men having joined the
Union forces. The refugee blacks and Indians suffered greatly. They had little
medical attention and inadequate food, shelter, and clothing, and throughout the succeeding months they struggled to survive in their camps at Neosho
Falls and elsewhere.[10]

INVASION OF INDIAN TERRITORY

In the summer of 1862, the forces of Brigadier General James G. Blunt
invaded the Indian Territory, but retreated shortly thereafter, taking
thousands of loyal Seminoles, Cherokees, and Creeks with them as far as
Baxter Springs. In April 1863, Colonel W. A. Phillips reoccupied and
fortified an enclosed area at Fort Gibson, where he remained in command
of the Indian troops north of the Arkansas River until the end of the
war.[11] Many of the Indians and blacks, anxious to return home, followed
the army to Fort Gibson. Their lot, however, was little better than that
of those who remained in the refugee camps in Kansas. Some of the Seminole blacks joined the First Kansas Colored Infantry, organized early in
1863, and participated in the battles of Cabin Creek and Honey Springs,
the two most important battles in the Indian Territory.[12]

Meanwhile, the southern Seminoles and their blacks were clustered on
the Washita below Fort Washita and up the Red River from the mouth of
the Washita in the Choctaw and Chickasaw Nations. They, too, suffered
greatly. The slave owners among them, on both sides of the Red River,

during February and March 1864, ran their slaves to the Brazos in Texas. By that time, the rebels were less concerned with repossessing the Indian Territory than with holding the Red River valley, as the slaves of refugees were "drifting in the direction of the Brazos."[13]

When the war was over, the United States government was exacting regarding terms of peace with the Five Civilized Tribes. In the fall of 1865, a board of commissioners was sent to meet with the Indians at Fort Smith. The board consisted of D. N. Cooley, the commissioner of Indian affairs; Elijah Sells, the superintendent for the Southern Superintendency; Thomas Wistar, a leader among the Society of Friends; Brigadier General W. S. Harney of the United States Army; and Colonel Ely S. Parker of General Grant's staff. At this time there were an estimated 2,000 Seminoles. Those at Fort Gibson were anxious to go to their own country, but the agent felt that matters had not sufficiently settled to allow them to do so. Altogether, about 1,000 of them were drawing rations from the government, and all were very poor and destitute.[14] Perhaps for that reason, more than any other, the Seminoles were the most anxious of all the tribes to negotiate with the government.

POSTWAR COUNCIL AT FORT SMITH

When the council convened at Fort Smith on September 9, 1865, the disloyal Indians had not yet arrived. Nevertheless, D. N. Cooley presented the President's message that he wished to renew alliances with the Indians. The Indians were told that by aligning themselves with the Confederacy, they had forfeited all rights due them under the treaties with the United States and must consider themselves at the mercy of the government. While this applied to the loyal as well as disloyal factions, the commissioners assured them that they were determined to recognize the loyalty of those who had fought for the Union and had suffered in its behalf.[15]

The loyal Seminoles were represented by John Chupco, Pascofar, Fo-hut-she, Fos Harjo, and Chucote Harjo, with Robert Johnson and Caesar Bruner, both blacks, as interpreters. The Seminoles had been unaware of the purpose of the council when they came and wanted time to consult. When the conference reconvened late that afternoon, the Seminoles said that they were not ready to do business. They had come to Fort Smith to attempt a reunification with the Seminoles who had gone with the South, not to make a treaty, which they felt they could not do without consulting their people.[16]

On the second day, Cooley reviewed the fact that treaties had been made with the Confederate States by the various tribes. By those treaties, the tribes had forfeited and lost all of their rights to annuities and lands. The President was anxious to renew relations with the Indians, but in the new treaties to be negotiated, he insisted on certain stipulations, among them that the institution of slavery be abolished, that steps be taken for the unconditional emancipation of all persons held in bondage and for the incorporation of the blacks into the tribes on an equal footing with the original members, or that they be otherwise provided for. A further stipulation would provide that slavery or involuntary servitude would never exist in the tribes except as punishment of a crime. However, Cooley insisted that those who had remained loyal, even though their Nation may have gone over to the enemy, would be liberally provided for.[17]

The third day of the council was used in hearing anything which the assembled delegates had to say about their position in the negotiations. Pascofar reiterated that the Seminoles were unprepared to treat until they had had time for further consideration. However, he stressed that the Seminoles desired to come to some terms and have a treaty.[18]

On the fourth day, the Seminole delegation addressed the commissioners. They had considered the statements made by the commissioners and fully endorsed the propositions made except that they wanted the third article of the proposed treaties revised to admit only those blacks held in bondage by the Seminole people and those free blacks who had resided in the Nation before the war. They wrote, "We are willing to provide for the colored people of our own nation, but do not desire our lands to become colonization grounds for the negroes of other States and Territories." While they felt it necessary to conclude a treaty with the United States, more important to them was coming to some satisfactory understanding with the disloyal faction. They therefore intended to go home, call a meeting, and elect a delegation to meet with the commissioners to conclude a treaty.[19]

After a few days of the council, the commissioners became convinced that no final treaties could be concluded until the differences between the loyal and disloyal factions were resolved. Therefore, they drafted a preliminary treaty to be signed by those delegates present, rejecting treaties with all other parties, reaffirming their allegiance to the United States, and agreeing to reestablish peace with them. The fifth day of the council was spent in reading the treaty of peace. The Seminoles agreed to sign it on the following day and submitted a statement of the circumstances under which some of the Seminoles had signed a treaty with the Confederacy.[20] On the following day, they signed the treaty as they had promised.

On the eighth day, a delegation from the southern faction of Seminoles arrived, and on the next day, the loyal and disloyal factions issued a joint statement that they had agreed to settle their differences and were willing to subscribe to all of the propositions which the commissioners had proposed to write into any treaties finally negotiated with the United States. They requested permission to go home to care for their families until the time that the government might call them to a treaty council. At that time, they would have the power from their people to enter such a treaty.[21]

On the eleventh day, the southern delegation, including John Jumper, George Cloud, and James Factor, rescinded their action of two days earlier, saying that they had signed the joint statement without being aware of all it involved. Especially did they rescind, among others, those propositions providing for the emancipation of the slaves and their incorporation into the tribe. They wrote, "We know the abolition of slavery to be a fact throughout the United States. We are willing to recognize that fact by the proper acts of our Council. But the proposition to 'incorporate' the freed negro with us on an 'equal footing with the original members' of the Seminole tribe is presented to us so suddenly that it shocks the lesson we have learned for long years from the white man as to the negro's inferiority. We honestly think that both the welfare of the Seminole and the freed negro would be injured if not destroyed by such 'incorporation.' The emancipated black man must, of necessity, be 'suitably provided for.' Such provision requires time and consultation as to how it shall best be done, and we, consequently, beg the indulgence of further time before we decide. We, however, bind ourselves to agree in good faith to any wise plan which shall be deemed just and equitable to all parties."[22]

The council lasted two days longer and accomplished little more than making arrangements for delegations from both factions to go to Washington at a later date and work out a treaty.

RETURN TO INDIAN TERRITORY

In October 1865, Superintendent Elijah Sells reported that about one half of the refugee Seminoles had returned to the Indian Territory, living on the Creek and Cherokee lands near Fort Gibson. About five hundred, consisting mainly of the families of those who had volunteered for the Union army, still remained in Kansas near Neosho Falls. Plans were under way to unite them with the rest of the Seminoles south of Fort Gibson. Living with the Seminoles were large numbers of blacks, whom Sells claimed, despite the disloyal faction's objections, the Seminoles desired to have incorporated into the tribe "as citizens, with equal rights." Besides these groups, there were about 950 disloyal Seminoles still on the Red River, supposedly "anxious to return to their former homes."[23]

These latter had received their last annuities from the Confederacy in March 1865. They were destitute by fall, when they appealed to the government for relief. They were preparing to remove to their own lands from their camps in the woods of the Washita. They knew that they would find nothing there, no houses and no food.[24]

As the Seminoles and other Indians returned to the Indian Territory, it became apparent to the government that the freedmen of all tribes must be protected until their status was established. Thus, in late October 1865 the Adjutant General's office assigned Brevet Major General John B. Sanborn, of the U.S. Volunteers, to the duty of "regulating the relations between the Freedmen in the Indian Territory and their former masters as the Secretary of the Interior may indicate," and the War Department directed post commanders and officers of the Quartermaster's Department to furnish Sanborn with escorts, transportation, and supplies.[25]

Sanborn's orders were explicit. Where he found relations between the freedmen and their former masters amicable and satisfactory to both, he was not to interfere or disturb them. But where he found rights denied or abuses existing, he was to give immediate relief. He was to discourage idleness among the freedmen and encourage them to support themselves by making contracts with persons who were willing to hire them as laborers either for wages or as sharecroppers. The contracts, which were to cover a period of no more than one year, were to be written and duly filed. The Indian agents were to cooperate with Sanborn in seeing that the freedmen were allowed to occupy lands of their own so that they could realize the profits of their own labor. Sanborn was to stress upon the Indians the justice of admitting the freedmen to equal rights of persons and property in the Indian nations and to broach the idea of the Indians' granting to the freedmen an equal enjoyment of civil rights, using the arguments that in doing so, the Indians would be following the example of the whites as well as increasing the strength of their nations.[26]

RELATIONS WITH FREEDMEN

At the time of Sanborn's appointment, rumors were rife in the Indian Territory that murder and other violence were being perpetrated upon the freedmen. Some of them complained to General H. J. Hunt at the Frontier District army headquarters at Fort Smith, yet they were not able to testify firsthand to the murders. Hunt ascribed the rumors to the general feeling of uneasiness which gripped the freedmen. Some Indians told them that they were free, while others told them that they were still slaves. In answering them, Hunt took the safe route, telling them that they would certainly be freed by the treaties then being negotiated. Meanwhile, he told them to support themselves and to work quietly with their present owners, making contracts when they were offered suitable wages. He told them to bear as well as they could the evils that attended "their change of condition." Hunt found that they were very reasonable concerning what he told them and seemed contented with the prospects held out to them. When he sought an official opinion on the freedmen's status, Commissioner Cooley told him that "the constitutional number of states having ratified the anti-slavery amendment, there is not, in fact, a slave within the limits of the United States."[27]

However, in early December, Seminole Agent George Reynolds reported from Fort Gibson that the southern Seminoles had all returned home destitute and were not acting in good faith toward their freedmen. In fact, Reynolds said that in every instance they still held the blacks as slaves and intended to do so as long as they could. They left the freedmen destitute by taking the crops they had made. The loyal and southern factions were wrangling over the rights of the southern sympathizers. The loyals claimed that they must come under the laws of the loyal faction and recognize John Chupco as chief. Reynolds recommended that if the southern Seminoles ever acquired any rights under the government, they should be required to pay the blacks for their labor during the preceding three or four years.[28]

General Sanborn arrived at Fort Smith on December 24, bringing with him certain preconceived ideas concerning the status of the freedmen of the Indian Territory. These views differed widely from those of General Hunt, who believed that the Emancipation Proclamation did not apply to the Indian Territory and that slavery would exist there until otherwise provided by law. Sanborn believed, mistakenly, that the blacks of the Indian Territory were not legally slaves before the war and that they were voluntary slaves who had the right to leave their masters and go anywhere. If they escaped to a free state, he reasoned, they could not have been returned by process of court. Sanborn disagreed with Hunt's idea that it would be disastrous to inform the blacks that they were now free. Hunt argued that they would abandon their old homes and haunts and go to the military posts where they would become completely dependent on the government. Sanborn felt that if they were told what rights would obtain to them among the Indians, the freedmen would remain where they were. They would have to be told sometime, he argued, and the sooner the better. To Sanborn, the best course for the government was to consider the blacks as part of the tribes to which they belonged and to give them freedom of choice to stay or to leave. Those who stayed should have all the rights, interests, and annuities that were given to the Indians. It was important to confer at once upon the freedmen the right to hold and acquire property, which would make them feel responsible for the contracts they made, making their property liable to loss if the contracts were broken.[29]

Sanborn established his headquarters at Fort Smith and made his policies known through circulars, the first of which he released on January 1, 1866. It contained his orders from the department and directed the agents to impress upon the Indians the correct idea of the new relation which existed between them and their former slaves and that the freedmen were now invested with all the rights of free men. The government was committed to the protection of the freedmen in their persons; an outrage upon a freedman would be considered an outrage upon the United States. The circular instructed the agents to see that contracts were made and that fair wages were paid for labor; all contracts for periods longer than a month were to be in writing.

The circular also announced that the system of polygamy which had always existed to some extent among the Indians and had been therefore practiced by some of the freedmen would no longer be tolerated by the government. No freedman thereafter would be allowed to take more than one wife; those cohabiting at that time would be considered legally married. Marriages which had been solemnized by Indian custom were considered binding and valid, and until provision was made, the agent could take the mutual pledges of a couple and give them a certificate. Finally, Sanborn's first circular stressed that every effort was to be made to remove all prejudice on the part of the Indians against the freedmen.[30] This latter point reflected the obvious naïveté of the department in pretending that the absorption of the freedmen into the Indian tribes could be effected without any discrimination or social and racial prejudice. Their expectations might have been fulfilled to some degree by the Seminoles and to a lesser degree by the Creeks, but it never was by the Chickasaws, Choctaws, and Cherokees.

Sanborn issued Circular No. 2 on the following day. It authorized Indian agents to sign ration returns for destitute freedmen of their respective tribes and authorized commissaries of subsistence to issue rations "in cases of great destitution."[31]

On his first visit to the Indian country, Sanborn found the freedmen "the most industrious, economical, and, in many respects, the more intelligent" segment of the population. He found that the freedmen of most tribes wanted to remain in the Indian country on land set apart for their exclusive use. The matter of segregated lands had been much discussed in the Indian Territory, and the freedmen were therefore inclined to do no more work than was necessary in improving the lands they occupied because they expected to be relocated. Sanborn urged that some decision be made before spring, for plowing and planting would begin as early as the first of March. If they were not to be resettled, they should know at once. Sanborn felt that they could survive by themselves because most of them had ox teams and among their numbers were blacksmiths, carpenters, and wheelwrights. He found that the Seminoles looked upon the freedmen as their equals in right and were in favor of incorporating them into their tribe with all the rights and privileges of native Indians.[32] Sanborn no doubt referred to the loyal faction of Seminoles, whom he apparently regarded as spokesmen for the tribe, for according to Agent Reynolds, the southern faction treated the blacks badly.

Sanborn soon made another tour of the Indian country and became convinced that land should be set aside for the exclusive use of the freedmen. Each male over twenty-one should be able to enter a homestead of 160 acres, with no power to sell the property. Second, there were a large number of freedwomen who had had from one to several children during slavery but had never had a husband. It would be difficult for them to find husbands under freedom, so Sanborn recommended that they be allowed to enter 160 acres as a head of a household. Finally, he recommended that four sections in every township of freedman land be set aside for school lands for freedmen children.[33]

In Circular No. 4, Sanborn authorized the freedmen to remain in the nations and cultivate the lands they occupied. He instructed Major Pinkney Lugenbeel at Fort Gibson to report the name of every Indian who denied those rights or whose conduct indicated an unwillingness to allow the freedmen to possess and cultivate land during the present season. The right of the freedmen to remain on the farms where their cabins were built and where they had been held as slaves would be maintained in all cases where their masters had abandoned the farms during the war and had gone south. It was important that as large a crop of corn and other cereals as possible be produced that season; thus, through Circular No. 6, Sanborn encouraged the freedmen to enter upon any unoccupied land which was not likely to be occupied by any Indians during the season and to make a crop. He requested the military officers to protect the freedmen who thus settled and to enforce contracts in which the freedmen owed part of the crop to the Indians.[34]

By April, Sanborn considered the existing relations between the freedmen and their former masters "generally satisfactory." The rights of the freedmen were acknowledged by all, fair compensation was paid for their labor, a fair part of crops to be raised was being allowed, there was plenty of work for the freedmen to do, and nearly all of them were self-supporting. Only 150 in the entire Indian Territory applied to Sanborn for assistance during April, and many of those had been taken south by their masters and were just returning to their old homes. Things were going so well that he saw little reason to continue his commission beyond the tenth of May. There might be a few abuses which it would be necessary to correct, and a general supervision of freedman matters would be more necessary at the time the crops matured and contracts were due. The continuance of his commission depended much on the treaties then being negotiated in Washington, but Sanborn felt that the agents, under proper instructions, could attend to and perform all the duties that pertained to his office. Sanborn was mustered out of service on April 30, 1866.[35] The matter of freedman relations was put in the hands of Elijah Sells, the superintendent of Indian affairs for the Southern Superintendency.

EQUAL FOOTING WITH SEMINOLES

Meanwhile, the future of the Seminole freedmen was being profoundly affected by events in Washington. In December 1865, a delegation of northern and southern Seminoles had gone to Washington with their agent to negotiate a new treaty with the government. They found that among the points of particular concern to the government was the relation which the freed blacks would thereafter hold to the Indians. The treaty, which was concluded on March 21 and proclaimed on August 16, provided for, among other things, abolishing slavery and placing the freedmen on equal footing with the Seminoles. According to the commissioner of Indian affairs, "This equality was the more easily accomplished in the case of the Seminoles, since there had already been a considerable intermingling of the races before the tribe removed from Florida, and several of the interpreters accompanying the delegation representing the tribe appeared to be of purely African blood." The Seminoles also ceded their lands—over two million acres—and bought from the Creeks a new reservation of 200,000 acres between the Canadian and the North Fork, about fifty-five miles west of their junction.[36] Thus, the freedom which the government had promised many of the Seminole blacks before removal was finally guaranteed by treaty. But it had come twenty years too late for many of them.

As soon as the treaty was concluded, a great number of the Seminoles removed to their new homes, and the rest prepared to remove in the fall. With them went the blacks who had survived the war and had been able to return. Those who had remained with the loyal Seminoles during the war, which was by far the great majority of them, numbered 333 in 1867. They settled Seminole fashion in bands—the Jim Lane Band and the John Brown Band—and took as surnames the names of their fathers or former owners.[37] To the citizenship rolls of the Seminole Nation were added the family surnames of Abraham, Cudjo, Dindy, Primus, and Sandy, names borne by their descendants today. Under the rights granted them by the treaty, they set about building a new life as free men.

NOTES

1. Henry M. Rector to John Ross, January 29, 1861, 38 Cong., 1 Sess., *House Executive Document 1,* Pt. 3, 345.

2. S. S. Scott to Choctaws, et al., December 26, 1862, 38 Cong., 1 Sess.,

House Executive Document 1, Pt. 3, 342; John T. Cox to W. G. Coffin, March 18, 1864, 38 Cong., 2 Sess., *House Executive Document 1,* 477; Edwin C. McReynolds, *The Seminoles* (Norman: University of Oklahoma Press, 1957), 289-290.

3. McReynolds, 292; Muriel H. Wright, "Seal of the Seminole Nation," *Chronicles of Oklahoma,* 34 (Autumn 1956), 266.

4. McReynolds, 292-294.

5. Dean Trickett, "The Civil War in the Indian Territory," *Chronicles of Oklahoma,* 18 (December 1940), 268-269, 270-279; McReynolds, 297-302; John Bartlett Meserve, "Chief Opothleyahola," *Chronicles of Oklahoma,* 9 (December 1931), 446-450. The battle of Round Mountain was fought south of the Cimarron River just above its juncture with the Arkansas; the battle of Chustolasah occurred about three and one half miles southeast of Sperry, Oklahoma; and the battle of Chustenahlah occurred on Hominy Creek west of Skiatook, Oklahoma. See "Oklahoma Historic Sites Survey," *Chronicles of Oklahoma,* 36 (Autumn 1958), 291.

6. Official Report of the Proceedings of the Council with the Indians of the West and Southwest, Held at Fort Smith, Arkansas, in September, 1865, 39 Cong., 1 Sess., *House Executive Document 1,* 516 (hereafter cited as *Official Report*); Report of the Secretary of the Interior (1863), 38 Cong., 1 Sess., *House Executive Document 1,* 145; Report of the Secretary of the Interior (1864), 38 Cong., 2 Sess., *House Executive Document 1,* 174.

7. George Reynolds to Elijah Sells, December 5, 1865, National Archives Microfilm Publications, *Microcopy M234*(Records of the Office of Indian Affairs, Letters Received)-837, S13-66; *Microcopy M234* is hereafter cited as *M234,* followed by the roll number. Evidence of Cooper's intent to capture slaves can be found in the affidavits in National Archives Record Group 75 (Records of the Bureau of Indian Affairs), *Records Relating to Loyal Creek Claims, 1869-70,* and McReynolds, 311.

8. Reynolds to Sells, October 2, 1865, and Sells to D. N. Cooley, October 16, 1865, 39 Cong., 1 Sess., *House Executive Document 1,* 467, 440.

9. Scott to Choctaws, et al., December 26, 1862, 38 Cong., 1 Sess., *House Executive Document 1,* Pt. 3, 342-343.

10. Report of the Secretary of the Interior (1864), 38 Cong., 2 Sess., *House Executive Document 1,* 174; McReynolds, 302-305.

11. Wiley Britton, *Memoirs of the Rebellion on the Border, 1863* (Chicago: Cushing, Thomas & Co., Publishers, 1882), 93, 154; McReynolds, 305-306.

12. A. V. Coffin to Colonel W. G. Coffin, September 25, 1863, Smith to W. G. Coffin, July 16, 1863, A. G. Snow to W. G. Coffin, September 4,

1863, and Milo Gookins to W. G. Coffin, October 17, 1863, 38 Cong., 1 Sess., *House Executive Document 1*, Pt. 3, 307-309, 329, 330, 303-304, 339; Britton, 154, 277, 316-326, 334, 356-361; McReynolds, 307-308, 311; General James G. Blunt to Colonel W. A. Phillips, April 30, 1863, and May 30, 1836, and Blunt to Major General John M. Schofield, June 26, 1863, *The War of the Rebellion: A Compilation of the Official Records of the Union and Confederate Armies* (Washington: Government Printing Office, 1880-1901), i, XXII, Pt. 2, 262, 297-298, 337 (hereafter cited as *Official Records*, followed by the series and volume numbers); A. V. Coffin to W. G. Coffin, August 25, 1864, 38 Cong., 2 Sess., *House Executive Document 1*, 451-452. Details of the battles in which Seminole blacks engaged can be found in *Official Records*, i, XXII, Pt. 1, 378-382, 447-456; *Official Records*, i, XXII, Pt. 2, 292, 763; and McReynolds, 309-311. Details concerning the black units in which Seminole blacks served appear in *Official Records*, i, XXII, Pt. 2, 292; *Official Records*, i, XVIII, Pt. 1, 258-259; and *Official Records*, iii, V, 660.

13. Phillips to W. P. Dole, March 22, 1864; Phillips to Major General S. R. Curtis, March 17, 1864; and Cox to W. G. Coffin, March 16, 1864, 38 Cong., 2 Sess., *House Executive Document 1*, 472, 473, 476.

14. Report of the Secretary of the Interior (1865), 39 Cong., 1 Sess., *House Executive Document 1*, 202, 206.

15. Report of Cooley, October 30, 1865, and Report of the Secretary of the Interior, 39 Cong., 1 Sess., *House Executive Document 1*, 482, 202; Annie Heloise Abel, *The American Indian Under Reconstruction* (Cleveland: The Arthur H. Clark Company, 1925), 189.

16. *Official Report*, 497, 499, 500.

17. Report of the Secretary of the Interior, and Report of Cooley, October 30, 1865, 39 Cong., 1 Sess., *House Executive Document 1*, 482-483, 202; Abel, 189.

18. *Official Report*, 503.

19. *Ibid.*, 508-509; Report of the Secretary of the Interior, 39 Cong., 1 Sess., *House Executive Document 1*, 203; Abel, 192.

20. Report of the Secretary of the Interior, 39 Cong., 1 Sess., *House Executive Document 1*, 203; *Official Report*, 515-516.

21. *Official Report*, 526; Abel, 206.

22. *Official Report*, 534-535; Abel, 206.

23. Sells to Cooley, October 15, 1865, 39 Cong., 1 Sess., *House Executive Document 1*, 440.

24. Reynolds to Sells, October 2, 1865, 39 Cong., 1 Sess., *House Executive Document 1*, 467; *Official Report*, 535-536.

25. James Harlan to Cooley, November 18, 1865, *M234*-836, I1382-65.

26. Circular No. 1, January 1, 1866, in *M234*-836, I56-66.

27. General H. J. Hunt to Cooley, November 28, 1865, *M234*-836, H1323-65; Cooley to Hunt, December 15, 1865, National Archives Record Group 393 (Records of the United States Army Continental Commands, 1821-1920), *Frontier District,* Seventh Army Corps and Department of Arkansas, Letters Received, 1865-1866.

28. Reynolds to Sells, December 5, 1865, in *M234*-837, S13-66.

29. General John B. Sanborn to Cooley, December 26, 1865, *M234*-837, S101-66.

30. Circular No. 1, January 1, 1866, in *M234*-837, I56-66.

31. Sanborn to James Harlan, January 10, 1866, *M234*-837, S91-66.

32. *Report of the Secretary of the Interior* (Washington: Government Printing Office, 1866), 283-284.

33. *Ibid.,* 286.

34. Sanborn to Major Pinkney Lugenbeel, April 7, 1866, and Circular No. 6, March 27, 1866, in *M234*-837, S216-66 and S203-66.

35. Sanborn to Cooley, April 13, 1866, in *Report of the Secretary of the Interior,* 287; E. D. Townsend to Sanborn, April 11, 1866, *M234*-837, I237-66.

36. *Report of the Secretary of the Interior,* 321, 8-9.

37. *Ibid.,* 320-321. A census of the loyal blacks can be found in National Archives Microfilm Publications, *Microcopy M574*(Special Files of the Office of Indian Affairs, 1807-1904)-11, Special File 87: Loyal Seminole Claims.

10

Conclusion

For fifty years preceding the Civil War, the Africans had been perhaps the single most significant shaping force in Seminole affairs. Every major treaty or agreement affecting the Seminoles from the Treaty of New York in 1790 to the Treaty of 1866 had resulted in part from the presence of Africans among them, and most of the documents contained explicit provisions regarding the blacks. The presence of slaves and free blacks among the Indians had related directly to Seminole participation in the First and Second Seminole Wars and in the American Civil War and had been of major concern to military and civilian officials responsible for removing the Indians from Florida.

BLACKS AND SEMINOLES

After removal, the blacks continued to play a major role in Seminole affairs as they sought to reestablish the semifree status they had enjoyed among the Seminoles before the Second Seminole War or struggled to achieve the status of free men that in their understanding had been promised to most of them when they surrendered to the Americans in Florida. Their struggle was long and bitter. Common distrust and fear of the Americans and Creeks had unified the blacks and their Seminole masters or allies, creating a sense of reliance and trust between the races. After removal, the blacks were caught between the Seminoles and Creeks in their political wrangling, which, compounded by the duplicity of proslavery public officials, undermined the alliance between the Africans and Seminoles.

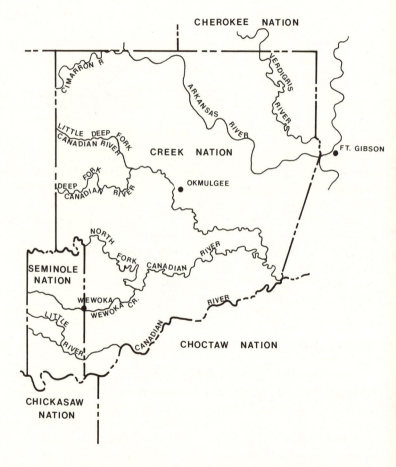

Seminole and Creek Lands Following the Treaties of 1866

Significant, however, is the fact that in the West the exigencies of war, which had contributed to the dependence of the groups on each other, no longer existed. Thus, in two decades the Indians moved from friendship and affection for the blacks, which had often resulted in intermarriage, to the prejudicial view, at least among those who were pro-Confederate, that the blacks were racially inferior.

The extent of racial prejudice among the Seminoles is not known. During treaty negotiations in 1865, the disloyal faction said that the Seminoles had learned well the lesson in racial hatred from the whites. Their statement seems to support William G. McLoughlin's theory that the Indians' system of slavery had at its base something "less deliberate, more unconscious" than simply frontier politics—i. e., an "acquired racial prejudice."[1] Yet Seminole records contain no such overt statements of racism as the southern faction expressed and give no indication that racial prejudice was widespread. It must be remembered, too, that when they made their statement, they were making excuses to representatives of the government for having aided in the rebellion.

The destruction of Seminole affection for the blacks was more the result of pressure from Indian neighbors, especially the Creeks and Cherokees, than from an "acquired racial prejudice." Indeed, the institution of slavery as it existed among the latter tribes, as well as among the Choctaws and Chickasaws, had resulted in little more than a transfer of the Seminoles' problems from the East to the West. Instead of American planters who wanted the enclaves of blacks broken up, it was Creek and Cherokee slaveholders and planters who had put pressure on the Seminoles to change. Their antagonism to the status of both slaves and free blacks among the Seminoles finally helped destroy the close relationship between Africans and Seminoles, who ultimately found it politically inexpedient to maintain the former relationship.

BLACKS IN OTHER NATIONS

Of course, the most direct political pressure came from the Creeks. They were not as far along the road to acculturation as were the Cherokees, Choctaws, and Chickasaws, but the influence of their changing slave code points in one direction: a system of slavery, complete with racial generalizations, more aligned with that of the other tribes and the Anglo-dominated society. The contrasting attitudes of these tribes and of the Seminoles toward slavery had direct bearing upon the condition of the blacks when they finally achieved the status of free men among the Indians.

A census of the Creeks taken in 1832 listed 502 slaves, with only a few Creeks owning more than ten. By 1860, there were 1,532 slaves. The 1832 census also listed a number of free blacks who were heads of households. They were removed with the Creeks, and by the time the Civil War began, some of them owned businesses such as boardinghouses and stores. Others were blacksmiths and interpreters. Except on the plantations of a few mixed bloods, slavery at first appeared to be a "convenience" to the Creeks. Slaves were allowed to accumulate property, by means of which they purchased their freedom, and there was little prejudice against intermarriage between Indians and blacks. However, by 1824, the Creeks had written a code which began to restrict the activities of their blacks. This code prescribed death to any black who killed an Indian or another slave, forbade inheritance by the offspring of Indians and Africans because it was "a disgrace to our Nation for our people to marry a Negro," prohibited slaves from owning property, provided for emancipation of slaves by their owners, appointed a receiver of runaway slaves, and relieved masters of any obligation made by their slaves. After removal, efforts of the mixed bloods resulted in stricter laws regarding blacks. Free blacks were subjected to property taxes, intermarriage was punished by whipping, aiding fugitive slaves was punished by fines and whippings, emancipation of slaves was permitted if the master took them out of the Nation, and a school law of 1856 prohibited the employment of abolitionists.[2]

The Cherokees held a greater number of slaves than any of the other tribes in the Indian Territory. In 1835, on the eve of removal, they owned 1,592, and by 1860 they had 2,511. Historians agree that slavery among the Cherokees was little different from that in the white South and that the status of slaves and free blacks among them declined after removal as laws became more severe. In 1839 the Cherokees wrote a constitution in which they admitted to citizenship the descendants of Cherokee women and black men but excluded the descendants of Cherokee men and black women. However, all persons of "negro or mulatto parentage" were excluded from holding public office. A few days after the adoption of the constitution, the Cherokee council passed a law prohibiting free citizens from marrying "any slave or person of color" who was not a citizen. Punishment could not exceed fifty lashes. A convicted black male, however, received one hundred. A law of 1840 prohibited free blacks, not of Cherokee blood, and slaves from holding improvements and other property in the Nation. Such property then held by blacks was ordered sold to the highest bidder. The same law forbade free blacks to sell spirituous liquors in the Nation. An 1841 law created "patrol companies" to capture and punish any slaves caught off their masters' premises without a pass and to give up to thirty-nine lashes to any black not entitled to Cherokee privileges and found carrying a weapon of any kind. The same council passed a law prohibiting the teaching of slaves and free blacks not of Cherokee blood to read or write. In the aftermath of the slave revolt of 1842, the council passed an act which ordered all free blacks not freed by Cherokee citizens to leave the Nation by January 1, 1843. Any who refused to leave were to be reported to the agent for expulsion. The same act provided that if a Cherokee citizen freed his slaves, he was responsible for their conduct as free blacks. If he died or left the Nation, the free blacks were to give "satisfactory security" to one of the circuit judges for their conduct. The act also stated that any free black found guilty of "aiding, abetting, or decoying" slaves to leave their owners was to receive one hundred lashes. An 1848 law prohibited the teaching of any black to read or write. An 1855 law prohibited the hiring of teachers with abolitionist sentiments, and finally, in 1859, the council passed an act requiring all free blacks to leave the Nation. This bill, however, was vetoed by Chief John Ross.[3]

The Choctaws also held great numbers of slaves. An 1831 census listed only 512 slaves and eleven free blacks. Most of the slaves were held by mixed bloods. In 1860, however, the Choctaws owned 2,349 slaves. From removal until 1855, the Choctaws and Chickasaws lived under one government, the latter having settled on the western lands of the former. Choctaw laws prevailed. In 1838, they forbade cohabitation with a slave, the teaching of a slave to read or write without the owner's consent, and the council's emancipating slaves without the owner's consent. In 1844, they passed a law which said "that no free negro unconnected with Choctaw blood should ever be allowed to draw any money from the Choctaw annuity." After 1855, the Choctaws passed laws which reaffirmed the laws against intermarriage and emancipation of slaves by the council. Others said that slaves brought to the Indian Territory would remain slaves, that owners should treat their slaves humanely, and that no person of African descent could hold public office.[4]

Before the removal period, the Chickasaws did not hold large numbers of slaves. Outstanding exceptions were Chickasaws named Colbert, several of whom owned more than twenty and one of those owning 150. At the

time of removal, a great many Chickasaws sold their homes and the reservations which had been granted them under former treaties and invested
their money in slaves whom they moved to the West. In 1860, Chickasaws
owned 975 slaves. In their new country, the mixed bloods opened large
plantations and farms and used their blacks in agricultural labor. Generally,
the relations between slave and master were relaxed, but there was little
mixture of the races. For the most part, the Indians treated their slaves
humanely. However, the Chickasaws emerged as "the aristocracy of the
Five Civilized Tribes, who regarded their slaves in the same manner as
white owners."[5] In their constitution of 1855, the Chickasaws forbade
the council's emancipating slaves without the owner's consent. In the late
1850s they passed laws prescribing harsh penalties for harboring runaways
and providing for the exclusion of free blacks from their limits. County
judges were authorized to order such blacks out of their respective counties.
Those who refused to go were to be sold to the highest bidder as slaves
for periods of one year, until they agreed to leave the Nation.[6]

ACCULTURATION AND BLACK CITIZENSHIP RIGHTS

The Indian tribes suffered a great reduction of their numbers between
removal and 1860. The Cherokees declined by an estimated 31 percent,
the Choctaws by 27 percent, the Chickasaws by 18 percent, the Creeks by
43 percent, and the Seminoles by 53 percent. The same period witnessed
an increase in the number of whites who had married into the tribes or
had been adopted by them. In 1860, there were 716 among the Cherokees,
804 among the Choctaws, 148 among the Chickasaws, 596 among the
Creeks, and thirty-five among the Seminoles. Thus, the number of whites
and slaves increased greatly, while the Indian population declined, in all
tribes except the Seminoles. While their numbers declined, the number
of slaves declined, and there was no significant increase in the number of
whites.[7] These figures reflect the degree of acculturation taking place in
the tribes, for there is a direct correlation between the increase in the
numbers of whites and blacks and the increasing severity of the slave
codes. Thus, while the other tribes were undergoing rapid changes
toward acculturation, the Seminoles remained an exception.

The degree of acculturation and racial antipathy reached by each tribe
before the Civil War directly affected the status of blacks as free men in
the Indian Territory. Again, the Seminoles stand as an exception. The

United States forced all of the tribes to adopt similar measures regarding the blacks during treaty negotiations in 1866. The Seminoles, Creeks, and Cherokees adopted their blacks immediately. The Choctaws resisted adopting theirs until 1885, and the Chickasaws refused to adopt theirs at all. The rights enjoyed by the freedmen differed at extremes. The Chickasaw freedmen had no rights, except to occupy and improve small plots of land. Life was little better for the Choctaw freedmen, and many of the Cherokee freedmen were excluded from rights because they had failed to return to the Nation within the six-months' limitation set by the Cherokee treaty. In contrast, the Creek freedmen were settled in three towns, with representatives in both houses of the Creek National Council, and enjoyed full rights of citizens. However, they became involved in the political factionalism that kept the Nation unsettled for a number of years following the war.[8]

Only in the Seminole Nation did the blacks have full rights of citizens and enjoy as well a life relatively free of political difficulties. In 1869, the superintendent of Indian affairs for the Southern Superintendency wrote, "Accepting fully the results of the war, and granting to the freedman unconditional citizenship, the Seminoles are living in a state of more perfect peace than any other tribe within the superintendency."[9] Thus, the long struggle for freedom which had begun in Florida had finally ended. The blacks' lives as free men among the Seminoles spanned four decades, after which they were given allotments of land in severalty and citizenship in the United States.

NOTES

1. William G. McLoughlin, "Red Indians, Black Slavery and White Racism: America's Slaveholding Indians," *American Quarterly,* 26 (October 1974), 370.

2. Antonio J. Waring, ed., *Laws of the Creek Nation,* University of Georgia Libraries Miscellaneous Publications No. 1 (Athens: University of Georgia Press, 1960), 21; Michael F. Doran, "Population Statistics of Nineteenth Century Indian Territory," *Chronicles of Oklahoma,* 53 (Winter 1975-76), 501; National Archives Record Group 75 (Records of the Bureau of Indian Affairs), *Creek Removal Records,* Census, 1833. A list of blacks who filed claims for improvements abandoned in the East during removal appears in B. Marshal et al, to W. Medill, April 2, 1848, National Archives Microfilm Publications, *Microcopy M234* (Records of the Office of Indian Affairs, Letters Received)-228, M215-48; examples of records relating to free blacks among the Creeks in the West appear in

National Archives Record Group 393 (Records of the United States Army Continental Commands, 1821-1920), *Fort Gibson,* Volume "Indian Affairs,"* 29, 39; Records of Scipio Barnett and Monday Durant, store owners, and Sarah Davis, a boardinghouse keeper, e.g., appear in National Archives Record Group 75, *Records Relating to Loyal Creek Claims, 1869-70,* Claim Numbers 113, 177, 966; Angie Debo, *The Road to Disappearance* (Norman: University of Oklahoma Press, 1941), 115-116, 126-127.

3. Kenneth Wiggins Porter, *The Negro on the American Frontier* (New York: Arno Press and The New York Times, 1971), 109; Grant Foreman, *The Five Civilized Tribes* (Norman: University of Oklahoma Press, 1934), 54, 83, 420; McLoughlin, 380-381; R. Halliburton, Jr., "Origins of Black Slavery Among the Cherokees," *Chronicles of Oklahoma,* 52 (Winter 1974-75), 496; *Laws of the Cherokee Nation: Adopted by the Council at Various Periods* (Tahlequah, Ind. Ter.: Cherokee Advocate Office, 1852) [Pt. 2], 7, 19, 44, 53, 55-56, 71, 173-174, 381; James W. Duncan, "Interesting Ante-Bellum Laws of the Cherokees, Now Oklahoma History," *Chronicles of Oklahoma,* 6 (June 1928), 179; J. B. Davis, "Slavery in the Cherokee Nation," *Chronicles of Oklahoma,* 11 (December 1933), 1066-1067.

4. National Archives Record Group 75, *Choctaw Removal Records,* Census Roll, 1831 (Census of North West District); Doran, 501; 49 Cong., 1 Sess., *Senate Report 1278,* Pt. 2, 493; Arrell M. Gibson, *The Chickasaws* (Norman: University of Oklahoma Press, 1971), 226; Wyatt F. Jeltz, "The Relations of the Negroes and Choctaw and Chickasaw Indians," *Journal of Negro History,* 33 (January 1948), 31-32.

5. National Archives Record Group 75, *Chickasaw Removal Records,* Census and Muster Rolls, 1837-39; 50 Cong., 1 Sess., *Senate Executive Document 166,* 9; Jeltz, 29-31; Gibson, 125, 226; Doran, 501.

6. *Constitution, Laws, and Treaties of the Chickasaws* (Tishomingo City, Ind. Ter.: E. J. Foster, 1860), 57-58, 115.

7. Doran, 498, 501. Doran cites a contemporary observer's estimate that there were 1,000 slaves in the Seminole Nation in 1860, but the evidence presented above does not support that figure.

8. No adequate histories of the freedmen of the Five Civilized Tribes exist. Porter (527) points out the lack of scholarship. However, information on the freedmen of the various tribes can be found in Debo's *The Road to Disappearance* (regarding the Creeks) and *The Rise and Fall of the Choctaw Republic* (Norman: University of Oklahoma Press, 1934), Gibson's *The Chickasaws,* and Morris L. Wardell's *A Political History of the Cherokee Nation, 1838-1907* (Norman: University of Oklahoma Press, 1938).

9. 41 Cong., 2 Sess., *House Executive Document 1,* Pt. 3, 842.

Appendix

LIST A

Registry of negro prisoners captured by the troops commanded by
Major General Thomas S. Jesup, in 1836 and 1837,
and owned by Indians, or who claim to be free.

(From 25 Cong., 3 Sess., *Executive Document 225*, pp. 66-69)

No.	Names	Sex	Tribe, town, or owner	Estimated age Years	Months	Remarks
1	Jacob	Male	Toon-a-hi-ka	25		Wounded in right knee
2	Rina	Female	Mic-a-po-to-ka	18		Wife and Children to Jacob;
3	Venice	Female	Mic-a-po-to-ka	2		Claudia died May 27, 1837
4	Claudia	Female	Mic-a-po-to-ka		2	
5	Jane	Female	Mic-a-po-to-ka	40		Mother to Rina and Molly
6	Molly	Female	Mic-a-po-to-ka	23		Mother and Son
7	Billy	Male	Mic-a-po-to-ka	12		
8	Chloe	Female	Mic-a-po-to-ka	19		Sister to Jacob;
9	Suah	Female	Mic-a-po-to-ka	2		mother and children
10	Dennis	Male	Mic-a-po-to-ka	1		
11	Pompey	Male	Mic-a-po-to-ka	70		Husband and wife
12	Dolly	Female	Mic-a-po-to-ka	50		
13	Lilla	Female	Mic-a-po-to-ka	20		Mother and children
14	Tom	Male	Mic-a-po-to-ka	11		
15	Bella	Female	Mic-a-po-to-ka	9		
16	Hagar	Female	Mic-a-po-to-ka	30		
17	Ned	Male	Mic-a-po-to-ka	3		

	Name	Sex		Age	Remarks
19	Charles	Male	Mic-a-po-to-ka	6	
20	Margaret	Female	Mic-a-po-to-ka	4	
21	Sylvia	Female	Mic-a-po-to-ka	-	
22	Buno	Male	Mic-a-po-to-ka	19	
23	Peggy	Female	Mic-a-po-to-ka	45	Daughter to Pompey and Dolly; mother to Hagar
24	Bob	Male	Mic-a-po-to-ka	30	
25	Margaret	Female	Mic-a-po-to-ka	21	
26	Cyrus	Male	Mic-a-po-to-ka	13	
27	Rose	Female	Harriet Bowlegs	70	Grandmother to Jacob and Chloe; sold by Mr. Forrester, of Six-mile creek, to Bowlegs, several years since; Juba cousin to Jacob
28	Juba	Female	Harriet Bowlegs	20	
29	Ned	Male	Harriet Bowlegs	19	
30	Noble	Male	Harriet Bowlegs	23	
31	Phebe	Female	Na-a-scholy-katta	33	Jacob's uncle's wife; mother and children
32	Toney	Male	Na-a-scholy-katta	11	
33	Argus	Male	Na-a-scholy-katta	7	
34	Nelly	Female	Mic-a-po-to-ka	20	Mother and children
35	Scipio	Female	Mic-a-po-to-ka	3	
36	Sandy	Male	Mic-a-po-to-ka	1	
37	Elsey	Female	Mic-a-po-to-ka	25	Mother and child
38	Katy	Female	Mic-a-po-to-ka	3	
39	Dick	Male	John Hicks	55	Said to be the property of Colonel Humphreys
40	Tena	Female	Micanopy	50	Mother and children, raised with the Indians
41	Susa	Female	Micanopy	14	
42	Nancy	Female	Micanopy	9	

LIST A (Continued)

No.	Names	Sex	Tribe, town, or owner	Estimated age Years	Months	Remarks
43	Linda	Female	Micanopy	8		
44	Mary	Female	Micanopy	24		Daughter to Tena, and mother
45	Pussy	Female	Micanopy	10		to the children
46	Ishmael	Male	Micanopy	6		
47	Cyrus	Male	Micanopy	5		
48	Tamar	Female	Micanopy	3		
49	Scipio	Male	Micanopy	1		
50	Patty	Female	Micanopy	33		Mother and children; daughter to
51	Lucy	Female	Micanopy	7		Tena
52	Pompey	Male	Micanopy	4		
53	Matilda	Female	Micanopy	3		
54	Katy	Female	Micanopy	25		
55	Eliza	Female	Micanopy	20		
56	Ben	Male	Micanopy	40		Father (one of the most important
57	Jane	Female	Micanopy	35		and influential characters among the
58	Flora	Female	Micanopy	13		Indian negroes), mother, and children;
59	Patty	Female	Micanopy	12		never had a white master
60	Charles	Male	Micanopy	11		
61	Polly	Female	Micanopy	9		
62	Joe	Male	Micanopy	7		
63	Betty	Female	Micanopy	4		
64	Elsey	Female	Micanopy	3		
65	Robert	Male	Micanopy		½	

No.	Name	Sex	Band	Age	Remarks
66	Betsey	Female	Micanopy	45	
67	Washington	Male	Micanopy	11	
68	Rachel	Female	Micanopy	25	
69	Hetty	Female	Micanopy		
70	Fanny	Female	Micanopy		
71	Joseph	Male	Micanopy		
72	Ino*	Male	Micanopy	45	Husband (the commander of the negro force on the Withlacoochee; the chief counsellor among the negroes, and the most important character), wife, and children
73	Eliza	Female	Micanopy	35	
74	Toby	Male	Micanopy	20	
75	Catherine	Female	Micanopy	12	
76	Nancy	Female	Micanopy	1	Rachel's child
77	Katy	Female	Jumper	25	Mother and child, cousin to Murray (a defect in Katy's right eye; said to be the property of Colonel Humphreys.)
78	Fanny	Female	Jumper	2	
79	Susan	Female	Micanopy	30	
80	Ben	Male	Ho-lah-too-chee	22	
81	Jacob	Male	Ho-lah-too-chee	24	
82	Mundy	Male	Mic-co-po-to-ka	20	
83	Murray	Male	Mic-co-po-to-ka	35	Owned by Colonel Crowell, and claimed by Nelly Factor; the best guide in the nation
84	Prince	Male	Mic-co-po-to-ka	24	
85	Tony	Male	Mic-co-po-to-ka	25	
86	Toby	Male	Mic-co-po-to-ka	32	Hostile; either qualified to take the lead in an insurrection
87	Peter	Male	Mic-co-po-to-ka	15	
88	Pompey	Male	Mic-co-po-to-ka	60	
89	Jacob, 2d	Male	Sa-uath-ith-ka	20	

*Apparently a mistake; the description fits Juan.

LIST A (Continued)

No.	Names	Sex	Tribe, town, or owner	Estimated age Years	Months	Remarks
90	Daley	Male	Sa-uath-ith-ka	22		
91	Mundy	Male	Mic-co-po-to-ka	1	6	Died May 11, 1837
92	George	Male	Mic-co-po-to-ka	1		Died May 23, 1837
93	Philip	Male	Mic-co-po-to-ka	4		Died May 17, 1837
94	Morris	Male	Mic-co-po-to-ka	1		Died May 31, 1837
95	Lydia	Female	Noc-sa-loc-se	60		Died May 11, 1837
96	Abraham	Male	Claims to be free	50		The principal negro chief; supposed to be friendly to the whites
97	Toney Barnett	Male	Claims to be free	36		Said to be a good soldier, and an intrepid leader. He is the most cunning and intelligent negro we have here. He is married to the widow of the former chief of the nation.
98	Polly Barnett	Female	Claims to be free	36		
99	Beckey	Female	Claims to be free	2		
100	Grace	Female	Claims to be free	6		
101	Lydia	Female	Claims to be free	5		
102	Mary Ann	Female	Claims to be free	3		
103	Martinas	Male	Claims to be free	1		

LIST B

Negroes brought in by August and Latty at Fort Jupiter,
to General Jesup under a proclamation by him offering freedom
to all who should separate from the Seminoles & surrender.
(From National Archives Record Group 94,
Records of the Office of the Adjutant General,
General Jesup's Papers, Box 15)

No.	Names	Indian Owners	Remarks
1	July	Nelly Factor	Killed in Florida
2	Tina	Nelly Factor	
3	Susan	Nelly Factor	
4	Nanny	Nelly Factor	
5	Nelly	Nelly Factor	
6	Sampson	Nelly Factor	
7	Kistooa	Nelly Factor	
8	Jenny	Nelly Factor	
9	Norata	Nelly Factor	
10	Pond	Nelly Factor	
11	Rosenta	Nelly Factor	
12	Kuntusee	Nelly Factor	
13	Phillis	Nelly Factor	
14	Robert	Nelly Factor	
15	Joe	Nelly Factor	
16	Sandy	Nelly Factor	Dead
17	Lucy	Nelly Factor	
18	Dembo	Nelly Factor	
19	Thomas	Nelly Factor	
20	Elsy	Nelly Factor	
21	Rose	Nelly Factor	
22	Mique	Nelly Factor	
23	Hannah	Nelly Factor	
24	Frank	Nelly Factor	
25	July Jr.	Nelly Factor	
26	Liddy	Nelly Factor	
27	Sandy	Nelly Factor	
28	Hetty	Micanopy	

No.	Names	Indian Owners	Remarks
29	Rofina	Micanopy	
30	Linda	Micanopy	
31	Nancy	Micanopy	
32	Rose	Micanopy	
33	Sarah	Micanopy	
34	Traphom	Micanopy	
35	Lewis	Micanopy	
36	Nancy	Micanopy	
37	Bacchus	Micanopy	
38	Susan	Micanopy	
39	Thomas	Micanopy	
40	Jessee	Micanopy	
41	Monday	Micanopy	
42	Tom	Micanopy	
43	Old Primus	Micanopy	
44	Flora	Micanopy	
45	Queen	Micanopy	
46	Abia	Micanopy	
47	Sarah	Holatoochee	
48	Dick	Holatoochee	
49	Ismael	Holatoochee	
50	Peggy	Holatoochee	
51	Tamer	Holatoochee	
52	March	Holatoochee	
53	Kokee	Holatoochee	
54	Hager	Holatoochee	
55	Pussey	Holatoochee	
56	Dosha	Holatoochee	
57	Harriet	Holatoochee	
58	Tennibo	Old Abram	
59	Long Bob	Jumper (free)	Dead
60	Old John	Miccopotpka or Miccologa	
61	Flora	Miccopotpka or Miccologa	
62	William	Miccopotpka or Miccologa	
63	Jim	Miccopotpka or Miccologa	

No.	Names	Indian Owners	Remarks
64	Rose	Miccopotpka or Miccologa	
65	Milly	Miccopotpka or Miccologa	
66	Cesar	Miccopotpka or Miccologa	
67	Eve	Miccopotpka or Miccologa	
68	Phillis	Miccopotpka or Miccologa	
69	Jeffrey	Miccopotpka or Miccologa	
70	Milly	Miccopotpka or Miccologa	
71	Nanny	Miccopotpka or Miccologa	
72	Betsy	Miccopotpka or Miccologa	
73	Joe	Miccopotpka or Miccologa	
74	Titus	Miccopotpka or Miccologa	
75	William	Miccopotpka or Miccologa	
76	Cudjo	Miccopotpka or Miccologa	
77	Ben	Miccopotpka or Miccologa	
78	Rudy	Miccopotpka or Miccologa	
79	Jim	Miccopotpka or Miccologa	
80	Charlotte	Miccopotpka or Miccologa	
81	Harriet	Miccopotpka or Miccologa	
82	Hannah	Miccopotpka or Miccologa	
83	Nancy	Miccopotpka or Miccologa	
84	Sancho	Miccopotpka or Miccologa	
85	Fanny	Miccopotpka or Miccologa	
86	Prince	Miccopotpka or Miccologa	
87	Ned	Miccopotpka or Miccologa	
88	Ned 2nd	Miccopotpka or Miccologa	
89	Jack	Miccopotpka or Miccologa	
90	Rose	A Hallec Hadjo	
91	Plenty	A Hallec Hadjo	Dead
92	Sally	A Hallec Hadjo	
93	Rachael	A Hallec Hadjo	
94	Jack	A Hallec Hadjo	Sold to Jim Casey, who sold him to Alexander, a Trader
95	Cesar	A Hallec Hadjo	
96	Jesse	A Hallec Hadjo	
97	Quaco	A Hallec Hadjo	

No.	Names	Indian Owners	Remarks
98	Boy (Charles)	A Hallec Hadjo	
99	Tina	William Bowlegs	
100	Rose	William Bowlegs	
101	Bob	William Bowlegs	
102	Wan	William Bowlegs	
103	Diana	William Bowlegs	
104	Hester	William Bowlegs	
105	Fanny	William Bowlegs	
106	Lizzy	William Bowlegs	
107	Frederick	William Bowlegs	
108	Rina	William Bowlegs	
109	Peggy	William Bowlegs	
110	Bella	William Bowlegs	
111	Judy	Free	
112	John	Harriet Bowlegs	
113	Polly	Harriet Bowlegs	
114	Amy	Harriet Bowlegs	
115	Davis	Harriet Bowlegs	
116	Jim	Harriet Bowlegs	
117	Rofin	Harriet Bowlegs	
118	Dolly	Harriet Bowlegs	
119	Eliza	Harriet Bowlegs	
120	Dewitt	Harriet Bowlegs	
121	Jack Bowlegs	Harriet Bowlegs	
122	Beck	Waxsi Hadjo	
123	Maria	Waxsi Hadjo	
124	John	Waxsi Hadjo	
125	Fanny	Echo Hadjo	
126	Jenny	Echo Hadjo	Sold
127	Fay	Echo Hadjo	
128	Leah	Echo Hadjo	
129	Liddy	Echo Hadjo	Sold to Dick Toney
130	John	Echo Hadjo	Sold to John Smith
131	Latty	Echo Hadjo	Eufala Tusteenuggee
132	Hester	Echo Hadjo	Eufala Tusteenuggee

No.	Names	Indian Owners	Remarks
133	Ben	Echo Hadjo	
134	Molly	Echo Hadjo	
135	Caty	Colcocholky	
136	Nancy	Colcocholky	
137	Israell	Colcocholky	
138	Betty	Colcocholky	
139	Milay	Colcocholky	
140	Sam Mills	Colcocholky	
141	Toney Philpot	Charley Emathla	
142	Dinah	Charley Emathla	
143	Joni	Charley Emathla	
144	Tom	Charley Emathla	
145	Mary	Charley Emathla	
146	Thursday	Charley Emathla	
147	Linda	Charley Emathla	
148	Hester	Charley Emathla	
149	Nancy	Charley Emathla	
150	Wannah*		Wife and children of
151	Daphney*		Sam Mills.†
152	Andrew*		
153	Limus*		In possession of
154	Sarah*		Osias Hardridge.

*These names are written in Jesup's handwriting and were probably added in 1845, when Jesup was at Fort Gibson; at that time Limus and Sarah were in Hardridge's possession.

†This notation applies to numbers 150-154.

A further notation in Jesup's hand reads, "Holatoochee was to retain his negroes during his life, but they were never to be sold or separated and were to be ultimately free. This was understood to be with their own consent. That chief who rendered us important services is now dead."

LIST C

List of Seminole Indians and Negroes sent from Fort Jupiter to
Tampa Bay for emigration to the West.

(From 25 Cong., 3 Sess., *Executive Document 225*, pp. 74-78)

No.	Names	Age	Sex	Owner's name	Remarks
	Indians				
1	Pah-see-chee	48	Female		
2	Cho Hadjo	24	Male		Son of the above
3	Is-tim-mah-pe-he-yay	18	Male		Son of the above
4	Yo-pot-ho-he-yay	12	Female		Daughter of the above
	Negroes				
1	Jack Bowlegs	36	Male	Harriet Bowlegs	
2	Nancy	30	Female	Micco Potokee	Wife of Jack
3	Sancho	8	Male	Micco Potokee	Son of Nancy
4	Harriet	6	Female	Micco Potokee	Daughter of Nancy
5	Fanny	4	Female	Micco Potokee	Daughter of Nancy
6	Joe	2	Male	Micco Potokee	Son of Nancy
7	Diana	35	Female	Tommy	Wife of Sam Bowlegs
8	Hester	18	Female	Tommy	Daughter of Diana
9	Fanny	15	Female	Tommy	Daughter of Diana
10	Lizzy	9	Female	Tommy	Daughter of Diana
11	Frederick	7	Male	Tommy	Son of Diana
12	Rhina	6	Female	Tommy	Child of Diana

13	Peggy	Female	5	Tommy	Child of Diana
14	Bella	Female	3	Tommy	Child of Diana
15	Possy	Male	60	Free	
16	Fanny	Female	34	Sock-ah-wah-pee	Wife of Possy
17	Elsy	Female	20	Sock-ah-wah-pee	Daughter of Fanny
18	Jenny	Female	19	Sock-ah-wah-pee	Daughter of Fanny
19	Fay	Male	18	Sock-ah-wah-pee	Son of Fanny
20	Leah	Female	15	Sock-ah-wah-pee	Daughter of Fanny
21	Liddy	Female	10	Sock-ah-wah-pee	Daughter of Fanny
22	Lotty	Female	9	Sock-ah-wah-pee	Daughter of Fanny
23	Hester	Female	3	Sock-ah-wah-pee	Daughter of Fanny
24	Dick	Male	25	Ho-lah-too-chee	Husband of Elsey
25	Ben	Male	5	Sock-ah-wah-pee	Son of Elsey
26	Molly	Female	3	Sock-ah-wah-pee	Daughter of Elsey
27	Judy	Female	1	Sock-ah-wah-pee	Daughter of Elsey
28	Winny	Female	9 mo.	Sock-ah-wah-pee	Daughter of Jenny
29	Ned	Male	40	Mocco-Potokee	
30	Maria	Female	28	Harriet Bowlegs	Wife of Ned
31	Polly	Female	11	Harriet Bowlegs	Daughter of Maria
32	Amy	Female	10	Harriet Bowlegs	Daughter of Maria
33	Davy	Male	7	Harriet Bowlegs	Son of Maria
34	Rophile	Male	5	Harriet Bowlegs	Son of Maria
35	Jim	Male	4	Harriet Bowlegs	Son of Maria
36	Charles	Male	60	Nelly Factor	
37	Katy	Female	40	Kool-kie-chah-way	Wife of Charles
38	Jim	Male	21	Kool-kie-chah-way	Son of Katy
39	Nancy	Female	24	Kool-kie-chah-way	Daughter of Katy
40	Hardy	Male	26	Nelly Factor	Husband of Nancy
41	Sally	Female	2	Kool-kie-chah-way	Daughter of Nancy

LIST C (Continued)

No.	Names	Age	Sex	Owner's name	Remarks
42	Plenty	37	Male	Micanopy	
43	Rose	35	Female	Hallek Hajo	Wife of Plenty
44	Wan	15	Male	Plenty	Son of Rose
45	Jack	13	Male	Plenty	Son of Rose
46	Sally	12	Female	Hallek Hajo	Daughter of Rose
47	Rachael	11	Female	Hallek Hajo	Daughter of Rose
48	Caesar	7	Male	Hallek Hajo	Son of Rose
49	Jesse	6	Male	Hallek Hajo	Son of Rose
50	Jesse	22	Male	Micanopy	Brother of Plenty
51	Nancy	37	Female	Micanopy	Sister of Plenty
52	Bacchus	20	Male	Micanopy	Son of Nancy
53	Sue	18	Female	Micanopy	Daughter of Nancy
54	Thomas	3	Male	Micanopy	Son of Nancy
55	Carolina	34	Male	Micanopy	Brother of Plenty
56	Teenar	28	Female	William	Wife of Carolina
57	Rose	5	Female	William	Daughter of Teenar
58	Bob	4	Male	William	Son of Teenar
59	Rophile	36	Male	Free	
60	Hetty	33	Female	Micanopy	Wife of Rophile
61	Belinda	15	Female	Micanopy	Daughter of Hetty
62	Nancy	14	Female	Micanopy	Daughter of Hetty
63	Rose	12	Female	Micanopy	Daughter of Hetty
64	Sarah Ann	11	Female	Micanopy	Daughter of Hetty
65	Straffar	9	Male	Micanopy	Son of Hetty

	Name	Sex	Age	Owner	Relationship
66	Primus	Male	60	Micanopy	
67	Sandy	Male	65	Nelly Factor	
68	Lucy	Female	55	Nelly Factor	Wife of Sandy
69	Hernar	Female	36	Nelly Factor	Daughter of Lucy
70	Rose	Female	21	Nelly Factor	Daughter of Lucy
71	Hannah	Female	19	Nelly Factor	Daughter of Lucy
72	Elsy	Female	16	Nelly Factor	Daughter of Lucy
73	Thomas	Male	14	Nelly Factor	Daughter of Lucy
74	Dembo	Male	30	Nelly Factor	Son of Lucy
75	Juby	Male	40	Nelly Factor	Son of Lucy
76	Suzy	Female	19	Nelly Factor	Husband of Hernar
77	Nanny	Female	17	Nelly Factor	Daughter of Hernar
78	Sanson	Male	14	Nelly Factor	Daughter of Hernar
79	Nelly	Female	12	Nelly Factor	Son of Hernar
80	Kistoba	Male	9	Nelly Factor	Daughter of Hernar
81	Jenny	Female	5	Nelly Factor	Son of Hernar
82	Mag	Female	2	Nelly Factor	Daughter of Hernar
83	Jack	Male	70	Ho-lah-too-chee	Daughter of Rose
84	Sarah	Female	55	Ho-lah-too-chee	Wife of Jack
85	Taymour	Female	27	Ho-lah-too-chee	Daughter of Sarah
86	Ishmael	Male	25	Ho-lah-too-chee	Son of Sarah
87	Phebe	Female	23	Ho-lah-too-chee	Daughter of Sarah
88	Cosar	Male	20	Ho-lah-too-chee	Son of Sarah
89	Peggy	Female	18	Ho-lah-too-chee	Daughter of Sarah
90	Charles (or Tenebo)	Male	34	Abram	Husband of Taymour
91	Hagar	Female	8	Ho-lah-too-chee	Daughter of Taymour
92	Pussy	Female	6	Ho-lah-too-chee	Daughter of Taymour
93	Harriet	Female	4	Ho-lah-too-chee	Daughter of Taymour
94	Hernar	Female	7	Ho-lah-too-chee	Daughter of Phebe

LIST C (Continued)

No.	Names	Age	Sex	Owner's name	Remarks
95	Ned	5	Male	Ho-lah-too-chee	Son of Phebe
96	Old John	60	Male	Micanopy	
97	Flora	50	Female	Micanopy	Wife of Old John
98	Jim	25	Male	Micanopy	Son of Flora
99	Rose	23	Female	Micanopy	Daughter of Flora
100	Milly	21	Female	Micanopy	Daughter of Flora
101	William	20	Male	Micanopy	Son of Flora
102	Hannah	18	Female	Micanopy	Daughter of Flora
103	Cosar	15	Male	Micanopy	Son of Flora
104	Eve	14	Female	Micanopy	Daughter of Flora
105	Dolly	12	Female	Micanopy	Daughter of Flora
106	Sam	11	Male	Micanopy	Son of Flora
107	Phillis	10	Female	Micanopy	Daughter of Flora
108	Jeffrey	6	Male	Micanopy	Son of Flora
109	Milly	3	Female	Micanopy	Daughter of Flora
110	John	25	Male	Harriet Bowlegs	Husband of Rose
111	Betsey	6	Female	Micanopy	Daughter of Rose
112	Joe	5	Male	Micanopy	Son of Rose
113	Titus	2	Male	Micanopy	Son of Rose
114	Tom	24	Male	Micanopy	Husband of Milly
115	Ben	5	Male	Micanopy	Son of Milly
116	Judy	3	Female	Micanopy	Daughter of Milly
117	Sam	53	Male	Micanopy	Brother of Flora
118	Judy	22	Female	Free	Wife of Jim

LIST D

List of Indians and Indian negroes enrolled for emigration to the West,
but who were prevented by sickness from accompanying the above to Tampa.

(From 25 Cong., 3 Sess., *Executive Document 225*, p. 79)

No.	Names	Age	Sex	Owner's name	Remarks
	Indian				
1	Soc-co-yi-chee	20	Male		Son of Pah-se-chee, retained with the army to act as guide
	Negroes				
1	Sam Bowlegs	30	Male	Harriet Bowlegs	Retained to act as interpreter
2	Scipio	28	Male	Harriet Bowlegs	Brother of Sam
3	Bess	30	Female	Micanopy	Wife of Scipio
4	Hard Times	10	Male	Micanopy	Son of Bess
5	Took-hear	9	Female	Micanopy	Daughter of Bess
6	Porris	8	Male	Micanopy	Son of Bess
7	John	7	Male	Micanopy	Son of Bess
8	Black	6	Male	Micanopy	Son of Bess
9	Long Bob	45	Male	Jumper	
10	Flora	33	Female	Micanopy	Wife of Long Bob
11	Eve	15	Female	Micanopy	Daughter of Flora
12	Jenny	6	Female	Micanopy	Daughter of Flora
13	Beck	36	Female	Sow-wee	Husband went off with Jumper
14	Maria	14	Female	Sow-wee	Daughter of Beck

LIST E

List of Negroes as turned over by Lieut. Terrett, 9th April 1838

(From National Archives Record Group 75, Records of the Bureau of Indian Affairs, *Miscellaneous Muster Rolls, 1832-1846*: Seminole)

No.	Names		Sex	Owners	Remarks
1	Plenty		Male	Timpokaitee	
2	Rose		Female	Ahalah Hajo	
3	Sally	Child		Ahalah Hajo	
4	Rachael	Child			
5	Caesar	Child			
6	Jesse	Child			
7	Wan	Child			Died at N.O. 17th May
8	Jack	Child			
9	Jesse		Male	Micanopy	
10	Rufile or Rafail		Male	Micanopy	
11	Hetty		Female	Micanopy	
12	Belinden	Child			
13	Nancy	Child			
14	Rose	Child			
15	Sarah Ann	Child			
16	Staffer	Child			
17	Eliza		Female		
18	Mary	Child			
19	Ledora	Child			
20	Mungo	Child			

No.	Name		Sex		Notes
21	Pussey	Child	Female	Sahtahlahkee	
22	Cumba	Child			
23	Lindy	Child			
24	Latty		Male	Echo Yohola	
25	Old Peter		Male	Thlas cha way	
26	Teena		Female		
27	Primus		Male		
28	Scipio		Male		
29	Daphne		Female		
30	Katy		Female	Thlas chah way	
31	Stephen				
32	Hackly		Male	Echo Fixico	
33	Fanny		Female		Died on board the steamer *South Alabama* 29th May
34	Elsy		Female		
35	Jenny		Female	Detained at Tampa Bay	
36	Leah		Female		
37	Fay		Male		
38	John	Child			
39	Lydia	Child			
40	Lotty	Child			
41	Esther	Child			
42	Ben	Child			
43	Molly	Child			
44	Judy	Child			
45	Winny	Child		Detained at Tampa Bay	
46	Dick		Male	Holatooche	
47	Jane		Female	Echo Fixico	Died on board the steamer *South Alabama* 3d June

LIST E (Continued)

No.	Names		Sex	Owners	Remarks
48	Sylla		Female		
49	Charles		Male		
50	Abram		Male		
51	Flora		Female	Harriet Bowlegs	Detained at N.O. by the Civil Authority
52	Abbey		Female	Harriet Bowlegs	Detained at N.O. by the Civil Authority
53	Jack		Male		
54	Nancy		Female	Micco Pictoca	
55	Sanko	Child			
56	Harriet	Child			Died on board the steamer *South Alabama* 26th May
57	Fanny	Child			
58	Joe	Child			Died at N.O. 25th April
59	Old John		Male	Micco Pictoca	
60	Flora		Female		
61	William		Male		
62	Annah		Female		
63	Caesar		Male		
64	Milly		Female		
65	Eve	Child			
66	Sam	Child			
67	Phyllis	Child			
68	Jeffrey	Child			
69	Milley	Child			
70	Ben	Child			
71	Rudy	Child			

No.	Name		Sex	Owner	Note
72	Old Sam		Male	Massah kee	
73	Peter Jumper		Male	Sillis hai	
74	Hannah		Female		
75	Tom		Male		
76	Friday		Male		
77	Ned	Child			
78	Fanny	Child			
79	Alexander or Allick	Child			
80	Daniel	Child			
81	Clara	Child			
82	Charles	Child	Male	Nelly Factor	Died on board steamer *South Alabama* 2d June
83	Katy		Female	Rulba Chaway	
84	Jim		Male		
85	Nancy		Female		
86	Judy		Female		
87	Hardy		Male	Nelly Factor	

LIST F

List of Negroes as turned over by Lieut. Mack U.S.A. 11th May 1838
(From National Archives Record Group 75, Records of the Bureau of Indian Affairs,
Miscellaneous Muster Rolls, 1832-1846: Seminole)

No.	Names	Owners	Remarks
1	Scipio	Harriet Bowleg	
2	Bessy or Bess	Micanopy	Died on board the steamer *South Alabama* 2d June
3	Hardtimes	Micanopy	
4	Poros	Micanopy	
5	Tuckya	Micanopy	
6	John	Micanopy	
7	Black	Micanopy	
8	Esther	Micanopy	
9	Romeo	Micanopy	
10	Cilla	Micanopy	
11	Peter	Micanopy	
12	Ceasar	Micanopy	
13	William	Micanopy	
14	Aaron	Micanopy	
15	Edsey	Micanopy	
16	Hetty	Micanopy	
17	Silla	Micanopy	
18	Pompey	Micanopy	
19	Billey	Micanopy	

20	Bob	Micanopy
21	Primus	Micanopy
22	Hagar	Harriet Bowleg
23	Delia	Harriet Bowleg
24	Fanny	Harriet Bowleg
25	Bella	Harriet Bowleg
26	Lucy	Harriet Bowleg
27	Adam	Harriet Bowleg
28	Toney	Polly
29	Towsdey	Polly
30	Dinah	Polly
31	Caty	Polly
32	Jinney	Polly
33	Sarah	Polly
34	Tepney	Polly
35	Tom	Polly
36	Lucy	Polly
37	Sam	Tuskeegee
38	Possey	Free
39	Diana	Tomy Bowleg
40	Hester	Tomy Bowleg
41	Fanny	Tomy Bowleg
42	Jim	Tomy Bowleg
43	Lizzy	Tomy Bowleg
44	Frederick	Tomy Bowleg
45	Rhina	Tomy Bowleg
46	Peggy	Tomy Bowleg
47	Bella	Tomy Bowleg

LIST G

List of Negroes received at Tampa Bay; no list turned over,
enrolled under the name of Masters represented by them.
(From National Archives Record Group 75, Records of the Bureau of Indian Affairs,
Miscellaneous Muster Rolls, 1832-1846: Seminole)

No.	Names	Sex	Owners	Remarks
1	Sandy	Male	Nelly Factor	
2	Dambo	Male	Nelly Factor	
3	Betsy	Female	Nelly Factor	
4	Eve	Female	Nelly Factor	
5	Nancy	Female	Nelly Factor	
6	Jane	Female	Nelly Factor	
7	Plenty	Male	Nelly Factor	
8	Lucy	Female	Nelly Factor	
9	Anna	Female	Nelly Factor	
10	Johnson	Male	Nelly Factor	
11	Ester	Female	Nelly Factor	
12	York	Male	Nelly Factor	
13	Timus	Male	Nelly Factor	
14	Nelson	Male	Nelly Factor	
15	Peter	Male	Nelly Factor	
16	Thomas	Male	Nelly Factor	
17	Elky	Female	Nelly Factor	

18	Hannah	Female	Nelly Factor
19	Lybby	Female	Nelly Factor
20	Aphy	Female	Nelly Factor
21	Rose	Female	Nelly Factor
22	Mikey	Male	Nelly Factor
23	Sandy	Male	Nelly Factor
24	Cuffy	Male	Micanopy
25	Pompey	Male	Micanopy
26	Robert	Male	Micanopy
27	Lucy	Female	Micanopy
28	Abby	Female	Micanopy
29	Suky	Female	Micanopy
30	Flora	Female	Micanopy
31	Bayal	Female	Micanopy
32	Carolina	Female	Micanopy
33	Eve	Female	Micanopy
34	Clara	Female	Micanopy
35	Carolina	Male	Micanopy
36	Sam	Male	Micanopy
37	Eliza	Female	Micanopy
38	Pussey	Female	Micanopy
39	Thomas	Male	Micanopy
40	Rose	Female	Micanopy
41	Robert	Male	Micanopy
42	Jim	Male	Micanopy
43	Easter	Female	Micanopy

Died on board the steamer *South Alabama* 26th May

LIST G (Continued)

No.	Names	Sex	Owners	Remarks
44	Bessy	Female	Micanopy	
45	Ester	Female	Micanopy	
46	Margaret	Female	Micanopy	
47	Titus	Male	Micanopy	
48	Cuffy	Male	Micanopy	
49	Rose	Female	Powas Tustanugge	
50	Teena	Female	Powas Tustanugge	
51	Wanna	Female	Powas Tustanugge	
52	Sarah	Female	Powas Tustanugge	
53	Bob	Male	Powas Tustanugge	
54	Tena	Female	Powas Tustanugge	
55	Sarah	Female	Powas Tustanugge	
56	Peggy	Female	Powas Tustanugge	
57	Jack	Male	Powas Tustanugge	
58	Peggy	Female	Powas Tustanugge	
59	Ismael	Male	Powas Tustanugge	
60	Phoeby	Female	Powas Tustanugge	
61	Nat	Male	Powas Tustanugge	
62	Harriet	Female	Powas Tustanugge	
63	Hagar	Female	Powas Tustanugge	
64	Pussey	Female	Powas Tustanugge	

65	Thomas	Female	Powas Tustanugge
66	Caesar	Male	Powas Tustanugge
67	Cornelia	Female	Powas Tustanugge
68	Pompey	Male	Powas Tustanugge
69	Jackson	Male	Powas Tustanugge
70	Maria	Female	Thle Hadjo & William
71	Beck	Female	Thle Hadjo & William
72	Tanneba	Female	Abraham
73	Robert	Female	Free
74	Hector	Female	Ufolla Hadjo

A note on the list reads, "One female Child Born 20th March, died 28th May."

LIST H

A List and Descriptive Roll of Refugee and Captured Slaves Belonging to
Colonel G. Humphreys of Alachua County, Florida,
Who Are in Possession of the Seminole Indians.
(From 25 Cong., 3 Sess., *House Document 225*, pp. 95-96)

No.	Name	Age	Remarks
1	Peter, first	45	Black, tall, straight and well made
2	Peter, second	45	Black, short and bandy-legged
3	Tom	55	Black, well made and gray
4	Sam	46	Black, tall and slender
5	Lancaster	28	Black, medium size
6	Morris	27	Black, stout make, pop eyes
7	Sampson	25	Black, tall, likely negro
8	Joe, first	23	Black, short, stout, and very well made
9	Andrew	21	Black, common size, well made
10	Dick	40	Black, tall, well made
11	Hardy	25	Yellowish, straight and slender, son of Peter, first
12	Worley	28	Black, tall and stout, lame in one foot
13	Ansel	24	Black, tall and large, prominent under lip and very large feet
14	Israel	20	Black, stout
15	Jim	18	Black, common size, brother of Israel
16	Cyrus	16	Black, common size, stammers badly
17	Mungo	45	Black, very tall, has but one hand
18	Joe, second	25	Black, rather tall, but well made
19	Cornelia	55	Black, middling size, mother of Lancaster, Morris, Sampson, Joe, first, Andrew, and Dick

20	Caty, first	60	Black, common size, gray, wife of Tom and decrepit
21	Jane	40	Black, common size, mother of Cyrus, Stepney, and Affy
22	Dolly	35	Black, common size, wife of Sam
23	Sophy	28	Black, tall and slender, wife of Morris
24	Beck	28	Black, good size and likely, wife of Lancaster
25	Amy	28	Black, tall and likely, wife of Peter, first, and mother of Nancy, Lymus, York, and Hester
26	Nancy	24	Black, short and well made, wife of Hardy
27	Hagar	24	Black, middling, daughter of Peggy and mother of Philip
28	Peggy	40	Brown, common size, mother of Hagar
29	Pamilla	45	Black, ordinary size, enticed away by an Indian who has her as his wife
30	Caty, second	24	Yellowish, ordinary size, has a defect in one eye; wife of Sampson
31	Lydia	35	Black, rather tall
32	Nancy	8	Black, common size, child of Peter, first, and Amy
33	Lymus	6	Black, common size, child of Peter, first, and Amy
34	York	4	Black, common size, child of Peter, first, and Amy
35	Hester	2	Black, common size, child of Peter, first, and Amy
36	Cooter	9	Black, common size, child of Lancaster and Beck
37	Tom	7	Black, common size, child of Lancaster and Beck
38	Frank	5	Black, common size, child of Lancaster and Beck
39	A girl	2	Black, common size, child of Lancaster and Beck
40	Stepney	7	Yellowish, ordinary size, child of Jane
41	Affy	5	Yellowish, ordinary size, child of Jane
42	Cyrus	5	Black, ordinary size, child of Sampson
43	Elsey	4	Black, ordinary size, child of Sampson
44	Philip	5	Brownish, ordinary size
45	Child of Hagar		
46	Child of Hagar		
47	Caty, third	50	Black, common size, mother of Nancy, Israel, and Jim

LIST I

List of Seminole Negroe Prisoners turned over at Fort Pike La the March 1838 to
Lieut J. G. Reynolds U.S.M.C. & Disbg. Agt. Ind. Dept. by
Bt. Major R. A. Zanzinger 2d Artillery in obedience to an order from
Major General E. P. Gains U.S.A. dated Head Quarters Western Division,
near New Orleans March 21st 1838. (From National Archives Record Group 75,
Records of the Bureau of Indian Affairs, *Miscellaneous Muster Rolls, 1832-1846: Seminole*)

No.	Names	Sex	Age	Ft.	In.	Owners	Remarks
1	Prince	Male	32	5	10	Micco Potoca	Detained at N.O. by the Civil Authority
2	Noble	Male	25	5	9	Sochtaika & Harriet	Detained at N.O. by the Civil Authority
3	Monday	Male	25	5	8½	Micco Pictoca	
4	Primus	Male	30	5	7	Humphreys & March	
5	Dick	Male	58	5	6½	So pic oc yie	
6	Ben	Male	40	5	10	Holachtoochee	
7	Joe	Male	25	5	8	Micco Pictoca	
8	Bunno	Male	18	5	7½		
9	Wann 1st	Male	75	5	7½	Sawakee, freed by her before her death	
10	Toby	Male	45	5	10½	Micco Pictoca	
11	Dailey	Male	18	5	5½	Than as lith kee	Detained at N.O. by the Civil Authority
12	Toney	Male	45	6	2½	Micco Pictoca	Detained at N.O. by the Civil Authority

No.	Name	Sex	Age			Owner	Remarks
13	Jacob 1st	Male	39	5	7	Holachtoochee	
14	Jacob 2d	Male	29	5	8¼		Detained at N.O. by the Civil Authority
15	Lewis	Male	55	5	6		Detained at N.O. by the Civil Authority
16	Sand 2d	Male	40	6	—	Betzy	
17	Sand 1st	Male	60	5	4	Cleohadjo	
18	Carolina	Male	35	6	—	Betsy	
19	Israel	Male	25	5	7	Betsy	
20	Peter	Male	70	5	6		
21	Wann 2d	Male	30	6	3	William	Detached for Tampa Bay 19th April by order of Genl. Jesup
22	Ned	Male	20	6	2	Harriet & Sochtaika	D tached for Tampa Bay 19th April by order of Genl. Jesup
23	Kibbitt	Male	25	5	4	Micanopy	
24	Fanny	Female	25	5	7	Micco Pictoca	Detained at N.O. by the Civil Authority
25	Juda	Female	30	5	4½	Sochtaika	Detained at N.O. by the Civil Authority
26	Hagah	Female	26	5	6	Micco Pictoca	Detained at N.O. by the Civil Authority
27	Katty 1st	Female	35	5	2	Queen Nelly	Detained at N.O. by the Civil Authority
28	Katty 2d	Female	35	5	2	Micco Pictoca	Detained at N.O. by the Civil Authority
29	Eliza 1st	Female	60	5	6	Has free papers	
30	Eliza 2d	Female	28	5	8¼	Micco Pictoca	Detained at N.O. by the Civil Authority
31	Jean 1st	Female	60	5	7	Micco Pictoca	
32	Jean 2d	Female	28	5	4	Timpokeetee	
33	Silla	Female	35	5	6½	Micco Pictoca	Detained at N.O. by the Civil Authority

LIST I (Continued)

No.	Names	Sex	Age	Ft.	In.	Owners	Remarks
34	Tunee	Female	58	5	—	Micco Pictoca	Detained at N.O. by the Civil Authority
35	Dollie	Female	75	5	4	Micco Pictoca	Detained at N.O. by the Civil Authority
36	Elsy	Female	26	5	2½	Micco Pictoca	Died at N. Orleans 18th April
37	Nelly	Female	30	5	3¾	Micco Pictoca	Detained at N.O. by the Civil Authority
38	Patty 1st	Female	33	5	3¾	Micco Pictoca	One female child born 30th April
39	Patty 2d	Female	10	4	6	Timpokeetee	
40	Flora	Female	12	4	2½	Timpokeetee	
41	Molley	Female	35	5	3¾	Micco Pictoca	Detained at N.O. by the Civil Authority
42	Rinee	Female	22	4	11	Micco Pictoca	
43	Mary	Female	30	5	5½	Micco Pictoca	Detained at N.O. by the Civil Authority
44	Rose	Female	70	5	2	Sochtaika	Died on board the steamer *South Alabama* 31st May
45	Peggy	Female	55	5	2	Micco Pictoca	Detained at N.O. by the Civil Authority
46	Suza	Female	45	5	4½	Micco Pictoca	One Birth a female Child 11th May
47	Linda	Female	10	4	5½	Micco Pictoca	
48	Nancy	Female	12	4	5¼	Micco Pictoca	
49	Pussey	Female	12	4	7½	Micco Pictoca	Detained at N.O. by the Civil

No.	Name	Sex					Notes
50	Sue	Female	16	5	1½	Micco Pictoca	
51	Lucy	Female	10	4	2½	Micco Pictoca	
52	Bessy	Female	50	5	—	Cleohadgo	
53	Wanna	Female	40	5	3	Betsy	
54	Millie	Female	18	5	4	Cleohadgo	
55	Polly	Female	15	5	—	Betsy	Died at N. Orleans 20th May
56	Daphney	Female	9	4	3	Betsy	
57	Lidia	Female	25	5	4	Micanopy	
58	Billy	Male	14	4	11	Micco Pictoca	Detained at N.O. by the Civil Authority
59	Johnny	Male	7	3	11	Micco Pictoca	
60	Toney	Male	14	4	5½	In nich yoe bee hee	
61	Thomas	Male	12	4	4½	Micco Pictoca	Detained at N.O. by the Civil Authority
62	Charles 1st	Male	9	4	2¾	Timpokeetee	
63	Charles 2d	Male	8	3	8	Micco Pictoca	Detained at N.O. by the Civil Authority
64	Ishmael	Male	8	3	11	Micco Pictoca	Detained at N.O. by the Civil Authority
65	Argus	Male	12	4	3½	In nich yo kee	
66	Pompey	Male	6	3	6	Micco Pictoca	
67	Scipio 1st	Male	5	3	5	Micco Pictoca	
68	Lyrus	Male	5	3	7½	Micco Pictoca	Detained at N.O. by the Civil Authority
69	Scipio 2d	Male	1½	2	4	Micco Pictoca	Detained at N.O. by the Civil Authority
70	Sandy	Male	3	2	11	Micco Pictoca	
71	March	Male	14	4	7	Holactoochee	
72	Doc	Male	9	4	—	Holactoochee	
73	Andrew at the breast						

LIST I (Continued)

No.	Names	Sex	Age	Ft.	In.	Owners	Remarks
74	Betty	Female	4	3	1	Timpokeetee	Detained at N.O. by the Civil Authority
75	Tamour	Female	3	3	2	Micco Pictoca	
76	Elsy	Female	3	2	10½	Timpokeetee	Detained at N.O. by the Civil Authority
77	Fanny	Female	4	2	9	Queen Nelly	
78	Katty	Female	5	3	6	Micco Pictoca	
79	Silba	Female	2	2	4	Micco Pictoca	The remark applied to Margaret also exists to Silba, being about one year old
80	Margaret	Female	10	3	11	Micco Pictoca	Left at N.O. by Lieut. Reynolds (with her mother) in consequence of youth, being about three years old instead of ten as here returned
81	Venus	Female	6	3	5	Micco Pictoca	
82	Matilda	Female	4	2	11½	Micco Pictoca	
83	Catherine	Female	5	3	–	Micco Pictoca	
84	Bella	Female	12	4	2	Wann's free	Detained at N.O. by the Civil Authority
85	Patty	Female	4	3	–	Micanopy	

List of Slaves Owned by Micco Potokee or Copiah Yahola,
April 29, 1835.* (From National Archives Microfilm Publications,
Microcopy M234, Roll 802, Seminole D153-56)

No.	Names and Comments
1	Pompey, an old man
2	His wife Dolly with children and grand children as follows:
3	Ned, a man
4	Bob, a man
5	Primus, a man
6-7	Nancy, with her youngest child
8-10	Silla, with two children, Tom and Bella
11	Caty
12-14	Nelly, with children Scippio and Sandy
15-17	Fanny, with children Charles and Margarett
18	Eliza
19	Boner, a boy, son of Nancy
20	Sancho, a boy, son of Nancy
21	Harriett, girl, daughter of Nancy
22	Jeane, oldest daughter of Pompey by former wife
23	John
24	Isaac
25	Toney
26	Pompey
27	Jack
28-29	Molly and child Billy
30	Susey
31-32	Riner and her child Venus
33	Old Tenah, her children and grand children as follows:
34	George
35	Monday
36	Sampson
37	Peter

List of Slaves Owned by Micco Potokee or Copiah Yahola,
April 29, 1835.* (From National Archives Microfilm Publications,
Microcopy M234, Roll 802, Seminole D153-56)

No.	Names and Comments
38-39	Elsey and her child Caty
40-43	Patty and her three children Lucy, Pompey, and small one Matilla
44-48	Mary and her four children Pompey, Ismael, Cyrus and Tayman
49-50	Sally and her child
51	Susey
52	Nancy
53	Linda
54	John, an old man, with his wife
55	Flora and their children and grand children as follows:
56	Jim
57	William
58	Caezar
59	Sam
60-62	Rose, with her children Betsy and Joe
63-64	Milly and her child Ben
65	Hannah
66	Dolly
67	Fillis
68	Jeffrey
69	Eaph
70	Peggy, with children and grand children as follows:
71	Joe
72-74	Hagar and her children Phillis and Ned

*This list was sworn to on April 24, 1835, by Coa Hajo, Billy Hicks, and Hotulsee
Emathla, who said they were in council at Big Swamp after the death of chief
Tuskenehau, when the council decreed that these slaves were the rightful property
of Miccopotokee or Copiah Yahola. However, testimony subsequent to this date
indicates that Miccopotokee received the slaves as guardian for Tuskenehau's
daughters. Compare this list to List L below.

LIST K

List of Negroes who surrendered under a proclamation of Major General Jesup when in command of the Army in Florida, who were entitled to freedom or were to accompany the Seminoles as a part of the Nation under the protection of the United States & were never to be separated or sold. Filed in the Adjutant's Office at Fort Gibson, C.N., July 24th, 1845, by General Thos. S. Jesup.*

(From National Archives Microfilm Publications, *Microcopy M574*, Roll 13, Special File 96: Seminole Claims to Certain Negroes, 1841-1849)

Negroes who surrendered to Genl. Taylor and were brought in by Capt. J. P. Taylor under a proclamation of Major General Jesup's offering freedom to all Seminole Negroes who would separate from the Seminoles and surrender.

No.	Names	By whom claimed	Remarks
1	August	Nelly Factor	Little River
2	Jno. Cowaya (Gopher John)	Free	Freed by old Cowaya; present
3	Old Peter	Micanopy	Present—Free
4	Tina	Micanopy	Dead
5	Pompey	Micanopy	Deep Fork
6	Primus	Micanopy	Little River
7	Dephney	Micanopy	Deep Fork
8	Caty	Micanopy	Present and daughter Fanny
9	Matilda	Micanopy	Absent—over Arkansas River
10	Rat	Micanopy	Present
11	Paris	Micanopy	Dead

LIST K (Continued)

No.	Names	By whom claimed	Remarks
12	Cyrus	Micanopy	Present
	John	Micanopy	Present
13	Sylla	Micanopy	Dead
14	Old Charles	Micanopy	Little River—Free
15	Hannah	Micanopy	Present and daughters Fanny and Sylla and son Peter
16	Old Simon	Micanopy	Little River—Free
17	Clary	Micanopy	Present
18	Elsey and child Dolly	Micanopy	Present
19	Ben	Micanopy	Present
20	Hetty	Micanopy	Sold to Dick Stinson, who sold her
21	Billy	Micanopy	August's sons—Present
22	Bob	Micanopy	Sold to John Drew
23	Peter, a big man	Micanopy	Dead
24	Cuffy	Micanopy	Present
25	Sukey	Micanopy	Present
26	Jim	Micanopy	Present
27	Colly	Micanopy	Present
28	Cesar	Micanopy	Present
29	Aaron	Micanopy	Present
30	Titus	Micanopy	Present

31	Pompey	Micanopy	Present
32	Calina	Micanopy	Present
33	Thomas	Micanopy	Present
34	Pussy	Micanopy	Present
35	Eliza	Micanopy	Present
36	Rosa	Micanopy	Present
37	Sam	Micanopy	Little River
38	Sarah	Micanopy	Present
39	Armstrong	Micanopy	Present
40	Eliza	Micanopy	August's wife—Little River
41	Mary	Micanopy	and Little River
42	Mungo	Micanopy	children Little River
43	Tina	Micanopy	Little River
44	Abbey	Micanopy	Deep Fork
45	Easther	Micanopy	Dead
46	Marguerette	Micanopy	Deep Fork
47	Robbin	Micanopy	Present
48	Jim	Micanopy	Deep Fork
49	Betsy	Micanopy	
50	Freeman	Micanopy	Deep Fork
51	Rabbit (Friday)	Micanopy	Present
52	Buck	Micanopy	Present
53	Aleck	Micanopy	Present
54	Daniel	Micanopy	Dead
55	Clary	Micanopy	Present
56	Latty	Micanopy	Sold
57	Dindy	Micanopy	Deep Fork
58	Cumba	Micanopy	Deep Fork
59	Romeo	Free	Mr. Dupeister paid for him by Congress

LIST K (Continued)

No.	Names	By whom claimed	Remarks
60	Lidda	Micanopy	Little River
61	Kivet	Micanopy	Present
62	Patty	Micanopy	Little River
63	Latty	Echo Hadjo	Present
64	Flora	Echo Hadjo	Deep Fork
65	Jane	Echo Hadjo	Deep Fork
66	Silla	Echo Hadjo	Present—children Mungo, Katy, Latty and Jane
67	Abraham	Echo Hadjo	Present
68	Cuffy	Echo Hadjo	No such person
69	Hager	Bill Bowlegs	Present
70	Boston	Bill Bowlegs	Present
71	Renty	Bill Bowlegs	Present and Free
72	Adam	Bill Bowlegs	Present
73	Lucy	Bill Bowlegs	Present
74	Quash or Quasse	Bill Bowlegs	Present
75	Delia	Bill Bowlegs	Present
76	Harkless	Bill Bowlegs	Deep Fork
77	Sarah	Bill Bowlegs	Present and Free
78	Pompey	Bill Bowlegs	Present
79	Wann	Bill Bowlegs	Absent in Texas

80	Cornelia	Bill Bowlegs	Present—2 children, Pompey and Isaac
81	Jim	Bill Bowlegs	Present
82	Sandy	Bill Bowlegs	Present and Free
83	Nanny	Bill Bowlegs	Present
84	John	Bill Bowlegs	Present
85	Tina	Bill Bowlegs	Present
86	Betsy and child Suky	Nelly Factor	Present
87	Sylla and child Plenty	Nelly Factor	Present
88	Affy and child Mary	Nelly Factor	Present
89	Silvia	Nelly Factor	Present
90	Eve	Nelly Factor	Present
91	Judy	Nelly Factor	Dead
92	John Wan	Nelly Factor	Present
93	Molly	Nelly Factor	Present
94	Phie	Nelly Factor	Present
95	Nancy and child Rose	Nelly Factor	Present
96	Sam Jane	Nelly Factor	Present
97	Bacchus	Nelly Factor	Dead
98	Kitty	Nelly Factor	Present
99	Bob	Nelly Factor	Present
100	Peter	Nelly Factor	Present and Free
101	Hardy	Nelly Factor	Present
102	Amy	Nelly Factor	Present
103	Nessey	Nelly Factor	Sold to Hill, a trader in the Indian Country
104	Limey	Nelly Factor	
105	York	Nelly Factor	
106	Johnston	Nelly Factor	
107	Peggy	Holatoochee	Dead
108	Jack	Holatoochee	Dead

LIST K (Continued)

Negroes brought in by August and Latty at Fort Jupiter

No.	Names	By whom claimed	Remarks
1	July	Nelly Factor	Killed in Florida
2	Tina and 2 children, Hanna and Julia	Nelly Factor	Present
3	Susan	Nelly Factor	Present
4	Nanny	Nelly Factor	Present – 2 children Cuffee and Kibbett
5	Nelly and child Murray	Nelly Factor	Present
6	Sampson	Nelly Factor	Present
7	Kistova	Nelly Factor	Present
8	Jenny	Nelly Factor	Present
9	Norreta	Nelly Factor	Present
10	Pond	Nelly Factor	No such person
11	Rosenti	Nelly Factor	Present
12	Robert	Nelly Factor	Present
13	Kuntessee	Nelly Factor	No such person
14	Phillis	Nelly Factor	Dead
15	Joe	Nelly Factor	Present
16	Sundy	Nelly Factor	Dead
17	Lucy	Nelly Factor	Present and Free
18	Dembo	Nelly Factor	Present
19	Thomas	Nelly Factor	Present
20	Elsey and child Rachel	Nelly Factor	Present
21	Rose	Nelly Factor	Absent at Little River
22	Mike	Nelly Factor	Absent at Little River

23	Hannah	Nelly Factor	Absent at Little River
24	Frank	Nelly Factor	Little River
25	July Jr.	Nelly Factor	Dead
26	Liddy	Nelly Factor	Little River
27	Sandy	Nelly Factor	Dead
28	Hetty	Micanopy	Little River
29	Rofile	Micanopy	Little River, Free
30	Linda	Micanopy	Little River
31	Nancy	Micanopy	Little River
32	Rode	Micanopy	Little River
33	Sarah	Micanopy	Little River
34	Traphom	Micanopy	Little River
35	Lewis	Micanopy	Little River
36	Nancy	Micanopy	Deep Fork
37	Bacchus	Micanopy	Deep Fork
38	Susan	Micanopy	Deep Fork
39	Thomas	Micanopy	Deep Fork
40	Jessee	Micanopy	Present
41	Monday	Micanopy	Deep Fork
42	Tom	Micanopy	Deep Fork
43	Old Primus	Micanopy	Deep Fork
44	Flora	Micanopy	Deep Fork
45	Queen	Micanopy	Present—2 children Bob and Hetty
46	Abia	Micanopy	Deep Fork
47	Sarah	Holatoochee	Dead
	Jack	Holatoochee	Present
48	Dick	Holatoochee	Little River
49	Ismael	Holatoochee	Little River
50	Peggy	Holatoochee	Deep Fork
51	Tamar	Holatoochee	Deep Fork

LIST K (Continued)

No.	Names	By whom claimed	Remarks
52	March	Holatoochee	Little River
53	Kokee	Holatoochee	Little River
54	Hagar	Holatoochee	Deep Fork
55	Pussy	Holatoochee	Present
56	Dosha	Holatoochee	Little River
57	Harriet	Holatoochee	Deep Fork
58	Tennibo	Old Abraham	Dead
59	Long Bob	Jumper (free)	Dead
60	Old John	Miccopotokee	Little River
61	Flora	Miccopotokee	Little River
62	William	Miccopotokee	Little River
63	Jim	Miccopotokee	Little River
64	Rose	Miccopotokee	Deep Fork
65	Milly	Miccopotokee	Deep Fork
66	Caesar	Miccopotokee	Little River
67	Eve	Miccopotokee	Little River
68	Phillis	Miccopotokee	Little River
69	Jeffrey	Miccopotokee	Dead
70	Milly	Miccopotokee	Deep Fork
71	Nanny	Miccopotokee	Deep Fork
72	Betsey	Miccopotokee	Little River
73	Joe	Miccopotokee	Dead
74	Titus	Miccopotokee	Deep Fork

75	Williams	Miccopotokee	Dead
76	Cudjo	Miccopotokee	Dead
77	Ben	Miccopotokee	Little River
78	Rudy	Miccopotokee	Deep Fork
79	Jim	Miccopotokee	Deep Fork
80	Charlotte	Miccopotokee	Dead
81	Harriett	Miccopotokee	Deep Fork
82	Hannah	Miccopotokee	Dead
83	Nancy	Miccopologa	Deep Fork
84	Sancho	Miccopologa	Deep Fork
85	Fanny	Miccopologa	Deep Fork
86	Prince	Miccopologa	Dead
87	Ned	Miccopologa	Little River
88	Ned (2nd)	Miccopologa	
89	Jack	Miccopologa	Deep Fork
90	Rose and child John	A Hallec Hadjo	Present
91	Plenty	A Hallec Hadjo	Dead
92	Sally and child Joe	A Hallec Hadjo	Present
93	Rachel	A Hallec Hadjo	Present
94	Jack	A Hallec Hadjo	Present and Free
95	Caesar	A Hallec Hadjo	Sold him to Jim Carey, who sold him to Alexander a trader
96	Cuffee	A Hallec Hadjo	Present and Free
97	Jessee	A Hallec Hadjo	Present
98	Quaco	A Hallec Hadjo	Present
99	Boy (Charles)	A Hallec Hadjo	Present
99	Tina	William Bowlegs	Present
100	Rose	William Bowlegs	Present
101	Bob	William Bowlegs	Present
102	Wan	William Bowlegs	Present

LIST K (Continued)

No.	Names	By whom claimed	Remarks
103	Diana	William Bowlegs	Dead
104	Hester	William Bowlegs	Present—3 children, Vina, Dinda and Colly
105	Fanny	William Bowlegs	Present
106	Frederick	William Bowlegs	Present
107	Lirry	William Bowlegs	Present
108	Rina	William Bowlegs	Deep Fork
109	Peggy	William Bowlegs	Little River
110	Bella	William Bowlegs	Present
111	Judy	Free	Burnt up at Deep Fork
112	John	Harriett Bowlegs	Deep Fork
113	Polly	Harriett Bowlegs	Little River
114	Amy	Harriett Bowlegs	Dead
115	Davis	Harriett Bowlegs	Little River
116	Jim	Harriett Bowlegs	Little River
117	Rofile	Harriett Bowlegs	Arkansas River
118	Dolly	Harriett Bowlegs	Little River
119	Eliza	Harriett Bowlegs	Little River
120	Dewitt	Harriett Bowlegs	Little River
121	Jack Bowlegs	Harriett Bowlegs	Little River
122	Beck	Waxsi Hadjo	Little River
123	Maria	Waxsi Hadjo	Little River
124	John	Waxsi Hadjo	Little River
125	Fanny	Echo Hadjochee	Dead

126	Tenny	Echo Hadjochee	Deep Fork
127	Fay	Echo Hadjochee	Present
128	Leah and child Lizzy	Echo Hadjochee	Present
129	Liddy	Echo Hadjochee	Sold to Dick Toney
130	John	Echo Hadjochee	Sold to John Smith
131	Latty	Echo Hadjochee	Eufale Tustanuggee
132	Hester	Echo Hadjochee	Eufale Tustanuggee
133	Ben	Echo Hadjochee	Little River
134	Molly	Echo Hadjochee	
135	Caty	Colcocholky	Claimed by Mrs. Leonard
136	Nancy	Colcocholky	Run off by traders
137	Israel	Colcocholky	Deep Fork
138	Betty	Colcocholky	Sold in Cherokee Nation
139	Milay	Colcocholky	Free and Present
140	Sam Mills	Colcocholky	North Fork
141	Toney Philpot	Charley Emartla	North Fork
142	Dinah	Charley Emartla	Dead
143	Dice	Charley Emartla	North Fork
144	Tom	Charley Emartla	North Fork
145	Mary	Charley Emartla	North Fork
146	Thursday	Charley Emartla	North Fork
147	Linda	Charley Emartla	Dead
148	Hester	Charley Emartla	North Fork
149	Nancy	Charley Emartla	Sold and run off
150	Limas	Wife and children of	Sold and run off
151	Sarah		Present
152	Wannah	Tom Mills	Present
153	Dephney	Child of Tom Mills	Present
	Katey	Jumper	Present
154	Andrew	Child of Tom Mills	

LIST K (Continued)

No.	Names	By whom claimed	Remarks
	Washington	Seminole Nation	Present
	Hannah	Seminole Nation	Present
	Joe	Seminole Nation	Present
	Mary	Seminole Nation	Present
	Flora	Seminole Nation	Present
	July	Seminole Nation	Present
	Dolly	Seminole Nation	Present

Negroes who came in at Peas Creek

No.	Names	By whom claimed	Remarks
1	Adam	Harriett Bowlegs	Present
2	Lucy	Holatoochee	Present
3	Dinda	Holatoochee	Dead
4	Rabbit	Holatoochee	Present (son of Lucy)
5	Fay	Holatoochee	Deep Fork
6	Peggy	William Bowlegs	Little River
7	Colby	William Bowlegs	Deep Fork
8	Scilla	William Bowlegs	Deep Fork
9	Toney	William Bowlegs	Deep Fork
10	Pussy	William Bowlegs	Deep Fork
11	Ned	William Bowlegs	Deep Fork

12	Abraham	William Bowlegs	Present
13	Andrew	William Bowlegs	Deep Fork
14	Jesse	William Bowlegs	Deep Fork
15	Mary	William Bowlegs	Deep Fork
16	Levi	William Bowlegs	Deep Fork
17	Isaac	William Bowlegs	Dead
18	Judy	William Bowlegs	Deep Fork
19	Jim	William Bowlegs	Dead
20	Jane	William Bowlegs	Deep Fork
21	Harkless	William Bowlegs	Deep Fork
22	Wally	Charley Emartla	North Fork
23	Pomilla	Charley Emathla	North Fork
24	Sarah	Creek Nation	

* The list is endorsed as follows: "The Seminole Negroes have been turned over to the Chiefs of that Nation in the presence of the Agent in accordance of the within list. Fort Gibson, C.N. January 2, 1849. W. G. Belknap, Brig. Genl. Bvt., Comdg." Two different handwritings appear on the list. The numbered names and most of the names of owners are in Jesup's handwriting, while the unnumbered names and most of the remarks are in another handwriting.

LIST L*

List of Negroes Belonging to Capitcha Micco,
According to Decision of Council.
(From National Archives Microfilm Publications, *Microcopy M234,*
Roll 802, Seminole D153-56)

No.	Name	Remarks
1	Old John	
2	Flora	
3	Jim	
4	Rose	
5	Milla	
6	William	
7	Hannah	
8	Caesar	
9	Eve	
10	Sam	
11	Phillis	
12	Jeffrey	
13	Jeffrey	
14	Ben	
15	Rose	
16	Betsy	
17	Titus	
18	Elsy	Sold
19	Toby	Sold
20	Monday	
21	Nancy	
22	Linder	Sold
23	Susy	
24	Jonny	
25	Samson	
26	Patty	

* This list was apparently made by Marcellus Duval in 1849; it was taken from a certified copy of the original, which was in the hands of Halleck Tustenuggee in 1855. Compare it with List J, above.

On the back of the list appear the following notes: "Caty—Assil's daughter; Eve—Cuffy's child; Fanny—Big Frances' sister; Sylvia—Big Frances' daughter; Jack Bowlegs—Big Frances' husband; Venus—Riner's daughter; Lucy—Pompey's daughter, Jim's wife, child of Venus; Sampson—Tiner's son; Phillis—Blind John's daughter; Sandy run off; Sarah—Primus' wife."

No.	Name	Remarks
27	Lucy	
28	Pompey	
29	Martilla	
30	Pussee	Sold
31	Silas	
32	Scipio	
33	Tamar	
34	Ismeal	Issue do not belong
35	Caty	
36	Fanny	
37	Eliza	Sold
38	Caty	Sold
39	Cillee	Sold
40	Nancy	
41	Nelly	
42	Bones	
43	Sanco	
44	Fanny	Sold
45	Thomas	Sold
46	Margaret	
47	Sylvia	
48	Scipio	
49	Sandy	
50	Hagar	Issue do not belong
51	Sampson	
52	Isaac	
53	Jack	
54	Sary	
55	Molly	
56	Riner	
57	Venus	
58	Billy	
59	Pompey	
60	Ned	Sold
61	Bob	
62	Sampson	
63	Charles	
64	John	
65	Small Girl	Daughter of Riner
66	Son of Sarah	

Bibliography

I. MANUSCRIPTS AND TRANSCRIPTS

Foreman Transcripts. Indian Archives Division, Oklahoma Historical
  Society. 7 vols.
Indian-Pioneer History. Indian Archives Division, Oklahoma Historical
  Society. 116 vols.
Records of the Bureau of Census (National Archives Record Group 29).
  Population Schedules, 1860: Arkansas [Slave Schedules] (National
  Archives Microfilm Publications, *Microcopy M653,* Roll 54).
Records of the Bureau of Indian Affairs (National Archives Record Group
  75).
  Chickasaw Removal Records: Census and Muster Rolls, 1837-39.
  Choctaw Removal Records: Census Roll, 1831 (Census of North West
  District).
  Copies of Records, ca. 1823-1860: Seminole and Seminole Emigration
  Creek Removal Records: Census, 1833.
  Documents Relating to the Negotiation of Ratified and Unratified
    Treaties with Various Indian Tribes, 1801-1869 (National Archives
    Microfilm Publications, *Microcopy T494,* Roll 9).
  Miscellaneous Muster Rolls, 1836-46: Seminole and Apalachicola.
  Records of the Commissary General Subsistence: Letters Received
    and Seminole.
  Records of the Office of Indian Affairs: Letters Received, Letters Sent,
    and Report Books (National Archives Microfilm Publications, *Micro-
    copy M234,* Rolls 225, 226, 227, 228, 289, 291, 800, 801, 802,
    806, 833, 836, 837, 923, and 924; *Microcopy M21,* Rolls 28, 30,

    31, 32, 33, 34, 35, 36, 38, 40, 41, 57, 58, 59, and 60; *Microcopy
    M348,* Rolls 2, 3, and 10).
  Records Relating to Loyal Creek Claims, 1869-70.
  Special Files of the Office of Indian Affairs, 1807-1904: Files 87, 96,
    and 277 (National Archives Microfilm Publications, *Microcopy M574,*
    Rolls, 11, 13, and 75).
Records of the Office of the Adjutant General (National Archives Record
  Group 94). General Jesup's Papers: Letters Received, Letters Sent,
  and Orders.
Records of the United States Army Continental Commands, 1821-1920
  (National Archives Record Group 393).
    Fort Gibson: Letters Received, Letters Sent, and Volume "Indian
      Affairs."
    Frontier District: Seventh Army Corps and Department of Arkansas,
      Letters Received, 1865-1866.
    Second and Seventh Military Departments: Letters Received and Letters
      Sent.
    Second Military Department: Letters Sent.

II. FEDERAL DOCUMENTS

Hodge, Frederick Webb, ed., *Handbook of American Indians North of
    Mexico.* 2 pts. Washington: Government Printing Office, 1907 and 1910.
Kappler, Charles J., comp., *Indian Affairs, Laws and Treaties.* 2nd ed.
    3 vols. Washington: Government Printing Office, 1904.
Official Opinions of the Attorneys General of the United States. Wash-
    ington, 1852-
Swanton, John R., *Early History of the Creek Indians and Their Neigh-
    bors,* Bureau of American Ethnology Bulletin No. 73. Reprint ed.
    New York: Johnson Reprint Corporation, 1970.
_____*The Indians of the Southeastern United States,* Bureau of Ameri-
    can Ethnology Bulletin No. 137. Reprint ed. New York: Greenwood
    Press, 1969.
United States Congress.
    25 Congress, 2 Session, *House Document 327.*
    25 Congress, 2 Session, *House Executive Document 381.*
    25 Congress, 3 Session, *House Executive Document 225.*
    25 Congress, 3 Session, *Senate Document 88.*
    26 Congress, 1 Session, *Senate Document 1.*
    26 Congress, 2 Session, *House Executive Document 2.*

27 Congress, 2 Session, *House Document 55.*
27 Congress, 2 Session, *House Executive Document 2.*
27 Congress, 3 Session, *House Executive Document 2.*
28 Congress, 1 Session, *House Executive Document 2.*
28 Congress, 2 Session, *House Executive Document 2.*
29 Congress, 1 Session, *House Executive Document 2.*
29 Congress, 2 Session, *House Executive Document 4.*
30 Congress, 1 Session, *House Report 724.*
32 Congress, 1 Session, *House Executive Document 2.*
33 Congress, 2 Session, *House Executive Document 15.*
38 Congress, 1 Session, *House Executive Document 1.*
38 Congress, 2 Session, *House Executive Document 1.*
39 Congress, 1 Session, *House Executive Document 1.*
41 Congress, 1 Session, *House Executive Document 1.*
49 Congress, 1 Session, *Senate Report 1278.*
50 Congress, 1 Session, *Senate Executive Document 166.*
United States Department of the Interior. *Report of the Secretary of the Interior.* Washington: Government Printing Office, 1866.
United States Department of War. *The War of the Rebellion: A Compilation of the Official Records of the Union and Confederate Armies.* 130 vols. Washington: Government Printing Office, 1880-1901.

III. BOOKS

Abel, Annie Heloise, *The American Indian Under Reconstruction.* Cleveland: The Arthur H. Clark Company, 1925.
Allsopp, Fred W., *History of the Arkansas Press for a Hundred Years and More.* Little Rock: Parke-Harper Publishing Company, 1922.
Britton, Wiley, *Memoirs of the Rebellion on the Border, 1863.* Chicago: Cushing, Thomas & Co., Publishers, 1882.
Coe, Charles H., *Red Patriots: The Story of the Seminoles.* Reprint ed. Gainesville: University Presses of Florida, 1974.
Constitution, Laws, and Treaties of the Chickasaws. Tishomingo City, Ind. Ter.: E. J. Foster, 1860.
Debo, Angie, *The Rise and Fall of the Choctaw Republic.* Norman: University of Oklahoma Press, 1934.
_____*The Road to Disappearance.* Norman: University of Oklahoma Press, 1941.
Foreman, Grant, *The Five Civilized Tribes.* Norman: University of Oklahoma Press, 1934.

———— *Indian Removal*. Norman: University of Oklahoma Press, 1932.

Gibson, Arrell M., *The Chickasaws*. Norman: University of Oklahoma Press, 1971.

Giddings, Joshua R., *The Exiles of Florida*. Columbus, Ohio: Follett, Foster and Company, 1858.

Hawkins, Benjamin, *Letters of Benjamin Hawkins, 1796-1806,* Collections of the Georgia Historical Society, Vol. 9. Savannah: The Morning News, 1916.

———— *A Sketch of the Creek Country in the Years 1798 and 1799,* Collections of the Georgia Historical Society, Vol. 3, Pt. 1. New York: William Van Norden Printer, 1848.

Hitchcock, Ethan Allen, *A Traveler in Indian Territory: The Journal of Ethan Allen Hitchcock, late Major-General in the United States Army.* Edited by Grant Foreman. Cedar Rapids, Iowa: The Torch Press, 1930.

Laws of the Cherokee Nation: Adopted by the Council at Various Periods. Tahlequah, Ind. Ter.: Cherokee Advocate Office, 1852.

Loughridge, R. M., comp. *English and Muskokee Dictionary*. Reprint ed. N. p., 1964.

McReynolds, Edwin C., *The Seminoles*. Norman: University of Oklahoma Press, 1957.

Mahon, John K., *History of the Second Seminole War, 1835-1842*. Gainesville: University of Florida Press, 1967.

Porter, Kenneth Wiggins, *The Negro on the American Frontier*. New York: Arno Press and The New York Times, 1971.

Potter, Woodburne, *The War in Florida*. Reprint ed. Ann Arbor: University Microfilms, Inc., 1966.

[Simmons, William Hayne] *Notices of East Florida*. Reprint ed. Gainesville: University of Florida Press, 1973.

Wardell, Morris L., *A Political History of the Cherokee Nation, 1838-1907*. Norman: University of Oklahoma Press, 1938.

Waring, Antonio J., ed., *Laws of the Creek Nation,* University of Georgia Libraries Miscellaneous Publications No. 1. Athens: University of Georgia Press, 1960.

IV. PERIODICAL MATERIAL

Arkansas Gazette, June 13, 1838, and June 27, 1838.

Davis, J. B., "Slavery in the Cherokee Nation," *Chronicles of Oklahoma,* 11 (December 1933), 1056-1072.

Doran, Michael F., "Population Statistics of Nineteenth Century Indian Territory," *Chronicles of Oklahoma,* 53 (Winter 1975-76), 492-515.

Bibliography

Duncan, James W., "Interesting Ante-Bellum Laws of the Cherokees Oklahoma History," *Chronicles of Oklahoma,* 6 (June 1928), 17⌐

Foreman, Carolyn Thomas, "Billy Bowlegs," *Chronicles of Oklahoma,* 32 (Winter 1955), 512-532.

_____"Early History of Webbers Falls," *Chronicles of Oklahoma,* 29 (Winter 1951-52), 444-483.

_____ "The Jumper Family of the Seminole Nation," *Chronicles of Oklahoma,* 34 (Autumn 1956), 272-285.

Graebner, Norman Arthur. "Pioneer Indian Agriculture in Oklahoma," *Chronicles of Oklahoma,* 23 (Autumn 1945), 232-248.

_____ "The Public Land Policy of the Five Civilized Tribes," *Chronicles of Oklahoma,* 23 (Summer 1945), 107-118.

Halliburton, R., Jr., "Origins of Black Slavery Among the Cherokees," *Chronicles of Oklahoma,* 52 (Winter 1974-75), 483-496.

Jeltz, Wyatt F., "The Relations of the Negroes and Choctaw and Chickasaw Indians," *Journal of Negro History,* 33 (January 1948), 24-37.

Littlefield, Daniel F., Jr., and Mary Ann, "The Beams Family: Free Blacks in Indian Territory," *Journal of Negro History,* 61 (January 1976), 16-35.

McLoughlin, William G., "Red Indians, Black Slavery and White Racism: America's Slaveholding Indians," *American Quarterly,* 24 (October 1974), 366-385.

Meserve, John Bartlett, "Chief Opothleyahola," *Chronicles of Oklahoma,* 9 (December 1931), 440-453.

"Oklahoma Historic Sites," *Chronicles of Oklahoma,* 36 (Autumn 1958), 282-314.

Porter, Kenneth Wiggins, "Negro Guides and Interpreters in the Early Stages of the Seminole War, December 28, 1835–March 6, 1837," *Journal of Negro History,* 35 (April 1950), 174-188.

_____ "Three Fighters for Freedom," *Journal of Negro History,* 28 (January 1943), 51-73.

Sturdevant, William C., "Creek into Seminole," *North American Indians in Historical Perspective.* Edited by Eleanor Burke Leacock and Nancy Oesterich Lurie. New York: Random House, 1971.

Trickett, Dean, "The Civil War in the Indian Territory," *Chronicles of Oklahoma,* 18 (December 1940), 266-280.

Wright, Muriel, "Seal of the Seminole Nation," *Chronicles of Oklahoma,* 34 (Autumn 1956), 262-271.

Index

Abolitionism, 156, 180, 201

Abraham, 10, 12, 22, 28, 39, 101, 125, 127, 193; character of, 171-172; as emissary, 28; as interpreter, 25, 74, 79, 86, 100, 101, 105, 111, 156; Jesup's promises to, 25, 30; loyalty of, 21; negotiations by, 18; slaves owned by, 50; treaty signed by, 18

Acculturation, 199-200, 202

Africa: proposed colonization in, 39, 121

Ah-halac Hadjoche, 53

Alachua, 7

Alachua band, 3

Alligator, 11, 20, 24, 57, 83, 89, 105, 107; claims of, 76; at Dade's Massacre, 28; as delegate to Florida, 76; emigration of, 45; surrender of, 28; in Washington, 86-88

Amalgamation, 171, 193, 200, 202

Annuities, 77, 90, 105, 188

Apalachee, 3

Apalachicola bands, 3, 30

Apalachicola Indians: blacks among, 49, 50, 54; blacks intermarried with, 53; emigration of, 50; removal of, 49; slave raids among, 54

Apopka, Lake, 16

Arbuckle, Gen. Matthew, 73, 74, 103, 104, 107, 112, 114, 126, 130, 131, 140, 145, 148, 155; blacks distrusted by, 48; blacks protected by, 106; and colonization, 121; Duval distrusted by, 141-142, 144; and slave claims, 44, 47, 71

Arkansans: Indians feared by, 44

Arkansas, 157, 173; blacks in, 171; blacks taken to, 164; Indian allies sought by, 180, 182

Armistead, Bvt. Brig. Gen Walker K., 123; command of, 50-52; war policy of, 50

Armstrong, William, 73, 76, 81, 87, 111; attitude of, toward blacks, 71, 81; as negotiator,

48, 90; and slave claims, 72;
and slave issue, 83
Army: blacks in, 184, 188
Army officers: blacks protected
by, 105, 106, 129, 139-140,
49; blacks supported by, 103-
105, 109, 112-113; sympathy
of, for blacks, 120
Aspberry, Daniel Boone, 166,
167, 168, 170, 172, 174;
slave claims of, 163-165
August, 26, 104, 134, 152; children of, 108; promises to, 27;
surrender of, 27

Barnet, Casena, 84
Barnet, David, 21, 74
Barnet, James, 82
Barnet, Polly (black), 21; family
of, 42-43, 63 n.42, 94 n.18
Barnet, Toney (black), 102, 109,
110, 125; claim of, 95 n.37;
Creek claims for, 74, 82; emi-
gration of, 50; family of, 50,
108; flight of, 82; as interpre-
ter, 74, 79, 82, 111; protec-
tion of, 84, 134; surrender of,
21
Barnet, William, 82
Battles. *See* locations of specific
battles
Baxter Springs (Kan.), 184
Beams family, 172, 173
Belknap, Brig. Gen. William G.,
142, 144, 146, 152, 154, 155;
blacks advised by, 149
Bell, John, 72, 73, 76
Bell, P. H., 155
Ben, 17
Ben (second), 17
Black Dirt, 68, 104

Blacks, Apalachicola: numbers
of, 50. *See also* Slaves
Blacks, Cherokee: numbers of,
200; as property owners, 201.
See also Free blacks; Freedmen; Slaves
Blacks, Chickasaw: numbers of,
201-202. *See also* Free blacks;
Freedmen; Slaves
Blacks, Choctaw: numbers of,
201. *See also* Free blacks;
Freedmen; Slaves
Blacks, Creek: as blacksmiths,
200; flight of, to Kansas, 183;
as interpreters, 200; number
of, 200. *See also* Free blacks;
Freedmen; Slaves
Blacks, Seminole: alliance of,
with Seminoles, 4-5; in army,
184, 188; bands of, 193;
blacks owned by, 50, 101,
127; as blacksmiths, 101, 191;
classification of, 15, 58-59,
75, 123; as captives, 16-17,
24, 25, 38, 150, 163, 165; as
carpenters, 191; as cause of
war, 10-11; colonization of,
39, 110-111, 121; Creek
claims for, 38, 39, 70, 74, 82;
crimes committed by, 113,
138, 152, 171; criticism of,
71, 122; disarmament of,
140-144, 147; emancipation
of, 54, 63 n.42, 102, 120,
134; emigration of, 43, 45,
49, 50, 51, 52, 53, 55, 56,
57-58, 155, 176; as farmers,
8, 31, 98, 121, 176, 191;
at Fort Gibson, 105-106,
107-108, 109, 110, 113, 119,
120, 130, 144, 183; as fugi-

tive slaves, 120; as guides, 25, 30, 34 n.40, 87, 116 n.7; harassment of, 103; hostility of, 25; as hunters, 8, 143; imprisonment of, 16; as interpreters, 6, 8, 18, 25, 27, 30, 45, 54, 55, 57, 58, 82, 87, 88, 100-101, 102, 104, 105, 107, 111, 127, 147, 156, 185; Jesup's appeal for, 87; Jesup's promises to, 87, 121, 125; Jesup's purchase of, 17; in Kansas, 183-184; loyalty of, 29; marriage of, to Indians, 42, 53, 63 n.42; and Mexico, 147- 148, 153; numbers of, 7, 8, 12, 27, 43, 50, 51, 176, 179 n.39; officials' distrust of, 21-22, 48; officials distrusted by, 101; as overseers, 152; passes received by, 134, 155; as plunder, 16; as prisoners of war, 23, 41; as property, 41; as property owners, 29, 84, 88, 107, 128, 129, 149, 171, 176; protection given to, 103-105, 109, 120, 129, 139-140, 149; relations with Seminoles severed by, 104, 105, 119; removal of, 19, 27, 30, 31, 41, 49; and removal policy, 10, 11-12, 18; return of, to servitude, 124-125, 132-133; in Second Seminole War, 49-55; and Seminole affairs, 197; Seminole attitudes toward, 12, 79-80, 138, 199; Seminoles defied by, 133, 134, 138-139, 140-141, 143; Seminoles influenced by,

9, 10, 11-12, 18, 47, 70, 172; separate towns for, 8, 121, 132; surrender of, 26; teaching of, 112, 121; as threats to slaveholders, 7, 9, 78, 79-81, 122; tribal adoption of, 186, 187, 193; unrest among, 130-131; as wheelwrights, 191; weapons carried by, 79, 84, 127, 130, 139, 140, 143; in warfare, 6-7, 12; war leaders among, 18, 20-21. *See also* Free blacks; Freedmen; Slaves

Blacksmiths, 101, 191, 200
Blake, Luther, 156
Blunt, 9, 49, 50
Blunt, Brig. Gen. James G., 184
Bob, 22, 25
Bonneville, Maj. B. L. E., 114
Bowlegs (Eneah Micco), 21, 57, 63 n.42; as slave owner, 42
Bowlegs, Billy, 145, 147, 156, 182, 183; emigration of, 175; slaves of, 151-152, 160 n.35
Bowlegs, Harriet, 156, 158, 165; as slave owner, 42, 111; slaves of, 50, 51, 118 n.27
Bowlegs, Jim (black), 148, 151, 155; as interpreter, 147; as overseer, 152
Bowlegs, Sam (black), 27
Brazos River, 147, 185
Bribery: to induce surrender, 50
Brooke, Gen. George M., 43, 152, 155
Broom, The, 105
Brown, Charley, 169
Brown, Isaac, 54
Bruner, Caesar, 185
Buchanan, James, 182

Buisson, Fred, 47
Bull, John, 50
Butler, Pierce M., 77, 101, 104,
    146; as negotiator, 90

Cabin Creek, Battle of, 184
Caddo Indians, 153
Call, Richard Keith, 24, 54
Canada, 165
Canadian River (Ind. Ter.), 193;
    Seminole settlement on, 68
Capers, Le Grand G., 51, 52, 58
Capichee, 150, 151
Capichee Micco. *See* Kinhijah
Carpenters, 191
Carr, Tom, 149
Casey, Lieut. John C., 22, 30,
    42
Cavallo, John (Gopher John),
    25, 26; capture of, 24; emi-
    gration of, 57; escape of,
    20, 25; as hostage, 19; nego-
    tiations by, 18; promises to,
    27; surrender of, 28. *See also*
    Gopher John
Charles, 21
Charlotte Harbor (Fla.), 25
Chattahoochee River (Ga.), 3
Cherokee Indians: Confederate
    appeal to, 180, 182; emigra-
    tion of, 45; influence of
    blacks feared by, 78, 79-81;
    peace delegation of, 25-26;
    pro-Union faction of, 184;
    racial prejudice among, 191;
    Seminole difficulties with,
    75-77; Seminoles influenced
    by, 199-200; as slaveholders,
    78, 108, 110, 180; slavery
    among, 12, 200-201; treat-
    ment of freedmen by, 203

Cherokee Nation: Seminoles
    in, 57, 68, 70-71, 75-76,
    78, 83, 95 n.32, 115 n.1
Cherokee Outlet, 175
Chiaha band, 3
Chickasaw Indians: Confed-
    eracy joined by, 182; Creeks
    attacked by, 182; racial prej-
    udice among, 191; slavery
    among, 13, 201-202; treat-
    ment of freedmen by, 203
Chickasaw Nation: Seminoles
    in, 183
Chiefs, Creek, 83, 128, 132;
    Seminole union opposed by,
    77; slave claims heard by,
    71, 84, 150, 163, 169-170;
    subagent influenced by, 83
Chiefs, Seminole: blacks received
    by, 131-133; land approved
    by, 70, loss of power feared
    by, 70; promises of, 133;
    slave claims heard by, 71, 84,
    104, 168; subagent distrusted
    by, 144
Chitto Harjo, 134
Chitto Larni, 170
Chocachatti, 3
Choctaw Indians: Confederacy
    joined by, 182; Creeks attacked
    by, 182; racial prejudice among,
    191; recruitment of, 23; slav-
    ery among, 13, 201; treatment
    of freedmen by, 203
Chucote Harjo, 185
Chupco, John, 182, 183, 185,
    189
Chustenahlah, Battle of, 183,
    194 n.5
Chustolasah, Battle of, 183,
    194 n.5

Civil War, 197; Five Civilized
Tribes in, 182-185; in Indian
Territory, 182-185
Clark, Maj. Isaac, 16, 40, 47, 52
Clarke, George W., 76
Clarksville (Ark.), 45
Clary, 129
Clifford, Matthew, 125
Clinch, Gen. D. L., 51
Cloud, George, 105, 143, 187
Cloud (Yaholoochee), 18, 20,
24, 26, 27, 71
Coa Hadjo, 11, 20, 71, 104; as
guide, 26; seizure of, 24; as
slave owner, 50
Cohabitation, 42, 201
Cohia, Charles, 57
Cohia, John. *See* Cavallo, John
Colbert family, 201
Colkeechowa, 108, 109; as
slave owner, 38
Collins, Nathaniel F., 46, 48,
49; as slave agent, 39, 43-44
Colonization: of blacks, 39,
110-111, 121
Comanche Indians, 146, 153
Confederate States of America:
agent appointed by, 183;
difficulties of, in keeping
promises, 183-184; Indian
allies sought by, 182;
Indian treaties with, 182,
186; negotiator sent by,
182
Conrad, Charles M., 157
Coody, Daniel, 110
Coody, Mrs. Susan, 108, 110
Cooley, Dennis N., 185, 186,
189
Cooper, Douglas H., 182
Coosa Tustenuggee, 50, 57

Corn; cultivation of, 76, 81, 89,
98, 121, 192
Cotsa Tustenucoochee, 76
Cotsee Tustenugee, 18
Cotton, 80
Council house, Seminole, 98,
175
Cowaya, John. *See* Cavallo,
John
Cow Bayou, 147
Cow Keeper, 3, 42
Cox, John T., 182
Crawford, T. Hartley, 48, 56,
70, 71, 72, 84, 86, 87, 88,
104
Creek Confederacy: bands of, 3,
4; Seminoles as part of, 5
Creek Indians: attitude of,
toward slaves, 119; com-
plaints of, about blacks, 112,
122; Confederacy joined by,
182; disputes of, with
Seminoles, 145, 149-150;
flight of, to Kansas, 182-183;
free blacks among, 144, 172;
interference of, in Seminole
affairs, 141, 144, 149; military discharge of, 17; pro-
Confederate faction of, 182;
pro-Union faction of, 182,
183; removal of, 17; Seminole
fear of, 10, 68, 70, 76, 81,
91; Seminole lands invaded
by, 154; Seminoles controlled
by, 91; Seminoles fought by,
7, 16; Seminoles influenced
by, 199-200; Seminole union
opposed by, 87; slave claims
of, 70, 74; slave codes of, 74;
slavery among, 5-6, 12, 200;
as slave speculators, 174;

treatment of freedmen by, 203
Creek War, 4
Crews, John, 58
Crowell, John, 17, 21, 126
Cudjo, 10, 28, 193; emigration of, 50; family of, 29; as interpreter, 29, 101, 105; loyalty of, 29; property losses of, 29; treaty signed by, 29
Cuffy, 132, 139
Cushing, Caleb, 173

Dade, Maj. Francis L., 11, 43
Dade's Massacre, 11, 28, 43
Daily, 43
Davenport, Col. William, 82
Davey (black), 45
Davis, Jefferson, 183
Davy, 49. *See also* Holatoochee
Dawson, James L., 85
Dean, Charles W., 172, 173, 174
Deep Fork River (Ind. Ter.): blacks settle on, 107, 133; Seminole lands on, 71; Seminoles settle on, 57, 68, 89
Dennis, 51, 156, 157
Dent, Capt. F. T., 150
Dexter, Horatio, 38
Dindy, 193
Dolly, 40, 41, 42, 72
Drennen, John, 142, 143, 156
Drew, Bill, 129
Drew, Dick, 149
Drew, John, 108, 110
Drew, Thomas S., 165, 166, 167, 168, 169, 171, 172, 177 n.26
Drew, William, 149
Duval, Gabriel, 149
Duval, Marcellus, 100, 106, 117 n.14, 134, 139, 147, 149,

150, 153, 169; attitude of, toward blacks, 107; downfall of, 155-157; emancipation opposed by, 120; military officials criticized by, 110, 111-112, 122-123, 148; personal motives of, 138, 139, 141, 143, 148; pro-slavery views of, 107, 110-111, 112, 119, 122-123, 139-140; protests of, concerning blacks, 110; slaving activities of, 120, 138, 142, 143, 148, 155, 156, 157, 162
Duval, William J., 143, 149, 162; Seminoles represented by, 120, 121; slave claims of, 142, 148, 150, 151
DuVal, William P., 9, 54

Echo Emathla, 76, 98
Echo Hadjo, 154
Econchatta Micco, 9; slaves of, 49, 50
Elk Creek (Ind. Ter.): Seminoles on, 89
Elsa, 106
Emancipation, 120, 201, 202; instances of, 42, 54, 63 n.42, 102, 134, 165; by treaty, 187
Emathlochee, 9
Emigration: of Apalachicolas, 50; of blacks, 43, 45, 49, 50, 51, 52, 53, 55, 56, 57-58, 155, 176; of Cherokees, 45; difficulties during, 45; of Seminoles, 43-44, 45, 49, 50, 51, 52, 53, 57-58, 175; as war policy, 56, 57
Eneah Micco. *See* Bowlegs
Estates: Seminole custom regarding, 167. *See also* Inheritance

Estelusti, 4
Euchee Billy, 24
Euchee Jack, 24
Euchee Indians. *See* Yuchi
  Indians
Eustice, Lake, 23

Factor, Billy, 152
Factor, Black, 53, 54, 171
Factor, Dembo (black), 108;
  stolen, 85, 103, 145
Factor, James, 187
Factor, Nancy, 171
Factor, Nelly, 53, 145, 152;
  slave claims of, 54; as slaveholder, 17
Factor, Rose Sena (black),
  30, 171, 177 n.26; claims
  for, 53-54, 65 n.60; emigration of, 53, 155; family of,
  50; manumission of, 54
Factor, Sally, 152; slaves sold
  by, 84
Factor, Sam, 53, 54
Factor, William (black), 54,
  55, 177 n.26; emigration of,
  55; family of, 53; as guide,
  25; as interpreter, 30, 53;
  as slavehunter, 171
Fanny, 38, 43, 152, 153
Farming: by blacks, 8, 31, 81,
  98, 121, 176, 191; by freedmen, 192; Seminole method
  of, 98; by Seminoles, 70, 71,
  98, 175
Ferry, 80
First Kansas Colored Infantry,
  184
First Seminole War, 7, 197
Flint, Lieut. F. F., 114, 142
Flood, 89
Flora: family of, 42

Florida: American settlement
  of, 8; cession of, 7; as haven
  for blacks, 7; as haven for
  Creeks, 3-4; Seminole delegations in, 73, 76, 147, 156
Fo-hut-she, 185
Forrester, A. J., 116 n.7; slave
  claim of, 55-57, 102
Fort Arbuckle, 153, 156, 171
Fort Bassinger, 28
Fort Coffee, 45
Fort Dade: negotiations at, 16
Fort Dade Agreement, 111, 123;
  collapse of, 20, 25; conflict
  over, 19-20; negotiation of,
  18-19
Fort Drane, 37
Fort Gibson: blacks at, 184,
  185; blacks given refuge at,
  89, 130, 132; blacks seek
  refuge at, 82, 105-106, 107-
  108, 110, 113, 183; construc-
  tion at, 105; as destination of
  blacks, 40; emigrants arrive
  at, 44, 45, 51, 52, 53, 58;
  Jesup visits, 105-106; reoc-
  cupation of, 184
Fort Jupiter, 26
Fort King, 24, 29
Fort Marion, 25
Fort Mellon, 26
Fort Peyton, 24
Fort Pierce, 52
Fort Pike, 16, 17, 18, 28, 38,
  39, 40
Fort Smith (Ark.), 73, 190;
  peace council at, 185-187;
  slaving raid at, 114
Fort Smith *Herald*, 157
Fort Washita, 184
Fos Harjo, 185
Fowl Town, 7

Free blacks: Cherokee, laws regarding, 81, 200-201
Free blacks, Chickasaw, 202
Free blacks, Choctaw, 173, 201
Free blacks, Creek, 144, 172; laws regarding, 200
Free blacks, Seminole: emigration of, 43, 50, 51, 52, 53, 57; as interpreters, 79; number of, 132; objections to, 124; passes given to, 134; as property owners, 129, 165; reenslavement of, 183
Freedmen: characteristics of, 191; contracts with, 188, 189, 190, 192; equal rights for, 189, 191, 193; as farmers, 192; homesteads proposed for, 191-192; lands occupied by, 188, 192; number of, 193; protection of, 188-192; relations of, with Indians, 188-192; separate lands proposed for, 191; tribal adoption of, 202-203; violence against, 189
Freeman, Lieut. W. G., 27
Friday (Jim), 51
Fugitive Slave Law, 173
Fushatchee band, 4

Gaines, Gen. Edmund P., 39, 41; lawsuit against, 40
Galt, Capt. P. H., 29
Garrett, W. H., 167, 168, 169, 172, 173
Gibbons, Lieut. John, 165
Gopher John, 103, 108, 112, 125, 127, 128, 132, 134, 138, 143, 148, 149, 153; attempted murder of, 88, 104; desire of, to emigrate, 120; emancipation of, 102; as interpreter, 57, 79, 88, 101, 104, 107, 127; Jesup's promise to, 57; as leader of blacks, 135, 139; migration of, to Mexico, 147; property of, 88, 107; in Washington, 104, 106-107
Grant, Ulysses S., 185
Gray, Archie, 150
Grayson, Watt, 169, 170
Grierson, William, 127
Guardianship, 42, 166; Seminole system of, 151
Guides, black, 25, 30, 34 n.40, 87, 116 n.7

Hadjo, Billy, 154
Hadjo, Toney, 50
Halleck Hadjo, 26, 27, 76
Halleck Tustenuggee, 106, 134, 146, 147, 151, 166, 167, 168, 169, 170, 183
Halpatch Hajo, 18
Hannah, 51, 66 n.60, 114
Hardridge, James, 21
Hardridge, Siah, 84, 85, 96 n.45, 103, 104, 109, 145, 148, 149
Hardy, 103
Harjo, Billy, 168
Harlock Harjo, 77
Harney, Brig. Gen. W. S., 45, 185
Harris, C. A., 20, 39, 40, 44, 46, 48, 123
Hatcheelustee Creek, Battle of, 16, 18
Hawkins, Benjamin, 6
Henshaw, Capt. John C., 156
Hernandez, Gen. Joseph, 24, 25

Hester, 152
Hill, James L., 73
Hillabee Square, 170
Hitchiti Indians, 25
Hitchiti language, 3, 4
Holata Mico, 11
Holatoochee (Davy), 151; as
    emissary in Florida, 28, 74;
    negotiations of, 18; as slave-
    holder, 17, 50. *See also* Davy
Honey Springs, Battle of, 184
Horse, John. *See* Cavallo, John;
    Gopher John
Horseshoe Bend, Battle of, 4
Horse stealing, 138, 152
Hospitake, 53
Hotalka Emathla, 76
Housing, 100
Humphreys, Gad, 152; as agent,
    9, 21; slave claims of, 36-37,
    43, 64 n.48; as slaveholder, 20
Hunt, Gen. H. J., 189, 190

Indian languages, 3, 4
Indian Removal Act, 10
Indian tribes. *See* names of indi-
    vidual tribes
Inheritance: Indian system of,
    42, 84. *See also* Estates
Intercourse Act of 1834, 37
Intermarriage: between blacks
    and Indians, 42, 53, 63 n.42
Interpreters: black, 8, 10, 18,
    25, 27, 30, 45, 53, 54, 55, 57,
    58, 82, 88, 100-101, 102,
    104, 105, 107, 111, 127, 147,
    156, 171, 185, 193, 200;
    Creek, 21
Isaac, 57
Istokpoga, Lake, 25
It-koh, 152

Jack, 112, 132
Jackson, Andrew, 4, 7, 10
Jacob, 17, 43
Jelka Hajo, 16
Jenny, 53
Jesse, 129
Jesup, Bvt. Maj. Gen. Thomas
    S., 39, 86, 109; blacks classi-
    fied by, 15; blacks distrusted
    by, 21-22, 29-30; blacks pur-
    chased by, 17; campaigns of,
    16, 25; command assumed
    by, 15; criticism of, 20, 83;
    Indian Territory visited by,
    105-106; intervention by,
    for blacks, 105-106; list of
    blacks made by, 105; nego-
    tiations by, 18; proclamation
    of, 26-27; promises made by,
    22, 28, 76, 85, 86-87, 106,
    114, 121; recruitment by, 23;
    resignation of, 30; rules of
    war violated by, 24-26; war
    policy of, 16, 23, 31, 72, 75
Jesup's Proclamation, 26-27, 82,
    101, 103, 104, 110, 122, 123,
    128, 156
Jim: at Battle of Okeechobee,
    109; slave claim of, 108
Jim (black), 54
Jim Boy, 47, 144; agreement
    with, 16
Jim Lane Band, 193
Joe, 51, 66 n.60, 114
John: claims for, 55; claims of,
    117 n.17
John Brown Band, 193
John Philip, 24, 33 n.28
Johnson, Robert, 185
Johnson, R. W., 172, 175
Jones, Adj. Gen. Roger, 103

Jones, Sam, 11, 20, 147, 156
Joseph, 102, 116 n.7
Juan (Whan), 8, 21
Judge, Thomas L., 83, 84, 104,
    117 n.14; attitude of, toward
    Seminoles, 81; union of
    tribes opposed by, 88, 89
Judy, 132
July: as black leader, 27;
    as guide, 34 n.40
Jumper, 18, 20, 24, 152
Jumper, Jim, 89, 134, 151, 156,
    162, 169; election of, as
    chief, 146; slaving activities
    of, 143
Jumper, John, 168, 182, 187

Kansas: blacks escape to, 183;
    Indians and blacks in, 183,
    184, 188; Indians escape to,
    182-183
Kan-tcati band, 3
Katy, 38, 43, 113, 152, 153
Kennedy, T. P., 34 n.28
Ketchum, Capt. W. S., 129
Kibbett, 113
Kichai Indians, 146
Kickapoo Indians, 146, 153,
    154, 155
King Bowlegs (Eneah Micco).
    See Bowlegs
King George's War, 3
King Payne, 8
King Philip, 11, 20, 24
Kinhijah (Capichee Micco), 150,
    169, 170; as slave owner,
    42, 150
Kirkham, Lieut. Ralph W., 107,
    108
Kissimmee River (Fla.), 25

Kitler Harjo, 76
Kith-lai-tsee (Eliza), 152
Kolomi band, 4

Latty (Lemo), 27, 110
Lea, Luke, 155, 157
Lewis, 152
Lewis, M. G., 146
Lewisburg (Ark.), 45
Limus, 108
Lincoln, Abraham, 180
Lipan Indians, 146
Liquor: prohibition of, 79
Little Doctor, 16
Little River (Ind. Ter.): blacks
    settle on, 107; Seminoles
    settle on, 68, 89, 98
Little Rock (Ark.), 43, 45
Livestock raising, 29, 88, 89, 98,
    107, 176
Lockahatchee, Battle of, 26,
    76
Logan, James, 72, 74, 77, 90,
    112, 113, 134
Long Bob, 21
Loomis, Col. Gustavus, 109,
    120, 128; blacks defended
    by, 112-113; blacks praised
    by, 121
Louis, 43
Love, Hugh, 150; slave claim of,
    40-43, 132
Love, John: slave claim of, 40,
    45, 46, 71-72, 92 n.12
Love, W. E., 131, 132
Lower Creeks, 3, 4
Lucy, 132
Lugenbeel, Maj. Pinkney, 134,
    152, 192

McHenry, James, 153
McIntosh, Chilly, 53, 169, 170, 174
McIntosh, D. N., 140, 148
McIntosh, Maj. James, 43
McIntosh, Roley, 71, 84, 109, 110, 132, 144, 149, 154; blacks demanded by, 82, 113; protest of, 77; slaving raids defended by, 129
McIntosh, Union, 114, 129, 149, 150
McLoughlin, William G., 6, 199
Mad Blue, 16
Mah-kah-tist-chee (Molly), 162, 163, 168, 169, 170, 172, 174; complaint of, 150-151; slaves of, 72
Mah-kah-tist-chee (Molly), 162, 169, 170; slaves of, 72
Maldonado, Col. Juan Manuel, 153
Manypenny, George W., 166, 172, 173, 174
Marcy, William L., 121, 126
Margaret, 129
Marriage: regulation of, 191, 200. *See also* Intermarriage; Polygamy
Marshall, Benjamin, 132, 142, 143
Mary (Maria Gracia), 51, 65 n.60
Mason, Col. Richard B., 88, 106; as supporter of blacks, 103, 104; in Washington, 104- 105
Mason, John Y., 122; opinion of, 123-125
Matlock, Gideon C., 100
Medill, William, 107, 111, 117 n.14, 127

Mexico, 176; blacks migrate to, 147, 148, 153; as refuge, 154, 165; Seminoles migrate to, 147, 148, 154; slaves escape to, 164 n.48
Micanopy, 11, 18, 20, 24, 27, 43, 71, 85, 86, 89, 101, 104, 105, 138, 146, 148, 150, 151; blacks defended by, 74; death of, 131, 146; executive council of, 98; in New Orleans, 40; recognition of, as chief, 47; seizure of, 26; settlement of, 50, 53, 129; surrender of, 19
Miccopotokee, 150; as guardian, 42; as slaveholder, 17
Mikasuki bands, 3, 25, 29, 49
Mikasuki towns, 7
Miles, Bvt. Lieut. Col. D. S., 130
Miller, Lieut. Col. Samuel, 22
Miller, Sam, 77
Miller, William, 53
Mills, Sam, 108, 138
Mix, Charles, 175
Molly. *See* Mah-ka-tist-chee
Morrow, J. S., 183
Mulatto King, 9, 50
Mundy, 17
Mungo, 38
Murray, 17, 113; capture of, 21; as guide, 25; Jesup's promises to, 25, 30-31, 38
Muskogee language, 3, 4

Nancy, 112
Neamathla, 9
Necksucky, 166
Ned, 18

Ned (second), 29
Negroes. *See* Blacks; Free
 blacks; Freedmen; Slaves
Negro Fort, 7
Nelson, William, 126
Neosho Falls (Kan.), 188
New Orleans: arrival of blacks
 at, 30-31; slave controversies
 in, 40, 45
Newspapers, 157
Noble, 42
Noble, George, 165
Nocose Yohola, 26, 71, 74;
 slaves of, 50
North Fork River (Ind. Ter.),
 175, 193; Seminole lands on,
 71; Seminoles settle on, 68,
 86
North Fork Town, 164, 182

Oconee band, 3
Octiarche, 82, 98, 146
Old-Bear, 105
Opothleyohola: agreement with,
 16; retreat of, 182; settlement
 of, 68
Osceola, 11, 20; family of, 25;
 seizure of, 24

Pacheco, Don Antonio, 43
Page, Capt. John, 74, 82
Papy, Miguel: slave claims of,
 51-52, 53-54, 65 n.60
Parhose Fixico: slaves of, 51
Parker, Col. Ely S., 185
Pascofar, 98, 185, 186
Pass Christian (Miss.), 17
Passes: blacks receive, 134, 155
Passockee, 108, 109
Passockee Yohola, 98, 134, 143,
 168, 169, 170

Patriot War, 6
Payne, Charles, 53
Pease Creek (Fla.), 25
Pellicer's Creek (Fla.), 24
Peter, 132
Phagan, John, 10
Philip. *See* King Philip
Phillips, Col. W. A., 184
Pierce, Franklin, 173
Pike, Albert, 182
Poinsett, Joel R., 17, 22, 27, 28,
 48, 73
Polk, James K., 120, 125
Polly: slaves of, 50
Polygamy, 190
Pompy, 40, 41; family of, 42
Pond Creek (Ind. Ter.), 175
Porter, J. M., 84
Porter, Kenneth Wiggins, 6
Potatoes, 89
Potostee, 113
Primus, 101, 114, 152, 193
Pryor, Cornelius D., 164, 172-
 173, 178 n.30. *See* Pryor
 Case
Pryor Case, 162-170, 172-173,
 175
Public officials: proslavery
 views of, 48, 106, 119, 143,
 162, 182, 197

Racial mixture. *See* Amalgama-
 tion
Racial prejudice, 6, 187, 191,
 199, 202
Rector, Elias, 175
Rector, Henry M., 180
Red River (Ind. Ter.): Seminoles
 on, 183, 184-185, 188
Red Sticks, 4, 7
Removal, 197, 202; of Apala-

chicolas, 49; black opposition
to, 11-12, 18; of blacks, 10,
19, 30, 31, 41, 49; of Creeks,
17; of Seminoles, 9-10, 12,
27-28, 49
Renown, 43
Revolutionary War, 5
Reynolds, George, 189, 191
Reynolds, Lieut. John G., 41;
blacks shipped by, 45, 46;
criticism of, 46; emigrants
accompanied by, 43-44
Rice: cultivation of, 81, 89, 98,
121
Rio Grande, 120, 145, 146
Roane, Sam C., 44
Robert, 168
Robertson, Ezekiel, 54
Robin, 127
Robinson, Tod, 47
Rockwell, J. A., 126
Romeo, 132
Rose, 104
Ross, John, 180, 201; protest of,
26; Seminoles assisted by, 76
Round Mountain, Battle of, 183,
194 n.5
Rufile, 132
Rutherford, Archibald H., 164

St. Augustine, 28
St. Marks (Fla.), 37
Sam, 53
Sampson, 57, 64 n.48
Samuel, 45
Sanborn, Bvt. Maj. Gen. John
B., 188-192
Sandy, 132, 193
Sarah, 108, 132
School lands, 192
Scott, S. S., 183

Sebastian, W. K., 171
Second Seminole War, 16-31,
73, 197; battles of, 12;
beginning of, 11; blacks in,
49-55; causes of, 9-11; Jesup
reports on, 121
Sells, Elijah, 185, 188, 192
Sells, John, 149
Seminole Indians: alliance of,
with blacks, 6-7, 199; attitude of, toward blacks, 4-5,
8-9, 79-80, 102, 111, 131,
138, 143; blacks' defiance of,
134, 138-139, 140-141, 143;
blacks' influence over, 47,
172; blacks married to,
63 n.42; blacks returned to,
132-133; blacks sold by, 131;
in Cherokee Nation, 68, 70-
71, 75-76, 78, 83, 95 n.32;
Creek antagonism toward, 5,
9, 16; Creek domination of,
91, 146; Creeks feared by,
10, 46, 68, 70, 76, 81, 91,
197; destitution of, 76, 77,
89; disputes of, with Creeks,
145, 149-150, 166, 167;
early history of, 3-4; emigration of, 43-44, 45, 49,
50, 51, 52, 53, 57-58; as
emissaries to Florida, 73,
76, 147, 156; factionalism
among, 145; farming by,
70, 71, 98, 175; flight of,
to Kansas, 183; at Fort Gibson, 188; guardianship
among, 42, 151, 166; inheritance customs of, 42, 84;
lands assigned to, 68, 71;
naming of, 3; other tribes'
influence on, 199-200; pop-

ulation of, 4; pro-Confederate
faction of, 182, 183, 186,
187, 188, 189, 193, 199; pro-
Union faction of, 182, 183,
185, 187, 189, 191, 193; racial
prejudice among, 6; removal
of, 9-10, 12, 27-28, 49, 197-
202; reservations for, 9; separate lands for, 87, 90, 174-
175, 193; slave owners
among, 17, 42, 50, 51, 53, 72,
129, 150; slavery among, 5,
37; slaves stolen by, 40;
system of slavery among, 37,
79, 80, 98, 119, 123, 173,
174, 199-200; town system
of, 98; treatment of freedmen
by, 203; treaty negotiations
by, 185, 186, 187, 192, 193;
union of, 77, 87; union of,
with Creeks, 39
Sharpkee, 170
Silla, 129
Slave claims: by Apalachicolas,
54; by Cherokees, 87, 110,
131; by Creeks, 38-39, 70,
74-75, 82-85, 103, 108, 131,
163-164, 169-170, 174; difficulties over, 38; removal
threatened by, 51, 53; by
Seminoles, 120, 132; tribal
disputes over, 74-75, 82, 83, 89,
102; by whites, 36-38, 40-44,
45-49, 51, 52, 55-57, 59,
64 n.48, 65 n.60, 71-74, 87,
92 n.12, 93 n.16, 103, 125,
131, 132, 148, 162-163, 164,
165, 173-174, 175. *See also*
Pryor Case
Slave codes: Cherokee, 78-79,
200-201; Chickasaw, 202;
Choctaw, 201; Creek, 6,

14 n.8, 74, 81, 83-84, 130,
140, 149, 200; Seminole, 199
Slave hunters, 20, 54, 84-85
Slave revolt: in Cherokee Nation,
80-81, 94 n.31, 201; in
Seminole country, 138
Slavery: abolition of, 186, 189,
193; characteristics of, among
Seminoles, 5, 8-9; among
Cherokees, 12, 201; among
Chickasaws, 12, 201-202;
among Choctaws, 13, 201;
among Creeks, 5-6, 12,
14 n.8, 200; national debate
over, 114, 120, 125-126;
reasons for, among Seminoles,
5-6; Seminole system of, 37,
79-80, 98, 119, 123, 173,
174, 199-200
Slaves: among Cherokees, 78,
108, 110, 180; among
Creeks, 80, 112, 147;
emancipation of, 42, 165,
187, 201, 202; guardianship
of, 42, 166; list of, 164; refusal of, to work, 111, 163;
in revolt, 80-81, 94 n.31,
138, 201; runaway, 5, 7, 9,
11, 37, 200; Seminole treatment of, 37; stealing of, 5,
85, 102; treaty agreements
concerning, 5; trial of, 80;
tribal conflict over, 74-75,
82, 83, 85, 89, 102. *See also*
Blacks
Slave speculators, 128-129, 141,
173
Slave trade: legality of, 37
Slave trading company, 173
Slaving raids, 84-85, 108-110; by
blacks, 170-171; by Cherokees, 129, 149; by Creeks,

102-104, 113, 129, 140, 145, 148-149, 150, 153, 163, 165, 166; at Fort Gibson, 113-114; tribal conflict over, 130; by whites, 144, 149-150, 153, 172

Slidell, Thomas, 40

Smith, J. M., 149

Smith, Joe, 129, 149

Smith, Joseph, 113

Smithson, B. H., 164

Solano, Don Filipe, 51

Solano, Matteo: slave claims of, 51-52, 53-54, 65 n.60

Sophia, 52, 64 n.48

South Alabama, 43

Spanish, the: Indian relations with, 3; relations of blacks with, 5

Spencer, John C., 51, 53, 56

Sprague, Lieut. J. T., 102

Steamboat travel, 43, 45, 79

Stephen, 148, 149

Stidham, Sally, 112

Sturdevant, William C., 4

Surnames, 193

Tallahassee band, 4, 25, 49

Tamathli band, 3

Tampa Bay: blacks assembled at, 16, 27; Indians assembled at, 20; removal parties at, 50

Taylor, Gen. Zachary, 28, 30, 70, 74, 77, 85, 101, 123; campaign of, 25; command of, 49-50; war policy of, 49

Texans: Creeks attacked by, 182

Texas, 154, 156, 157; Indians emigrate to, 49; slaves in, 185

Thomas, 129, 139

Thompson, Waddy, 120

Thompson, Wiley, 11, 54

Tiger, 105

Tiger Tail, 107

Toby, 17

Tom, 89

Tom (black), 50; as interpreter, 147

Toney, 17, 22, 28; as interpreter, 147

Tonkawa Indians, 146

Toucey, Isaac, 125

Traders, 73, 142, 164

Treaty of Colrain, 5

Treaty of 1845: commission appointed for, 86; negotiation of, 87, 89-90; provisions of, 90

Treaty of 1856, 174-175

Treaty of 1866, 193, 197

Treaty of Fort Gibson, 10, 11; provisions of, 68

Treaty of Moultrie Creek, 9

Treaty of New York, 5, 197

Treaty of Payne's Landing, 11, 29; provisions of, 39, 68, 75, 85; reaffirmation of, 19

Tribute, 167

Tuckabatchee Micco, 16

Tuskeegee, 26, 27, 28, 76

Tuskeneehau, 42, 72, 150, 169, 170

Tuskihadjo, 9

Tuskinia, 20

Tussekiah, 98

Tustenuggee, 107

Tustenuggee Micco, 76

Twiggs, Col. David E., 27

Tyler, John, 125

United States troops: requests for, 141, 142

Upper Creeks, 3, 4

Van Buren, Martin, 71
Van Buren *Intelligencer,* 157
Vandever, Joseph, 171, 177 n.26
Vann, Joseph, 80
Vann, Martin, 149
Vegetables: cultivation of, 81, 98
Vicksburg (Miss.). 43

Waco Indians, 146, 153
Walker, John, 49, 54
Walker Pachassee, 50
Walking Joe, 138
Wannah: family of, 108
War of Jenkins' Ear, 3
Wars. *See* names of wars
Washbourne, J. W., 166, 168, 170, 171, 173, 175
Washington, 101
Washington, D. C.: blacks in, 88-89, 104, 106-107; Indians in, 86-88, 104-105
Washita River (Ind. Ter.), 184, 188
Watson, James C.: blacks purchased by, 39; slave claim of, 43-44, 45, 47, 48, 49, 73-74, 93 n.16, 125-126
Watson, John H., 73
Weapons: carrying of, by blacks, 79, 84, 127, 130, 139, 140, 143
Webbers Falls (Ind. Ter.), 82; disembarkation at, 79; slaves revolt at, 80
Wewoka Creek (Ind. Ter.): blacks settle on, 133, 134, 149

Whan. *See* Juan
Wheelwrights, 191
White, P. H., 142, 143, 149
Whites: adoption of, 202
Whitfield, William, 129
Whitman, George, 47
Wild Cat, 20, 25, 33 n.28, 55, 83, 85, 89, 98, 105, 107, 127, 128, 134, 143, 148, 167, 173; captured, 24, 52; confederacy planned by, 146; dissatisfaction of, 145, 146-147; emigration of, 53, 76; migration of, to Mexico, 147-148; promises made to, 56; return of, to Indian Territory, 153-154; slaves of, 53; in Washington, 86-88
Wilkins, William, 87, 89
Willie Bob, 164
Wilmot, David, 126
Wistar, Thomas, 185
Withlacoochee, Battle of, 12, 16
Withlacoochee Creek (Fla.), 25
Women: condition of, 174, 191-192
Worth, Col. William Jenkins, 82, 123; command of, 52-57

Yaholoochee. *See* Cloud
Yamassee War, 3
Yohola Harjo, 89
Young Alligator, 89
Yuchi Indians, 25

Zantzinger, Maj. R. A., 18, 39